A Nation in Transition

Published in association with
Observer Research Foundation
New Delhi

Observer Research Foundation (ORF) is a public policy think-tank that aims to influence formulation of policies for building a strong and prosperous India. The ORF pursues these goals by providing informed and productive inputs, in-depth research and stimulating discussion. The Foundation is supported in its mission by a cross-section of India's leading public figures, academics and business leaders.

Jayshree Sengupta is a Senior Fellow at Observer Research Foundation, New Delhi. After graduating from Delhi University, she studied at the London School of Economics where she completed M.Sc. and M.Phil in Economics. She was a lecturer at Indraprastha College and Miranda House, University of Delhi (1966-1977). She was Senior Economic Writer at the Hindustan Times, New Delhi (1998-2004). She has been a consultant to the World Bank, Washington DC and OECD, Paris. She has published a number of papers, reports and a book, co-authored with Prof. S. Sideri, *The 1992 Single European Market and the Third World* (Frank Cass, London).

A Nation in Transition

Understanding
the Indian Economy

Jayshree Sengupta

ACADEMIC FOUNDATION

NEW DELHI

First published in 2007
by

ACADEMIC FOUNDATION
4772-73 / 23 Bharat Ram Road, (23 Ansari Road),
Darya Ganj, New Delhi - 110 002 (India).
Phones : 23245001 / 02 / 03 / 04.
Fax : +91-11-23245005.
E-mail : academic@vsnl.com
www. academicfoundation.com

in association with the

Observer Research Foundation, New Delhi

Cataloging in Publication Data--DK
  Courtesy: D.K. Agencies (P) Ltd. <docinfo@dkagencies.com>

Sengupta, Jayshree.
   A nation in transition : understanding the Indian economy /
Jayshree Sengupta.
     p.   cm.
   Includes bibliographical references (p.   )
   Includes index.
   ISBN-13: 9788171886241
   ISBN-10: 8171886248

   1. India--Economic conditions. 2. India--Economic policy.
   I. Title.

DDC 330.954   22

Typeset by Italics India, New Delhi.
Printed and bound in India.

CONTENTS

...CONTD. ...

1

India at a Glance

An Introduction

Many who visit India for the first time are baffled by the picture of sheer contrast presented to them. On the surface, India looks like any developing, Third World, country. But within, it has pockets of wealth and western modernism that visitors find perplexing. Curiosity aroused, the visitors find themselves asking what lies behind this face of modern India and how does its economy work.

There are books galore on the Indian economy, written by reputable Indian and western scholars. What is the need for another book on the subject? This book aims at explaining the workings of the Indian economy, not to the 'initiated', but to the intelligent reader who is interested in knowing more about India's changing economic pattern. How has India risen from being a poor developing country to a position of importance in world economy in a matter of five decades?

The book aims at presenting the various intricacies of the economic system of India simply and clearly, so that educated women and men would find the book useful in understanding what is going on around them in the world of finance and trade, as also the government's policies. Undergraduates interested in economic issues, would also find the book useful.

Though there are many business newspapers and TV channels, they too are for the initiated, often using jargon and technical terms too difficult even for the lay intelligentsia. This book attempts to fill this gap by clearly elucidating, in simple terms the Indian economic policies, past and present, so as to make it intelligible to the average reader.

The history of Independent India's development is only five decades old. Its future course seems to be bright but uncertain. India's emergence as a prominent economic power alongside China is indeed impressive and industrialised countries are taking more and more interest in this phenomenon.

One of the reason for this interest is India's huge population, second only to China. Its population is young and enthusiastic and will remain young for a long time. India's population policy has been discussed along with the formidable problem of raising India's human development profile in Chapter 2.

India's population is restless and on the move—from the villages to the cities in search of jobs and a better life. It is a country in transition and each of its cities bear the weight of a large transient population. Although in some aspects, India is visibly taking important strides forward for a position of prominence in the new Millennium, many gaps remain, reminding one that India is not yet treading confidently on a secure growth path. It has not reached the 'take off' stage and remains bogged down with formidable social problems, which keep the larger section of the population isolated from the growth process, as also depriving them of the benefits of that process.

These problems of poverty and inequity are nothing new for India. They are as old as the history of its fertile lands, wealth and the luxurious lives of its ruling class that attracted hoards of distant invaders and conquerors for over a thousand years. In very few eras in the past thousand years did ordinary people live happily and without threat from within or outside the country. The contrast between extreme wealth and extreme poverty has always been an ugly presence. Foreign tourists are well aware of India's past heritage of wealth, monuments and culture, *et al.*, but what they cannot fail to see is the all too omnipresent abject poverty in the midst of riches in cities and towns.

Perhaps in no other country in the entire South and Southeast Asian region, can one see such a vast canvas of deprivation, malnutrition and illiteracy. We shall discuss the causes of poverty as well as the Indian Government's poverty alleviation programmes in Chapter 3.

It is because of the widespread poverty in the villages that rapid urbanisation is taking place. People are leaving their villages and migrating to far away places just to earn a living. Even to a casual observer, it would be obvious that all big cities and towns have a substantial migrant population. They live in makeshift huts covered with plastic in shanty towns on the outskirts and sometimes right in the middle of big cities. Urbanisation is important for development but only up to a point. If it is not controlled and managed well it can lead to huge transient populations living in inhuman conditions. There is a pressure on urban infrastructure and children of migrant parents have special problems. We shall discuss urbanisation in Chapter 4.

Most educated Indians can speak English, especially in the cities—a lasting legacy of the British *raj*. Colonial architecture in Kolkata, Mumbai, New Delhi and Chennai tells its own story and the great Indian monolith, the bureaucracy, is also a fallout of the British administrative system. In many ways, India is going through industrialisation much like what Britain went through during the Industrial Revolution in the 19th century. We shall take up India's colonial legacy in Chapter 5.

Agriculture has been, is and will continue to be the most prevalent and important means of livelihood (65 to 68 per cent of the people are engaged in agriculture). Total dependence on monsoons has always been the main problem for the subcontinent's farmers. The transformation to a more dependable, modern, high productivity system of farming has been slow in coming. In fact, problems of Indian agriculture have its roots in the colonial past. The state of Indian agriculture today and its present problems as well as the government's struggle with assuring food security to the poor have been discussed in Chapter 6.

India has been industrialising rapidly and many more consumer goods are available in the shops and many of its products are of high quality today. India produces its own steel, cement, machinery, sophisticated equipment, armaments, planes and plenty of cars and bicycles. The number of cars, trucks, buses and auto-rickshaws on the roads amaze tourists. India is even exporting cars to Europe.

At the time of Independence, India's leaders, particularly its first Prime Minister, Pandit Jawaharlal Nehru, wanted to make India an industrial power. We have tried to trace the industrialisation experience from the beginning of the Five Year Plans, initiated by Nehru in 1950. The Five Year Plans and the resultant growth of India's national income and Gross Domestic Product (GDP) have been dealt with in Chapter 7. Right from the beginning, the focus was put on promoting capital goods industries. Perhaps, in doing so, exports were neglected. Heavy foreign exchange requirements led to an import substitution regime and the now infamous licence–permit *raj*.

Industrial growth started picking up in the 1950s after the First Five Year Plan and industries have been growing ever since, with intermittent setbacks. Industrial growth is the basis of GDP growth and Nehru's dream of industrialisation was given its first concrete shape in this era.

Another striking aspect of India's pattern of industrial production is that a significant bulk of its manufactures are made by small, self-employed producers and small enterprises. They make a large number of goods for the use of the common person or the *aam aadmi*. They belong to the unorganised or informal sector. India's industrial growth and the performance of industries, the organised, and the unorganised (informal) sectors and the public sector have been discussed in Chapter 8.

People from abroad, especially Non-Resident Indians (NRIs), find the economic and industrial infrastructure still too shaky and unreliable for their comfort. The state of India's infrastructure fits the label of an economy in transition. It is at best patchy in metro cities and in a dismal state in the villages and small towns. What are the major constraints to upgrading and improving infrastructure and, if foreign investment is so badly needed, how should it be attracted? From airports to ports, roads, power and railways, all need to be refurbished and revamped. Even if one stays in five-star hotels, one cannot escape environmental pollution, frequent power failures and bumpy roads. Problems of infrastructure are vast and even in a Mercedes Benz or BMW, the ride on an average Indian road is far from comfortable. The new National Highways are very different and smooth but to get to them, one has to travel on poorly maintained roads. The problems of infrastructure have been discussed in Chapter 9.

Even though the manufacturing sector has been taking rapid strides in recent years, it has not been able to absorb a significant number of jobseekers. And a considerable number of the work force is actually not contributing much either to production or sales of the enterprises they are working in. There are too many people in shops, offices and hotels who are idle. Many of the enterprises and establishments are overmanned with underemployed workers. Sometimes entire families sit in shops when only one or two persons are required. But, in their view, being underemployed is certainly better than being unemployed. Unemployment is one of the most serious problems facing the nation. There are large number of youths wandering around doing nothing. In rural areas, the situation is even worse and is the main cause of persisting poverty. Problems of employment have been discussed in Chapter 10.

India's savings rate is around 26 to 29 per cent of the GDP. It is not very low, but is lower than China's. In India, everyone saves money for the future and invests in financial assets, houses and gold. Savings have to be properly invested because investment brings about growth. Foreign Direct Investment (FDI) brings in technology and know-how along with the dollars. But foreign investment remains below its potential and nowhere near the Chinese level. FDI is needed for creating jobs and raising incomes all round, but what should be done to get a bigger amount of FDI? Indeed, due to FDI, many foreign brands of consumer goods and durables are now available in India. It is affecting the savings and consumption pattern of the people. Problems related to savings and investment including foreign investment, have been taken up in Chapter 11.

Many tourists come to India on a shopping spree, especially women, attracted by a plethora of items and exoticas for which India has become famous in the exports area.

The number one item is gems and jewellery. Another is textiles. India's foreign trade has a long history and some Indian goods were famous even in ancient times. India's foreign trade has become complex over time and the pattern has been changing. Earlier, the nation saw a slowdown in exports during certain periods and, in recent times, an increase in imports. As a result, there has often been deficits in the balance of payments. The salient facts regarding India's balance of payments since the 1960s have been elucidated in non-technical terms. Likely future trends have been outlined in the context of import liberalisation and the big reduction in import duties that had, till the 1990s, been kept high as a protectionist measure for our industries. What has been the impact of increase in imports on the domestic manufacturing industry? From being completely deprived of imported consumer goods, today the Indian consumer is flooded with them. The change is remarkable and has thrown a big challenge to Indian industries.

India's foreign trade, its exports, imports, Special Economic Zones (SEZ), its foreign exchange regime have been discussed in Chapter 12. India is a member of the World Trade Organization (WTO) and what it means for India in terms of compliance, has also been discussed in the same chapter.

The money market and the commercial banks have played a crucial role in India's economy since the British times. India's banking and financial system are pretty good, though perhaps not as fast or efficient as those in the industrialised countries. There are many banks and ATM machines all over big towns and cities. There are banks even in small villages. The banking system and the function of the Reserve Bank of India and its role with regard to interest rates policy has been discussed in Chapter 13. How does the RBI's monetary policy work? How is the RBI engaged in controlling the value of the rupee in terms of the dollar or euro? What impact does it have on exports and imports?

Next in importance for business is the stock market. How does India's stock market function? The intricacies of the capital market have been explained in Chapter 14 along with the problems of regulation. Many scandals, big and small are surfacing every once in a while. The two most infamous among them, Harshad Mehta and Ketan Parekh scams, have been dealt with. Also, the small investors' problems have been discussed because they have been at a loss as to where they should invest their money, especially after the Unit Trust of India (UTI) crisis let them down badly in 2001. Mutual funds and life and general insurances have been discussed from the point of view of small savers who invest in these instruments. These institutions with their access to huge long-term funds can be tapped for investment in the infrastructure.

Probably the most striking phenomenon India witnessed at the turn of the century is the mushrooming of several cyber cities and the software empires built by our own entrepreneurs—such as Narayana

Murthy and Azim Premji—impressing even the computer king, Bill Gates. The services sector (software, business process outsourcing) is really booming and is the fastest growing sector in the country. Problems in the services sector have been taken up in Chapter 15 along with software and tourism. India can become a major tourist hub in the world because of the variety it offers to tourists, but many problems remain and these have been identified.

A common feature of Indian cities and towns is the number of gold shops and new buildings that are coming up everywhere. How can so many Indians afford to buy so much gold and real estate? The answer is the presence of a huge amount of black money in the system and the difficulty that the government faces in making Indian citizens tax compliant. Like in many other fast growing cities, corruption and tax evasion is rife in India. It leads to less money available for development with the government in its budget. Also, more often than not, it is difficult for the lay man to understand the content and the effect (on them) of the Annual Budget, which the Finance Minister presents to Parliament. The basics of budget making and problems in the tax structure and tax collection as well as the introduction of VAT have been discussed in Chapter 16.

Today, Indian states are at different levels of development. Some are advanced in every way and others are miserably backward. Why is there such an imbalance—such highs and lows in performance among states? The many problems of state finance and the role of the Centre in Centre-State relations and the all important issues of governance have been discussed in Chapter 17. Many states are poorly governed and are not doing well even though they get the money they need from the Centre. The chapter also deals with the procedure of revenue transfer from the Centre to the States. Which are the forward and which are the backward states and why are they in that condition year after year?

Finally, people who are visiting India would be aghast to see the condition of the country's major hospitals. The public hospitals are overcrowded and pathetic in the way they cope with an overflow of patients daily. There is lack of space, amenities and even doctors. On the other hand, private hospitals are mushrooming everywhere and private healthcare is booming. Private healthcare is expensive and not always good and dependable. Similar is the case of government schools. Most of them are in a very bad state, dogged by the lack of teachers, classrooms and books. The social sector needs to be reformed first if India wants to join the league of industrialised nations. Problems in the social sector, in health and education have been tackled in Chapter 18.

The Indian knows well that his or her country is fast 'globalising', though it is not so obvious to a visitor in the beginning, except for the western mode of dress that women sport in cities, especially at discos and clubs where the rich young tend to throng. But NRIs who stay with their Indian relatives feel the deeper impact of globalisation on Indian society. There is a strong influence of NRIs on the Indian policy makers and on their families back in India. How India is globalising and what its impact is on the consumption pattern of Indians has been discussed in Chapter 19. A fast rate of economic growth and rise in the consumption standards, like having more cars, is causing serious damage to the the environment and urgent steps are needed to take care of this problem. What should be done to conserve water and keep it clean, free the air of pollution and maintain the delicate ecological balance? What should be done to prevent land degradation and soil erosion? The rampant felling of trees in the forest regions is a reality today, not just a future threat. What should be done through the environmental policy? These questions have been posed in the same chapter.

Many foreign investors and NRIs who want to invest in India would like to know how far India is prepared to go with economic reforms. The reforms were launched in 1991 and the process continues today in 2006-07, despite different political parties assuming power at the Centre. But to many, the pace of economic reforms has slowed down and this is affecting the investors' confidence in India. Economic reforms and the second generation reforms have been discussed in Chapter 20, as also the progress, successes and failures of these reforms. How far have they transformed agriculture, infrastructure, industry and the services sector? How far have they been instrumental in reforming public enterprises? What are the reasons for the resistance to reforms from the public sector and organised labour?

We end by discussing India and the SAARC (South Asian Association for Regional Cooperation) because many visitors to India are from neighbouring countries and peaceful economic relations is good for the region on the whole. India's neighbours are important for India's economy, its growth and prosperity as well as security. Peaceful relations, especially with Pakistan, would lead to more money being available for human and economic development. How India can assume a leading role in this attempt is discussed in Chapter 21.

In conclusion, the book outlines how India is pushing ahead in spite of a maze of problems, and its huge potential in becoming a powerful and economically strong nation cannot be denied by anyone today. It is amply evident in the *bazaars* buzzing with activity, the expanding markets of India and the relentless labour that people with ordinary salaries and wages are putting in daily, without fuss, to get ahead in life. It is reflected in the Bollywood cinema, which has become ever so popular not only in the Arab world but in New York and London and the popularity of Indian designs and cuisine around the world.

India's middle class that increasingly includes the rural well-to-do, are all aspiring for a higher standard of life for themselves and for their children. They are making their children seek better marks, learn new skills and get good grades—all in preparation to earn more, preferably by going abroad. In any case, all want their children to lead lives better than their own. Motivated by the glut of images fed by the media—especially electronic—about the high global standards of life, there is a wave of people trying to do their best in all walks of life to get ahead and perhaps catch up with the developed world's life style. It is the driving force behind the big push forward that can make India great in the future.

A very brief digression: who is this NRI who visits India regularly?

NRIs are important visitors for India and come regularly to visit their relatives and friends. There are around 20 million people of Indian origin in different parts of the world. Even people whose ancestors migrated in the 18th and 19th centuries to Africa and South America, like Nobel Laureate V.S. Naipaul, regularly visit India. For most NRIs, Indian culture is important and they some how have managed to preserve it wherever they live. They often come to imbibe the culture first-hand or give their children an exposure to Indian traditions.

Their influence has been important for the Indian economy, not only because they keep sending money and gifts to people back home, but also because they have invested in various foreign exchange deposit schemes that India has set up for NRIs, in real estate and in industries. They have also been the first to notice the various problems in the Indian bureaucracy and have for long been pressing for reforms. They are big shoppers and are good for Indian trade and commerce, especially for clothing, jewellery and food articles. The powerful NRIs have been a major force behind the liberalisation policies that India has been following in recent years. Today many software engineers are settled in the Silicon Valley in California and making important contributions to India's foreign exchange reserves. India has the highest flow of remittances from abroad in the world.

The NRIs are also the role models for families hosting them in India and their lifestyle and behaviour is often copied by the new generation family members and friends back home. NRIs have thus been instrumental in introducing globalisation in India many years ago and have given their relatives and friends a luxurious taste of imported goods. They have introduced the idea that consumption can be fun, over-riding the Gandhian ideal of simple living and high thinking. Indians today, as a result have a great appetite for consumer goods and all global companies are scrambling to establish their bases in India.

Yet, ironically, many NRIs, especially those who have gone to the US on short assignments, remain pretty frugal and save a large part of their incomes. They remain rather insular and dedicated to their work. They work very hard as compared to their local colleagues and go back to their traditional family atmosphere, eating Indian food, at the end of the day. No wonder they are so popular with their bosses! They save a lot of money because they have hardly anything they are tempted to spend on and feel obliged to send money home to parents and relatives. Many NRIs settled in the US, however, are living in an affluent style and have invested in huge palatial properties. Their median income is around $60,000 and there are 200,000 millionaires among them.

Despite their wealth, many NRIs nurse a desire to return to India and many have already done so. This is because they have come to realise that there is not much difference in the lifestyle of a wealthy

Indian and an NRI in America. The rich Indians today also shop abroad for clothes and drive swanky foreign cars and have all the good things in life, including many more personal services that are very expensive abroad.

To the foreigner or the NRI, India is a nation divided into two different worlds. One is the world in which the rich are setting new standards of good living and stylish acquisitions and the other in which the less fortunate commoner is managing to make two ends meet within their rather frugal means. But there is also the third world, the worst of them all, where millions are are living in grinding poverty in villages or in the cities' shantytowns. To many NRIs and foreign visitors, removing poverty would obviously be the number one priority. It has also been the much proclaimed goal of the series of Central Governments. But this has not happened as promises made by politicians have not been kept and millions, defeated by life, continue to live in misery.

It is not only the Central Government but the State Governments which has to take care of the many problems appearing on the economic front daily—especially those related to the welfare of the people not included in the process of globalisation and economic upliftment. The states have to look after those who have no stable incomes and are living from day-to-day, leading haphazard, vagrant and unstable lives. This hopelessness that afflicts many millions and leads to a life full of anxiety and hardship, is the dark side of India's rapid growth. This is what makes India a land of great, ugly contrasts and huge growing inequalities that shocks foreign visitors. This is what needs to be changed. The foremost task of the government and indeed, the more privileged people of the country, is to bring the underprivileged—hopelessly lost in hunger and malnutrition, joblessness and illiteracy—in to the fold of progress and economic emancipation, that is, into the 'other India' of confidence, hope and ambition, freeing them from the vicious circle of poverty. It is in this direction that this book attempts to make some suggestions.

2

Population

The one thing that has gone on increasing at a rapid pace in India since Independence is population. India's population has tripled since Independence: it is the second most populous country in the world. Population growth will slow down over the next two decades but it will continue to grow above one per cent. China has already managed to bring its population growth down to 1.1 per cent. A higher population growth and the two-child norm instead of the one-child norm of China has benefited India in one way. A few years hence, India's population will be relatively young while China's population will be ageing.

India was not always a populous country. It was only in 1921 that there was a turnaround in population growth due to a sharp decline in death rates, made possible through the discovery of new types of medicines. In the earlier part of the century, death rates were high due to famines, epidemics and malaria. After 1921, strides in science helped to control epidemics and the use of DDT helped to contain Malaria. (DDT resistant mosquitoes however have brought back malaria). The last famine was in 1943 which devastated West Bengal and led to the death of a million people; after that no more famines have occurred. The Malthusian checks like disasters, famines, diseases were thus brought more or less under control. According to Malthus, population, if not controlled, would lead to disasters because while it grows in geometric progression, food supply grows more slowly in arithmetic progression. Hence, natural calamities and diseases would automatically control population.

The theory of 'demographic transition' on the other hand began to be applicable to India from 1921 and from a high birth rate and high death rate scene, there was a transition to a low death rate and high birth rate scene. The last stage of this demographic transition would be low birth rate and low death rate. It can only be achieved through a conscious effort on the part of the population itself to control the birth rate. China has already reached the tail end of 'demographic transition' while India is reaching an interesting and positive stage where a huge chunk (83.4 per cent) of the population is young (below 45). Many governments at the Centre have played a part in population control but it has been seen that in India, the demand for contraception has to come from within families for any popular policy to be successful.

What has been the impact of the population explosion? Many towns have come up in the last few years that seem to be teeming with people. Mega cities have been established but nearly six million villages are relatively less populated. The density of population in towns, however, has increased in the last two decades of the 20th century, making many towns overcrowded and congested.

Since 1950, the decline in birth rate has been much slower than the decline in the death rate and that is why population started to grow at a phenomenal rate of 3 per cent and, for three decades, remained between 2.1 and 2.2 per cent per annum. India was, at the same time, also the first country in the world to officially promote family planning.

In the 1970s and 1980s, India's promotion of contraceptives was slower than in Bangladesh, Iran, Indonesia and Sri Lanka. This was because in India many of those who used sterilisation and other forms of contraception for birth control did so only after the age of 30. By 30, in the most fertile years, women already had an average of 4 children. In recent years, however, female sterilisation has become the most popular mode of birth control.

Since Independence, the rural population has grown faster than the urban population and both the death rate and the birth rate have tended to be lower in urban than in rural areas. In rural areas, there were few jobs to be found for the burgeoning population as employment growth in non-farm work was slow. It led to rapid urbanisation involving migration of labour from rural to urban areas because population growth in rural areas led to open unemployment. In the 1950s, 85 per cent of the population lived in the villages and today, the rural population has come down to 65 per cent. Today there are 741 million people residing in rural India and 285 million live in towns and cities. The urban population is around 30 per cent of the total population.

India's population had grown from 361 million in 1951 to over a billion by 2001. Though the compound annual rate of population growth has declined from 2.1 per cent between 1981-1991 to 1.9 per cent between 1991-2001 to 1.6 in 2004-2005, the population of India is likely to overtake that of China by 2035 when India's population will touch 1.46 billion. Between 1991 and 2001, 182 million people have been added and the population of India in the last census (March 1, 2001) was 1.029 billion. Currently, the age composition of the population is such that 58 per cent are between the age of 15-60 and as pointed out above, India has a relatively young population—a great advantage when the population in Europe and Japan is ageing. But by 2020, people above 60 years of age, will double. This will affect the composition of the workforce and the need for a bigger healthcare industry in the country will arise.

The average Indian's life expectancy has increased from 32 years at the time of Independence to 62.4 years in 1996. This has been due to a decline in death rate, better healthcare and a slowing down of the total fertility rate (measured as TFR—the average number of children born to a woman up to the end of her reproduction period). The TFR was 5.4 in 1988 and it has come down to 4.9 in 1993.

Some states like Bihar, Madhya Pradesh, Uttar Pradesh and Rajasthan have a higher population growth than others. These states also have a lower female literacy rate and lower average age of marriage for girls. These states need to bring down their population growth rate in order to reap the benefits of economic development.

The population explosion has been due to the fact that: (i) people, especially rural families, did not perceive a worsening of their living conditions as a result of an increase in their family size or a rapid growth of the village population; (ii) living conditions in villages improved despite population growth and though per capita availability of land in rural areas declined, people still did not see any danger in having large families; (iii) little use of contraceptives in low income family dwellings where there is hardly any privacy, has been another reason for unwanted births; and (iv) strong preference for boys has led to couples trying to have a boy even after three girls—

perhaps linked with insecurity in old age when they see sons as looking after them and also linked with the requirements of Hindu last rites which only sons can perform.

Indira Gandhi's younger son Sanjay Gandhi, who between 1975-1977 thought that rapid rise in population was one of the main causes for underdevelopment, initiated programmes for family planning that had some element of coersion. His sterlisation campaigns became counterproductive and led to corruption and bribery. There were terrible blunders that were widely publicised. Politicians soon realised that the demand for smaller families has to come from within the families. Nobel Laureate Amartya Sen has been emphasising the importance of female literacy and better healthcare, in the campaign for smaller families. With a rise in female literacy, it has been found that there would be a lower level of infant and child mortality and it could lead to a higher status for women; as a result, a lower fertility rate could be achieved. A higher status for women, through empowerment by education, would lead to women being able to exert a choice in the use of birth control measures. It would lead to a smaller family size and better-cared children. But many have argued that it would take a long time for female literacy to make big advances and India's population growth will continue unabated. Besides, primary education alone cannot empower women in a male dominated society.

Tamil Nadu's example can be followed where a decline in fertility rate was brought about by political support for raising the age of marriage for girls along with a programme for imparting 'information, education and communication' to women and girls.

The Government of India came out with a National Population Policy in 2000 which has many important features. First of all it aims at facilitating the access to contraception, healthcare and, especially, child healthcare. It aims at stabilising the population by 2045 at a level consistent with the requirements of sustainable economic growth, social development and environment protection. It also aims at bringing down the TFR from 4.9 to replacement level by 2010. The replacement level of fertility means that the net reproductive rate is of one or two children per couple and one daughter per mother.

There is no doubt that due to illiteracy, poverty and the general belief that more children, especially sons, are desirable, it would be hard to control the population growth rate in an effective manner in the next few years. The availability and affordability of contraceptives is key to population control. This has to be combined with late marriages for girls. Societal norms, however, are hard to change and early marriages (the average age is 19.4 years), are still widespread. There has to be a conscious, well-orchestrated movement that will help to change people's perception about the size of families and the need to have more sons. Social security measures for the poor that guarantee an income and healthcare in old age would definitely change the perception.

A high population growth rate would have been fine if there was human development alongside for each citizen. Indeed, India's huge population could have been transformed into a big asset if each person was well looked after in terms of job, healthcare and educational facilities. If each person could be granted social security, managing a big population would not be a problem. But with scarce resources, this is not currently feasible.

The pressure of population is adversely affecting the topsoil of farmland and 141 million hectares (43 per cent of total geographical area) of agricultural land in India is acknowledged as highly degraded subject to water and soil erosion (Central Water Commission, June 1996). There are 41 million people waiting to get jobs. The urban infrastructure is overstressed and every public place is overcrowded. There is a hassle in accessing simple things and queues are everywhere to be seen, especially for the lower income groups for accessing even basic amenities. There is a big problem of mounting air and water pollution and solid waste disposal. There are crowds everywhere, specially in marketplaces, which make them an easy target for terrorist attacks. There is absolutely no doubt that the population has to be checked so that every person can enjoy a better standard of life and more fulfillment.

In general, it is only through women's empowerment that there can be a sharp decline in the TFR; only then can women exercise their choices in all aspects of life. Instead of targeting groups of acceptors of family planning methods like IUD for women or sterilisation for men through incentives, the government should instead work on disincentives for having more children. Incentives have in the past led to corruption and mismanagement. Again, better health facilities for women would lower the fertility rate. All pregnancies have to be followed up in a systematic manner by health workers in villages and towns with the sequence of antenatal, intra-natal and post-natal care for both the mother and child. Family planning after the birth of the second child can be introduced to the mother by health workers, especially in rural areas.

Status of Women

The status of women has to change if the population programme of controlling the fertility rate is to succeed. The level of illiteracy among women still remains high, especially in the Hindi belt of Rajasthan, Bihar, Uttar Pradesh and Madhya Pradesh. The female literacy rate in India is only 45 per cent whereas in China it is 87 per cent. In some states like Kerala, female literacy is as high as 60 per cent though the overall literacy level is 58 per cent. In some backward states, it is as low as 20 per cent. Low literacy among women leads to their having a closed mind and believing in superstitions rather than in modern medicine. It also means that women end up by treating their own daughters and daughters-in-law not equal to their sons and discriminate against them. Many of the dowry deaths are brought about by the ill-treatment of women in the family towards young brides.

Low literacy among women has been responsible for the high rate of child mortality—about 15.3 per cent of those born in India may not survive till the age of 4. In fact, there is a positive correlation between the child population in the age group 0-6 and the decline in fertility. In some of the states where family planning has been successful, there has been a fall in the child population between the age of 0-6. In Kerala, Tamil Nadu, Andhra, Karnataka and Gujarat and states with successful family planning programmes, the child population has been reduced from 17.9 per cent to 15 per cent of the population between 1991-2001.

Low literacy of women has also contributed to their being unaware of the nutritional content of food. According to the World Bank, 47 per cent of under five-year olds are underweight compared to 10 per cent in China. Between the period 1990-1992 to 2000-2002, India was able to reduce the number of malnourished children only slightly—from 221 million to 216 million. One-fourth of all the malnourished people in the world live in India.

The low status of women is also reflected in the skewed gender or sex ratio of the country. The gender component is of interest because there are many states in which there are proportionately less women than men per thousand of population. The sex ratio (the number of females to 1000 males) is much better in industrialised countries (higher) and there are more females than males in the population. But the sex ratio in India shows that there are more males than females. There were 945 females/1000 males in 1991 and the ratio declined to 927 females/1000 males in 2001.

There are many reasons why there are more men than women in the Indian population; one of the reasons is female infanticide and general apathy towards the girl child after she is born. Female babies are often not taken to doctors on time, especially in villages, because it is considered a waste of resources. This imbalance in the sex ratio is of great concern and should be corrected. This deficit of women has been prominent in prosperous states like Haryana and Punjab. These states also are the ones in which the preference for sons is more pronounced in terms of boys being the contributors to the family income, providers for parents in old age and getting a big dowry at the time of marriage. A low sex ratio has also been caused by the widespread practice of female foeticide aided through amniocentesis or sex determination tests. Strangely enough, many women themselves agree to such tests and would want to abort female foetus because "only a male child brings them enhanced status."

More than half of India's female population is anaemic and maternal mortality rate is high at 540 per 100,000 as compared to 50 per 100,000 in China. This high rate of maternal mortality is due to neglect of women at childbirth especially in the villages. The village midwife cannot handle complicated pregnancies and the result is death. Girls dying at childbirth is considered to be a hazard about which little is be done. It is part of the general malaise of lack of healthcare at the village level in many parts of the country.

The discrimination against women continues in both towns and villages: girls do not get adequate nourishment in childhood or sent to private fee-paying schools where they could be better educated. Girls are often forced into marriage to boys who are not suitable matches, chosen by the parents and families, and are punished if they refuse. There is discrimination in the rights of ownership and succession. Though women are supposed to have equal property rights, access to property is denied through devious means, including cheating by brothers, uncles and other male members of the family. In freedom of movement taking important decisions and even in matters like dress and age of marriage, women are discriminated against and are not free to choose what they want. Mothers and mothers-in-law, through tyrannical ways, condition the aspirations of young women and make them submissive, compliant and obedient.

In towns and cities, women are discriminated at the workplace and often subjected to sexual harassment and eve teasing. In general, though half the population is women, they continue to have a low status in all matters. As pointed out above, this is especially pronounced in the villages and backward and remote regions. There has been an increase in crime against women in urban areas too and domestic violence and abuse have also risen in recent years all over India.

3

Poverty

A Village Mosaic

Poverty is widespread in many parts of the Indian countryside. Three-fourths of India's poor live in the villages. The poor keep pouring into towns and cities daily in search of work and live in inhuman conditions in the slums of big cities. Why have the villages remained stagnant and why has there been very little change in them in the last 50 years?

Poverty in Indian villages is rather invisible—unlike the slums of big cities. It is evident in many ways, especially in the slow pace of life and the stillness all around with very little activity in sight.

Just take a car ride from Delhi into nearby Haryana or Rajasthan or Uttar Pradesh—all within a short distance from the National Capital. Within an hour you will reach some places where conditions and attitudes have not changed for what seems like centuries. In village India, except for a few signs of modernisation like public phone booths (STD and even internet facilities are often available) and roadside cafes (*dhabas*) with beer and coke or a small bank tucked away somewhere, not much has changed. Many still live in mud huts and do not have any vestige of modern sanitation or drainage in their dwellings. Their houses are bare except for some pots and pans and some storage boxes.

Many of the houses in most villages around the country are not *pucca*. Often, a small part of the house would be built with bricks, and the rest of the place would be made of mud and thatch. Piped water is seldom available inside dwellings and women spend long hours fetching water from village tube wells, and other water sources like tanks and wells. Many villages in West Bengal have common tanks for adjacent dwellings and women wash their utensils and clothes in them. Using such water for cooking and washing affects the health of people and water-borne diseases continue to plague the countryside.

According to the National Full Household Survey II, 1998-99, 32 per cent of households had *pucca* houses at the national level and only one-fifth of households in rural areas were *pucca*. Having *pucca* houses depends on the income levels and the general prosperity of the village; in rich states like Punjab, 77 per cent of the households have *pucca* houses. Around 78 per cent of households at the national level had access to safe drinking water. At the state level, 77 per cent had access to tube wells/hand pumps and 18 per cent to *pucca* wells.

About 60 per cent of the households had access to electricity at the national level; 91 per cent of the population living in urban and 48 per cent of the rural had electricity connections in their houses. About 64 per cent of households had no access to toilets, though in Kerala 85 per cent households had access to toilets. If a visitor wants to go to a toilet in a typical Indian village, it would be hard to find one, especially one which has a door or a tap.

The Scheduled Caste and Tribes (SC/ST) households had even lesser access to all these amenities—electricity, toilets, safe drinking water. In 1991, 28 per cent of the SC and 45 per cent of ST had no amenities at all.

A visitor to the typical village would notice children running around happily but many are thin and quite obviously malnourished. Around half the child population in India is malnourished. Millions of children, especially girls, do not attend schools and instead help their mothers around the house. Many are working as child labour in other people's farms and establishments for small amounts. Many of the women are also malnourished and this affects the weight of the babies born to them. According to doctors, underweight babies do not have normal brain development. Malnourishment and anaemia are two most common ailments afflicting women in India, especially in the villages. It affects their longevity, general health and their ability to work and earn.

The picture of rural India is thus far removed from the throbbing metro cities and their modern urban society. A visitor will be again reminded of the two Indias—one 'modern' and gleaming with 'beautiful people' who seem to have everything in their well furnished, modern homes and the other, 'traditional, backward and poor,' that has stood more or less still in time over the last 50 years.

In some parts of India, amazingly, customs, dress and language have remained unchanged for centuries.

Many women are the main bread earners in villages because farm incomes are small and inadequate. If they go to towns, it is mainly to work as maids and they remain vulnerable to exploitation and abuse. They are also very active in farming. You see women toiling away in the fields but they get much lower wages than their male counterparts. Women are still doing a lot of work in the house that includes bringing water and wood for cooking, looking after the animals in the farm and taking care of the elderly.

Some women are also engaged in trading and go to nearby towns to sell their wares. Often one can see them in handicraft stalls in Delhi and other metro cities bringing in what they make in their spare time at home. One can see how little they are aware of what is in demand because they are repeating their old designs over and over again. Whatever they do, they end up earning very little because of lack of information about the market, capital and even new skills.

In some villages, however, women have become enterprising in seeking work for themselves. For women in some of the villages in West Bengal and Gujarat (which I saw), there were no jobs but they have been enterprising enough to organise themselves in groups, and, together, they have been able to earn a living whether through weaving, growing vegetables, *zari* work or working as farm labour. They are gradually forming self-help groups (SHGs) or joining NGOs like SEWA for bettering their prospects of income generation. Most lack skills and if some NGO imparts skills, offers microcredit and equipment for weaving cloth, women readily join. It is becoming a better deal for most women to engage in some sort of income generating activity than doing unpaid farm work around the year.

Village life centres around the local market and farmers have to take their produce to *mandis* soon after harvesting as many lack proper storage faciltiies. They still bring their produce, fruits and vegetables in bullock carts but in some of the affluent villages, they use tractors. They are not able to get the best prices because they have hardly any capacity to hold their produce and wait for prices to improve and, secondly, because of the middlemen who give them ready cash and buy cheaply from them. These middlemen keep a hefty margin for themselves when they sell the produce in the market. Farmers are also poorly informed of the market trends due to lack of reliable information.

Since most women and some men are semiliterate (they can barely sign their names), they are not able to cope with crop failures even though crop insurance schemes have been started in various villages. They fall victim to any adverse turn in the weather and have to borrow heavily in times of drought. They are unable to save their crops through alternate sources of irrigation. In Andhra Pradesh, farmers borrow to drill tube wells and when even that does not work and they cannot pay back the money, they commit suicide. Attack from pests and diseases, high cost of hybrid seeds and high indebtedness are also reasons why there has been a spate of suicides by farmers in recent times in some states. Lack of proper irrigation plays havoc with the lives of farming families and can perpetuate poverty.

Going inside any one of India's six million villages, one realises that millions of people have been left behind from the recent gains of development and though there are success stories in every village, the change that has been brought about by development policies and globalising forces, is slow and sometimes not obvious at all. The contrast between Indian villages and villages in the west is quite sharp because of the drastically different lifestyle that Indian villages have when compared with city life. In the west, villages are idyllic places with all the amenities of the towns and cities; the well-heeled and rich often decide to reside in villages.

People living in Indian villages are also still steeped deeply in their old ways, superstitions and traditions. Children are still being 'sacrificed' (murdered) on the 'advice' of magicians and practitioners of cults near the capital city of Delhi for propitiating gods. Some villages, specially in one of the backward regions, still have people steeped in superstitions and barbaric rituals from the medieval times.

Mostly it is the lack of modernisation and education that is responsible for this backwardness. Even in the 21st century, 1.24 lakh villages have not been electrified and many are still using kerosene as fuel and for lighting. The poorest are using biomass fuel for cooking which is dangerous for the health of women. There is very little improvement in the health facilities in most villages. This will be discussed below. The roads remain clogged and non-negotiable in the rainy season. There is often only an irregular bus service between the towns and the villages and the growing number of village youth have very little to do. Unemployment is a big cause for migration to urban areas. There are few industries in which young people who have passed high school can find jobs.

Many become school dropouts. Village schools across the country are of poor quality. Yet, down South, in some villages, children can be seen cramming books in order to pass exams; they become software engineers, fulfil the dreams of their parents and many migrate to the US. There is an eagerness to go abroad and earn dollars as many hear of the success stories of village boys making it big in the US.

But most village schools are hardly furnished with books and equipment. There is rarely a proper school structure in many of the villages and teachers are often absent. The degree of neglect is higher in case of schools for *Dalit* children. There is hardly any teaching done as all grades sit together and the dropout rate is high, especially among girls.

The poorest of poor cannot afford proper education for their children and as a result boys and girls who have received only a few years of inadequate education remain unemployable. From generation to generation, they are engaged in the lowest paid occupations because the schools meant for the poor and *Dalits* are the worst in village India in terms of staff and equipment.

Literacy campaigns and skill development along with a better communications network would allow women and the youth to leave their own villages and seek work in the neighbouring towns. If the state governments established more village based industries, it would also help. In changing the scene in rural India, more public investment and an active *panchayat* is required. Better execution of various government programmes meant for the poor can change village life. And wherever there is an active *panchayat*, villages are faring better. There is hope for a faster pace of change and social transformation only with better local level governance and involvement of the local people in designing and implementing poverty alleviation programmes.

Awareness of the outside world, however, is seeping through the villages of India, in some cases very rapidly, in others, very slowly. Hopefully, the realisation, about the outside world will bring about the need and urge for change and modernisation. Big business houses are fast realising the importance of rural markets because the rural population is consuming an increasing proportion of consumer goods. Rural India purchases a sizeable amount of durable products and fast moving consumer goods; various manufacturing companies are finding that the high volume of sales is very lucrative even though the margins may be low. Out of the 3.3 million retail shops in the country, 2.2 million shops are in the villages.

Why So Many Poor?

Returning from an Indian village, a visitor or observer would wonder, "Why has India remained poor for hundreds of years starting from the time of the collapse of the Moghul empire?" Its legendary wealth when it was called the 'Treasury of the World' vanished sometime in the 18th century when the Moghul empire disintegrated. Today in the 21st century, India has quite a few people who are members of the global billionaire's club but the fact remains that around 300 million people are still poor and are living in subhuman conditions, in towns and villages. Their life is one of deprivation, denial of opportunities to better their incomes and life prospects, and continuation of illiteracy, malnutrition and disease.

Backwardness in agriculture, on which a large proportion of the population is still dependent, has been one of the main reasons for widespread poverty. The causes of poverty are usually associated with lack of assets like land, capital and entrepreneurial skills; then there are problems arising from lack of social status and obstacles to social mobility for a large section of the population. It is also associated with rural indebtedness and people who cannot find jobs because they have no education or skills, poor health and large families with few resources between them.

Population pressure has led to the subdivision of land into small parcels and this abundance of tiny holdings has also been responsible for the spread of poverty. Division and subdivision of land has led to small size of agricultural holdings that cannot be used for growing large enough produce for the market. Small cultivators have, thus, become subsistence farmers and many just produce enough for their own consumption. Many small farmers have sold their land to big farmers and have became landless labour. Landless labour forms 47 per cent of the rural poor. Low agricultural productivity has impoverished many medium size farmers also because they use poor inputs and are dependent on the monsoons.

Women-headed households have also receded into poverty more quickly than households headed by men. This is because of the persistence of inequality of wages between men and women in the rural areas and the fact that women are finding it more difficult to gather food and fuel from the dwindling common property resources like pastures and forestland.

People belonging to the SC/ST have also found themselves disadvantaged from birth and there is hardly any way they can move up and better their lives. The number of such disadvantaged persons has been increasing over the years and today they form 80 per cent of the rural poor. They not only lack education facilities and healthcare but also, mainly due to illiteracy, are following archaic customs like child marriage, harassment of brides for dowry and other socially backward and cruel practices against women. They hardly have any land or guaranteed tenancy rights and seem to be in perpetual poverty.

Rural indebtedness is another cause for poverty. This is because the rural population undertakes excessive expenditure on marriages, medical treatment and funerals for which they borrow from local moneylenders. Many rural families are indebted due to illness in the family as they have to seek medical aid in faraway towns. This is because there is hardly any reliable treatment available locally. Borrowing at high rates of interest, the rural poor are reduced to penury because they have to pay back debts and also pay exorbitant interest charges.

The decline in handicrafts has also led to increase in poverty among artisans. Even though there exist, in every village, craft persons who are skilled at carving, weaving, painting, metal or inlay work, they are not earning enough money to pursue their crafts and make their children learn those crafts. They may still be practicing their crafts, but being a craftsperson is no longer a prestigious or paying occupation. Many are on the brink of starvation and have switched to other occupations. The craftsmen and weavers have not been able to upgrade the technology or the quality of the product or designs due to lack of capital and guidance. As a result their costs remain high and their products cannot compete with machine-made products.

Most makers of handicraft items, on their own, have not been able to change with the times in terms of style and marketability, and as their sales have dwindled, more and more people engaged in such crafts are leaving age-old professions. Those still practicing their crafts have become poor.

Handloom cloth that used to be made in the villages is being completely replaced by mill made cloth and synthetic fabrics. A weaver's son is rarely choosing to be a weaver anymore. India's crafts have not adapted to the new lifestyle requirements in towns and cities that are under the impact of globalisation, and have not got fully integrated with big business ventures for domestic consumption and exports. Some ingenious exporters are, however, sourcing their items from villages in specially set up workshops, and giving the artisans design options and raw materials, but such ventures have not spread much. Demand remains small and growth is slow.

This is unfortunate because crafts, which were an essential and integral part of rural economic and cultural life, are fast vanishing and along with them, the tradition of decoration and ornamentation of the home and objects of daily use. They not only provided employment but also enriched local cultural life.

Crafts that were often practiced by women and their products sold in *melas* and *haats*, are dwindling, reducing the incomes of families considerably. The village crafts and cottage industries have remained protected and subsidised because after Independence the government felt that these were a source of employment. Since they were unique in many ways, they needed to be preserved. About 875 items were reserved for cottage and small-scale industries. Exports of handicrafts and handloom cloth were encouraged but, over time, they lacked innovative designs and cost reducing simple technology. Except for those who really love handicrafts and ethnic arts in foreign countries, many find it difficult to blend these items with their interiors. Handicraft and handloom production has remained artisan-based and on a small-scale.

Individual efforts of some persons have helped to promote Indian crafts and the Festival of India in 1985 gave a boost to Indian handicrafts. But without aggressive promotion, their demand is growing quite slowly. Even though handicrafts have been encouraged by various government agencies, and more handicrafts are being exported every year, there is not enough demand to enable them to earn higher and sustainable incomes.

Strangely enough, while Indian village craftsmen themselves have remained poor, their designs have been copied in neighbouring countries. Many in Southeast Asia make elephants and boxes like Indian craftsmen and are selling them in tourist spots. And since they have a much heavier flow of tourist traffic, Indian looking items are being sold in Bangkok. The fine workmanship however gets diluted as such items have got too commercialised and too common. The uniqueness of Indian handicrafts has got lost in the process.

The demand for handcrafted decorative items within India is also declining because globalisation has led to an influx of a number of imported, often 'kitschy', decorative items which are increasingly favoured by the urban middle class. India's urbanised population increasingly seeks to decorate homes with imported knick-knacks instead of ethnic goods. Some handicrafts have actually died like handmade toys and ethnic jewellery. The workers have been absorbed in the unorganised or informal sector in towns.

People are receding into poverty due to lack of non-farm jobs in the villages. They have problems in getting loans from banks as few have collateral support. The poor remain poor because they are not seen as 'bankable'. Only microcredit and SHGs can help them to turnaround.

People engaged in some commercial activities are also not able to go to nearby towns easily to sell their wares because of lack of proper roads connecting villages with towns. If women are engaged in food processing like making pickles and *papads*, they sell them within the village and get very little profit. Lack of proper marketing channels is also responsible for poverty in the rural areas.

Many western observers have remarked that Indians lack the motivation to better their lives and it is one of the reasons why people of India, especially in the villages, have remained poor. People in India, according to them, are 'passive', 'complacent' and 'fatalistic'. But the same Indians, when they go abroad, many straight from the villages, show great enthusiasm for bettering their lives through hard work and enterprise. They accumulate wealth quite rapidly and are as interested in the good things of life as people in their host country.

In many of the prosperous villages in India, there is a distinct desire to move upwards, a growing demand for better education and healthcare facilities. There is a demand for relatively more expensive private education from women for their sons in nearby towns, especially those who are making a decent living through trading or some other jobs in the village. Thus, there are signs that they could easily be motivated to improve their lifestyle and quality of life, specially the lives of their children. But all depends on the availability of jobs and income generating activities in the villages. Many of the rural poor, who have special skills, have tried to set up clusters in which many workers are located in small workshops and use common infrastructural facilities. Studies have found that clusters of artisan based industries, when encouraged by the state governments, can generate a large number of jobs and much higher incomes e.g., Gujarat's diamond cutting industry or the Tirupur garment industry. They can help a big core industry and grow around it.

Indians who have migrated abroad from villages have shown entrepreneurial skills and have built, in quite a few cases, large empires starting from scratch. In India, it is mainly due to lack of equal opportunity that people with inherent entrepreneurial qualities have not been able to use their talents. The general lack of managerial skills is also responsible for the large number of failed ventures in villages which has forced many to remain poor. In general, the causes of poverty can be found mainly in the villages and it is by transforming Indian villages completely that poverty can be reduced. Fortunately, there are sparks of change that can be seen in some villages. How to modernise all the remote and backward villages, however, will remain the biggest challenge for any government at the Centre in years to come.

Measurement of Poverty—Rural and Urban

Economists have tried to measure the extent of poverty in the country since the 1950s on the basis of interviews with rural and urban poor. In fact, their calculations of poverty ratios give us important benchmarks regarding the progress of economic reforms. If there is a decline in poverty, it means that people are benefiting from the economic reforms initiated since 1991. It also gives us an idea of the number of people below the poverty line which is defined in terms of a threshold of income and consumption expenditure as well as caloric intake. The Planning Commission appointed an Expert Group under the chairmanship of Prof. D.T. Lakdawala in 1993. It defined the 'base' line as comprising of a monthly per capita expenditure of Rs. 49 for rural and Rs. 57 for urban at the all-India level, at 1973-74 prices. People living below that level of income were considered the real poor. In terms of daily per capita intake of calories, a person who was below the poverty line consumed less than 2400 calories in rural areas. The National Sample Survey defined the 'base' line as Rs. 211 for rural areas and Rs. 454 for urban areas in 1999-2000 and base caloric intake has been taken as 2250 calories per day.

The Planning Commission has been estimating the incidence of poverty at the national and state level. Using the methodology given by an Expert Group on Estimation of Proportions and Numbers of Poor (Lakdawala Committee), poverty ratios—the percentage of poor in the total population have been calculated. The methodology was applied to consumer expenditure data collected from large sample surveys conducted by the National Sample Survey Organsation (NSSO) at an interval of approximately five years between 1973-74 to 1999-2000.

Villagers were asked to recall their consumption expenditure in the last 30 days on various consumer items including clothing, food, tobacco, education, etc. On the basis of the data on consumption expenditure, the NSSO has found that the poverty ratio in 1999-2000 was at 27.09 per cent in rural areas and 23.6 per cent in urban areas. The incidence of poverty is expressed as a percentage of people living below the poverty line.

According to the latest poverty ratio figures, there has been a steady decline of poverty from 55 per cent in 1973-74 to 36 per cent in 1993-94 and to 26 per cent in 1999-2000.

It is also important to note that between 1973-1993, the number of poor remained stable at 320 million due to the fast growth in population that more or less neutralised the gains from development. The number of poor below the poverty line came down to 260 million out of a total population of 990 million in 2000. Thus, there has been a steady decline in the number of poor but in absolute terms, the number is still very large.

Naturally, for a vast country like India, there are different poverty ratios for different states in accordance with the level of development. For relatively richer or forward states, the poverty ratio would be lower than in the backward or less developed states. The rural poverty ratio has been found to be high in Orissa, Bihar, the North Eastern States and Uttar Pradesh. The urban poverty ratios were between 30 to 42.8 per cent in these states in 1999-2000. The poorest states are Bihar and Orissa; the combined rural and urban poor make for a high poverty ratio of 42.6 per cent in Bihar and 47 per cent in Orissa. There has been a significant reduction in poverty in Kerala, Jammu and Kashmir, Goa, Delhi, Andhra Pradesh, Gujarat, Tamil Nadu and West Bengal. Punjab and Haryana have reduced poverty through faster agricultural growth, Kerala has reduced poverty through human development and West Bengal has managed to do the same through land reforms and empowerment of the *panchayats*. In Andhra Pradesh, the state has intervened in the distribution of food grains to benefit the poor.

There is some controversy about the poverty ratios and some economists have questioned the change in the 'recall' period between the early times and in the recent rounds of data collection based on consumption expenditure. If a shorter period is used, the poverty figures turn out to be lower than if a 365-day recall period is used. In the early 1950s, till the 35th Round of NSSO, a 365-day recall period had been used.

In any case, even though there may be controversy surrounding the exact number of poor—which is very hard to ascertain—there is no denying the fact that much of India's affluence today has large circles of poverty surrounding it. This is most disturbing and even though empowering the poor has been tried out for decades through a multitude of poverty alleviation programmes, the poverty ratios are still high for many states. The poverty ratio cannot be reduced to zero because even the richest countries have pockets of extreme poverty. But the numbers do not add up to millions of people as is the case of India.

Poverty Alleviation Programmes for the Poor

Since employment creation is a sure way of absorbing the poor and reducing poverty, various centrally sponsored schemes have been in operation since the 1970s, when Indira Gandhi came up with her famous *"Garibi Hatao"* slogan. There have been and there still are many drawbacks of these schemes because of poor administration and the top-down approach that they invariably follow. Many beneficiaries are not out of poverty because the income generating assets that they collect from these schemes are sold almost immediately in the market for meeting their consumption expenditure. Sustained effort at training youth and women would go a long way in giving them regular income and employment.

In the 1980s, some poverty alleviation schemes were started like the Integrated Rural Development Programme, National Rural Employment Programme, Rural Landless Employment Guarantee Programme, Jawahar Rozgar Yojana, Employment Assurance Scheme, and Development of Women and Children in Rural Area (DWKRA).

New schemes have been devised in recent years, after the reforms were started, to help the rural poor and according to the Economic Survey 2004-05, rural housing would be undertaken under Valmiki Ambedkar Awas Yojna and Indira Awaas Yojna. Self-employment in rural and urban areas has been encouraged through the Prime Minister's Rozgar Yojana, Rural Employment Generation Programme, and Swarna Jayanti Shahari Rozgar Yojna. Wage employment has been assured though the National Food for Work Programme and Sampoorna Grameen Rozgar Yojana.

Basic services would be launched through Pradhan Mantri Gramodaya Yojana. Food distribution to the poor would be through the Antyodaya Anna Yojana and drought relief would be given through the Drought Prone Area Programme and Integrated Wastelands Development Programme. Rural connectivity would be provided through the Pradhan Mantri Gram Sadak Yojana. Credit needs of the poor would be looked after by the Swaranjayanti Gram Swarozgar Yojana.

Since 1951, the poverty ratio in the country has indeed gone down. The Green Revolution and the growth of the manufacturing sector are responsible for this but the role of the poverty alleviation programmes has also been important throughout. They could have been better implemented but they produced some clear benefits nevertheless. To reduce poverty in a significant manner, there is need for land reforms and assured tenancy rights for sharecroppers also. Better education opportunities and healthcare for the poor would empower them to find suitable jobs. Access to easier credit would reduce their debt burden and enable them to undertake business ventures. Basically, increase in employment opportunities for both men and women would be the best antidote to poverty. It is a big challenge for India to promote inclusive development that aims at drastic poverty reduction.

Growth will also reduce poverty through the trickle down effect. This will be taken up later.

4

Urbanisation

For many of the poor from the countryside, there is no option but to leave their hearth and home and seek jobs in cities and towns. This has resulted in a huge migratory flow outwards from villages. India's urbanisation pattern has been very rapid in recent years though it is still not one of the fastest in the world. Urbanisation usually accompanies economic transformation from an agrarian pattern of production to an industrialised pattern. But cities and towns have to grow to cope with it because as millions of migrants arrive, there is tremendous pressure on the infrastructure. Most migrants are always in search of jobs though some come for begging and scavenging. Since they arrive in big cities without much money, they end up living on pavements, slums and shanty towns which have sprung up all across big metro cities in India. In recent years, the rapid pace of migration has led to an increase in urban poverty.

The extent of urbanisation can be judged from the rise in urban population. It was only 17.3 per cent of the total population in 1951 and it has increased to 27.8 per cent in 2002. Of around 30 per cent of the country's population that lives in cities and towns, two-thirds of the urban population or 75 million people live in slums. Nearly half of the urban households are one room apartments only. Migrants go to modern cities like Bangalore in great numbers and service the new affluent sectors. About 20 per cent of the population of Bangalore lives in slums.

Contrast this growth of shanty towns with the mushrooming of huge farmhouses on the outskirts of big cities like Delhi where lavish parties are held for the urban elite and the rich. The glossy magazines are often full of stories about these parties in which all the well heeled, smart set want to be included. But the exclusion of millions from the high lifestyle is worrisome. People in slums see what is going on in their neighbourhood and are full of resentment and envy.

It has led to a rise in crime in big cities and contrasting lifestyles have fuelled extremist political movements in different parts of the country.

India has the second largest urban population in the world (307 million) and more than two-thirds of the urban population lives in urban agglomerations with a population greater than one million. There has been a steep growth in the number of people living in metro cities due to the bigger scope for commercial activities and an increase in job opportunities.

In the past, urbanisation has been marked by the influx of refugees from Pakistan with their settlements primarily in the urban areas of northern India; building of new administrative cities like Chandigarh and Bhubaneshwar, construction of new industrial townships near major cities, rapid growth of metro cities and a decline in small towns. As a result of all these changes in the last five decades, there has been a massive increase in shanty towns and slums in the metro cities, and the emergence of an urban-rural fringe.

From among the slum dwellers, many children and women take to begging and rag picking. Foreigners are aghast to see people in big cities move about ignoring semi-clad, often deformed beggars. Sometimes people toss coins at them from cars and, more often than not, shoo them off. But most Indians have got used to these daily sights and regard the same faces turning up at their car windows with indifference. Most people regard able-bodied beggars with disdain because there are organised gangs who beg and steal; children are made to knock on windows of Mercedes or BMWs to beg. But there may also be those who are genuinely poor, who tried but could not find work for lack of skills and education.

Even though the squalor of urban slums is quite shocking, the availability of electricity, safe drinking water and toilet facilities to low income households in India is much greater than in rural areas. But there is increase in noise and air pollution and problems of solid waste disposal and sewerage that are unique to urban India. There is an acute shortage of low cost housing in Mumbai and almost half of the population is made up of either slum dwellers and the homeless who are occupying six per cent of the city's land. About 60 per cent of the *chawls* and huts are one room units.

In the whole of India 20 to 25 per cent of the urban households in the country are in slums, refugee colonies and squatter settlements. Over 35 million people needed housing in the 1990s out of which only about 7 million have been covered so far by the various schemes under the Five Year plans. The urban landscape however is heavily centred around posh colonies as in Delhi in which many five-star hotels and exclusive clubs are located. When you go to a five-star hotel in New Delhi—to one of the clubs on the roof top—you can easily mistake it for one located in some rich western country and not in India. Every item in their well-decorated interiors is carefully chosen to compete with the best clubs in the world. Only the waiters are Indian. Foreigners who come from airports in tinted glass limousines and check into one of these hotels would never be able to guess that India is a country with so much poverty and deprivation. They see the recently acquired posh face of India and tall buildings of steel and glass and the 'swish' set in hotel lobbies. Perhaps it is a good thing that they see only glamour and style because if they were to see the wretched conditions in which millions of the urban poor live, they would not be inclined to bring new investment for fear of a possible political upheaval.

Urbanisation is however conducive to modernisation and change of archaic attitudes and superstitions because through the large concentration of population, various prejudices and caste barriers can be broken. There can be greater scope for communication and interaction between different communities in India and the participation of people of all sections in the economic development of the country can take place more easily. There is, however, an urgent need for both rural industrialisation and urban planning. Rural industrialisation will increase rural employment through agro-based industries and food processing factories and this may stem the flow of migration to towns. Urban planning will have to take care of the infrastructural problems involving the Centre, the States and the NGOs. There has to be systematic upgradation of energy, infrastructure, and the communications network in order to have better cities. The involvement of the private sector and the local user groups is also very important.

Unfortunately, urban poverty is more glaring and though people in the cities may have more amenities, the urban poor are living in extremely stressful conditions. In Delhi alone, with its 13 million population, there are 1,500 shanty colonies that house over 3 million people. And the average population density in a shanty town is 300,000 persons per square kilometre. One water pump, on average, serves 1000 persons. Many of the slums do not have latrine facilities and in some areas that have latrines, one latrine serves 27 households.

Rapid urbanisation has brought about an increase in child labour as migrant parents are unable to get children admitted to local schools. They often lack a permanent address which goes against the children's admission in schools. There are around 40,000 child labourers in Delhi and 100,000 children as part-time or full-time domestic helps. They are involved in strenuous work like stone breaking or arduous jobs like working as cleaners in motor workshops or restaurants. About 75 per cent of the men and 90 per cent of the women in the shanty towns are illiterate.

Apart from the rapid growth of slums, urbanisation has led to traffic congestion, water shortage and power cuts. Due to excessive demand for basic amenities, the urban infrastructure is feeling the strain. Power is often stolen by the rich and the poor alike, leading to shortages in the summer months. Even privatisation of distribution of power has not helped in any way.

One of the ways out from the distressing contrasts between rural and urban population is to have PURA model that involves Providing Urban Amenities in Rural Areas. The flow of migrants would definitely be abated if there were more job opportunities in villages.

A number of villages can be linked with a network of roads and all the villages in a particular cluster could have a common ring road around it so that each village has access to it. Besides roads, provision of electricity and transport facilities as well as banks and training facilities, would also have to be included.

Basically, if jobs and amenities could be available in the villages, few would be tempted to come out to the urban areas by the trainloads everyday and live a deprived life which is without human dignity. Everyone is more comfortable on his or her own home ground. If transportation can be improved, commuting to work would increase instead of migration.

The PURA idea has come from the President of India, Abdul Kalam, who has said that PURA is one of the mechanisms which could be utilised for making our villages into productive economic zones. It will, however, need a huge amount of investment which has to come mainly from the central and state governments. The Centre's allocation of Rs. 3 crore for each cluster development may not be sufficient. Since not much private sector involvement may be expected, it is the state governments that would have to supplement the financial needs and undertake to develop the PURA model. Along with improvement in physical infrastructure, the social infrastructure has to be improved to make the village population stable and more self-sufficient.

5

Colonial Legacy

When the British left in 1947, India was largely an agricultural nation with pockets of legendary wealth concentrated among a number of feudal rulers and it had an educated layer of Indian civil servants who ran a big bureaucracy. On the industrial side, there were a small number of private capitalists and business leaders in traditional industries like cotton textiles and jute. Coal mining got a fillip because of an increase in demand from mills for coal generated power. Indian industries were started after World War I during the Great Depression of the 1930s when protection against imports was allowed after much debate and deliberation in the British Parliament.

But in the 18th and early 19th centuries, the de-industrialisation of Indian industry had taken place through a vigorous promotion of British manufactures in Indian markets, and this led to the loss of livelihood of many rural artisans and handicraft workers. Even though India's craftsmanship was famous in the past, village artisans and weavers could not stand the competition from machine-made goods and, consequently, there began a decline of crafts as machine-made cloth gradually came to replace the traditional handloom cloth.

The East India Company had started out by trading in Indian goods like muslin, calico, chintz, silk, indigo and spices. British imports originating from East India Company increased from 1.5 million pound sterling in 1750-51 to 5.8 million pound sterling in 1797. Indian textiles were the rage in Britain. But by 1800, England was on the threshold of completing a revolution in the cotton textile industry. Instead of importing cotton piece goods from India, the British rulers wanted to make India a major market for its textile manufactures. Thus, curiously, British rulers followed a policy of *laissez-faire* till the middle of the 19th century in order to allow the imports of British goods to come in freely to India but did not encourage its exports of cotton textiles. From an exporter of fine textiles, *shawls* and handcrafted luxury goods, India began to import British goods. The high customs duty levied on Indian textile imports into England facilitated the Industrial Revolution as well as, acted as a deterrent to their growth in India. India was encouraged to supply raw silk and jute. Britain imported cotton mainly from America because the short staple cotton from India was not suitable for mill-made cloth produced in British mills.

There was a switch to growing commercial crops like indigo, jute and opium and better quality, irrigated land was diverted from food to commercial crops. The switch to commercial crop farming, however, did not lead to capital-intensive farming with improved technology and higher quality inputs. But from the second half of the 19th century, commercial farming of cotton and jute led to the gradual development of modern industry in India. Cotton, tea and jute industries were established and at the time of Independence, other industries like cement, paper and sugar also developed.

Thus, after the British government took over from the East India Company in 1858, the tables were completely turned and India was encouraged to become a provider of agricultural goods like food grains and raw materials only. This pattern of exports continued till Independence and between 1935-1939, food, drinks, tobacco and raw materials constituted 68.5 per cent of Indian exports and manufactured goods constituted 64.4 per cent of imports.

The decline of handicrafts and handlooms during the period of free trade had an adverse impact on the village economy and its self-sufficient nature as many involved in the traditional crafts lost their livelihood and fell back on agriculture. They had no alternatives available like migrating to towns because there was no industrial revolution taking place and towns could not absorb surplus labour like in Britain.

Agriculture was also not helped by the new tenurial system of Permanent Settlement introduced by the British as it promoted absentee landlordism and rack-renting. Wherever there was *zamindari* system, the landlords who were given the ownership rights extracted higher and higher land revenues that left very little surplus with the peasants. The *zamindars* spent virtually nothing on the development of agriculture and their exploitation of farmers led the latter to fall into the clutches of moneylenders. Landlords controlled 70 per cent of the land along with the moneylenders and the colonial state appropriated more than half of the total agricultural production.

Many farmers sold off their land and became landless labour. By 1931, the proportion of population dependent on agriculture increased to 72 per cent. The *zamindari* and *ryotwari* system ultimately led to the creation of a huge number of subsistence farmers who became part of the impoverished peasantry.

For most of the colonial period, landlessness had been rising; the number of landless agricultural labour grew from 13 per cent of the agricultural population in 1871 to 28 per cent in 1951. Increase in tenant farming and sharecropping and overcrowding of agriculture was followed by frequent subdivision of land into small-size holdings. Fragmentation of land into non-contiguous parcels led to low productivity that made farmers recede into subsistence farming.

The colonial state's interest was to collect land revenue and to spend as little as possible on improving agriculture. There was very little investment in irrigation and rural roads. The lack of purchasing power in the hands of rural people, at times of monsoon failure, led to high food prices and famines. There were several famines during the British period and the last was in 1943 in which, officially, 1.5 million died. But parallel estimates of the number of dead in the Bengal famine were put around 3.5 million. Enquiries revealed that the famine was created by hoarding and speculation that led to an artificial rise in food prices which people without any purchasing power or cash could not afford. Secondly, the severeness of famine could have been curtailed had the government stopped exporting food grains during the lean years.

It was during the British times that the rural population was not made the focus of development and their needs were neglected. No design for agricultural development was introduced in a consistent manner and industrialisation was postponed till very late.

Britain's own industrial revolution, however, flourished as its larger capacities got ready supply of raw materials from India and a huge market awaited their finished goods. Indian industries, on the other hand, were handicapped through lack of experience in management of joint stock companies and lack of financial institutions. British managing agents took over the task of managing the new industries and took away as commission a large share of the profits. India also did not experience rapid industrialisation because it lacked a capital goods industry. It imported all its machinery from England. Whatever industrialisation took place, it was not uniform and it was confined only to certain parts of the country like Bombay, Calcutta and Ahmedabad.

The British, instead of investing the surplus revenue in India, transported it back as home charges. For the first time India's rulers were sending back money to the 'home' country. The other conquerors had always stayed back and ruled from within the country or they plundered and left. But a very large part of India's economic surplus was appropriated by the colonial state and a very small part was spent on the development of agriculture and industry, social infrastructure or on nation-building activities such as education, sanitation, health.

The British did help to establish an administrative network and also laid out railways with imported equipment. It connected all corners of India but it was mainly meant to facilitate the export and import of goods. India, in any case, was underdeveloped, agrarian, primitive as far as the development of capitalist form of production was concerned, and so was unprepared for industrialisation according to some economic historians but all evidence suggests that it had the potential of becoming an industrialised nation alongside the developments that were taking place in other Western nations. But without adequate investment in infrastructure, health and education, banking, technology, it remained laggard in many ways and became only a trading nation.

The rapid growth in population had already led to a large number of poor in rural areas at the time of Partition. The majority of people were without education and proper healthcare and the country lacked a well functioning infrastructure.

The *rajas* and *maharajas* were patrons of the 'arts' and 'builders' of magnificent palaces during British times but did not help their subjects to get educated and there were few job opportunities in their stagnant agrarian states. Many allied themselves with the British and got protection. But native rulers, on the whole, were busy accumulating personal wealth that was based on the exploitation of the poor farmers.

The British, thus, left behind a technologically backward agriculture with hardly any innovations and agricultural growth declined to 0.72 per cent per year during 1911-1941. Industries remained underdeveloped because even the railways did not have backward linkages with any indigenous suppliers and it only encouraged steel and machine making industries in Britain. It was only after World War I that several consumer industries started. The multinational companies also made an entry into India after 1918 but the growth of foreign capital was slower than the growth of Indian capital.

The Nationalist Movement that started around the end of 19th century emphasised the development of the heavy capital goods sector. Several indigenous entrepreneurs emerged and demanded protection from cheap imports. This was the origin of the Bombay Club. The Nationalists opposed the entry of foreign capital and they wanted to prohibit by law foreign ownership, management and control over key areas of the economy.

It was from the pre-Independence era that state ownership of large-scale industries was stressed and Pandit Jawaharlal Nehru, in his memorandum of June 1939 to the National Planning Committee, laid down the ideal of the Congress and foundation of 'our plan', which was not socialism but the creation of an egalitarian society in which all citizens had equal opportunities and a civilised standard of life.

6

Agriculture

Through the ages, India has been primarily an agricultural country and in 1947, about 70 per cent of the population was dependent on agriculture. Though Nehru laid emphasis on agriculture in the First Five-year Plan, subsequently, agriculture has relatively been neglected. The lack of modernisation and low productivity of Indian agriculture over the years have finally surfaced clearly before the government as the main obstacles towards achieving a higher rate of economic growth. Rapid agricultural growth would make the per capita income of 235 million people dependent on agriculture higher; and it is because of the backwardness of agriculture that rural India has remained more or less unchanged.

As pointed out above, most of India's poor live in the villages and no government at the Centre so far in the last four decades has made agriculture its main focus, though every government has highlighted its importance and promised to increase agricultural productivity.

Agriculture has continued to be the biggest source of employment in the country and it is the provider of wage goods, in the form of food grains, for the country's labour force. Every leader so far has realised agriculture's potential for controlling inflation because food prices are the main items of importance in the calculation of the consumer price index. If food prices rise, all prices rise alongside. But still, scant and uneven attention has been paid to the rapid development of agriculture since Colonial times.

Due to continued stagnation and backwardness of agriculture during British rule, India had many devastating famines. And, unlike in the industrialised countries, there was no agrarian revolution preceding industrialisation in India. The agrarian revolution preceded the Industrial Revolution in Britain and agriculture supplied labour and capital for the factories in Britain. In most other rich nations, it was agriculture that transformed the economy first, giving the process of industrial development a firm base that generated a demand for industrial goods.

In India, since agriculture remained underdeveloped, farmers' incomes remained low and they had to borrow for meeting various needs. Even in rich agricultural areas, small farmers have been burdened by debt and lack of innovative practices and the result has been low agricultural productivity. The poverty in the countryside evident even today in the 21st century (as discussed above) is also a legacy of the past when the British rulers used India as a supplier of raw materials and foodstuffs for export to Britain. As a result of continued neglect, the crop yields hardly rose between 1911-1941. High rates of land revenue further robbed farmers of money that they could have spent on farms.

But since 1951, efforts have been made to introduce certain changes to modernise agriculture, at least partially. Yet the rate of agricultural growth has not been spectacular. From 1949-50 to 1973-74 agriculture grew at 2.7 per cent. However food crop production halved from 3.2 per cent per annum in the 1980s to 1.7 per cent in the 1990s. During 2000-01, agricultural growth dipped to 0.9 per cent per annum. In 2002-03, it was negative and in 2003-04, it was suddenly high at 9.6 per cent because of the low base line figure of the previous year and also due to good monsoons. But in 2004-05, again agricultural growth remained modest at 1.1 per cent. The long-term growth of agriculture has been 1.6 per cent between 1970 and 2000.

Imports of foodgrains were required between 1950-1965, because while demand for foodgrains increased at 3 per cent, foodgrain production increased at 2.4 per cent per annum. There was a severe drought in 1964-65 and food production did not grow fast enough to meet the demand and food imports continued till 1974-1976. After 1974, however, there was a policy turnaround and a new food policy was announced in which the state was to procure wheat from the farmers through the Food Corporation of India. Wheat procurement prices were announced as well as the 'issue price' (the sale price) by the government at every cropping season.

The 1970s saw some drastic changes and the Green Revolution was started by introducing high yielding varieties (HYV) of wheat.

1970-71 was the golden year of the Green Revolution which included the use of better seeds, more water availability through the use of pumps, fertilisers and pesticides. But it covered only one-fifth of the total cropped area. Some states like Punjab and Haryana benefited and productivity increased but, in many states, stagnation in production continued through the 1980s. Also, the bigger farmers benefited more than the small farmers as they took advantage of all the subsidies and inputs, including pumps.

The area under wheat increased by 92 per cent between 1965-2002 while the area under rice increased only by 22 per cent. Overall, the picture changed slowly: from a food importing nation, India emerged as a food exporting nation with huge food stocks with the Food Corporation of India by the 1990s. It was not a mean achievement for a country which was the world's second largest importer of food in 1966! The closing food stocks reached 65 million tonnes in 2002 but were reduced to 40 million tonnes in May 2003 and to 22 million tonnes in November 2003 due to higher domestic offtake through the Public Distribution System (PDS) and release to the market due to drought conditions. About 10 million tonnes were also exported. Again, by 2005-06, India has started importing wheat.

Since Independence, the overall average rate of agricultural growth did not keep pace with population growth. While the Indian population has grown at around 2.2 per cent over the last four decades, agricultural growth has been much slower, at an average of around 2 per cent. There has also been a slight change in the cropping pattern (diversion to non-food crops) and while foodgrain production still remains important and 75 per cent of the land is under food crops, commercial crops have also become prominent. The biggest increase has been in potato production. Between 1951-2004, there has been a 300 per cent increase in potato production.

Wheat and rice still remain the main crops because farmers are guaranteed minimum support prices (MSP) that is attractive because it offers them the security of the produce getting lifted. Millions of farmers have stuck to the safe option of producing wheat and rice. As a result, there has been a problem of having too much stock of wheat and rice because of the big increase in production. Moreover, political lobbies try and hike procurement prices every year. But in other types of crops like oilseeds and pulses, India is not self-sufficient. Even in rice and wheat, productivity per hectare is pretty low as compared to India's competitors. There is an urgent need for diversification of crops, especially towards the production of coarse crops, requiring less water, as they are in demand from the poorer sections of the rural population. There can also be diversification to horticultural crops and commercial crops.

Unfortunately, many problems in agriculture still remain unresolved. One main problem has been the slow pace of land reforms. These aim at providing security of tenure, fixing of rents at reasonable levels and conferring ownership to tenants. But since agriculture is a state subject, only a few states have carried out land reforms while others have done nothing much. The lack of progress in land reforms front has resulted in a huge number of small land-holdings, compounded by the continued subdivision and fragmentation of land between family members. The average size is less than two hectares or five acres. It is because of the lack of alternative job opportunities and population pressure that too many people are still dependent on agriculture and this has resulted in a very high land to man ratio that leads to lower productivity; too many people are working on small parcels of land that are uneconomic in size.

The slow application of agricultural innovative practices is another problem. Agriculture is a highly competitive field and modern scientific knowledge is constantly being applied to it in rich countries. The lack of education among farmers, and belief in age-old agricultural practices and superstitions, has led to a closed mind in general. Farmers are reluctant to use better seeds, fertilisers or farm implements, sometimes due to lack of knowledge and unwillingness to take risks. Agricultural research, though developed over the years in a growing number of universities, has not been adequately applied to farms for enhancing productivity. All this has led to low profitability of agriculture as the latest discoveries in tissue culture, biotechnology and high value crop production, are not much known to the Indian farmers.

Instead of farmers getting richer over time as in the US, there are many who have become 'subsistence farmers' in recent years. Due to subdivision of land and low productivity, they can barely subsist on what they grow. Irrigation is one of the main problems in agriculture. Many projects were started soon after Independence with great gusto and the quantum of irrigated land has increased three-fold. But 63 per cent of the agricultural land is rainfed and is dependent on monsoons. If the rains fail or are below normal, the farmers hardly have any alternative source of irrigation. Successive droughts, though not occurring uniformly all over the country at the same time, have also played havoc as also has the distribution of food and relief to the drought stricken areas. Drought relief has not been free from corruption either.

Agricultural production from rainfed land contributes to 45 per cent of the agricultural production and though irrigation canals have been dug in the drought prone areas in recent years, it is still the scarcity of regular water supply in the fields that has been one of the main causes of low productivity in India. The Green Revolution also bypassed these rainfed areas. As a result, vast tracks are without irrigation facilities and as one travels across many of the states, what is striking is the aridity of land.

Around 78 per cent of the available potential for irrigating 81.4 million hectares from minor irrigation sources (consisting predominantly of groundwater resources), has been exploited already. Further progress towards the exploitation of the remaining potential depends on the availability of electric pumps, especially in the eastern region, where there is considerable amount of unexploited groundwater resource. In any case, water use efficiency in India is very low and water conservation and its proper use is called for.

Just as drought is a problem in some parts of India, excessive rainfall is a problem in others. Floods also destroy crops and water-logging is a problem in some states.

Another problem is the inefficient use of natural resources and degradation of land. Heavy tilling of soil due to population pressure has adversely affected the top soil of the farm land. Today, over 110 million hectares of agricultural land in India is regarded as 'degraded'. Farmers are also not able to switch to better paying crops because of the low quality of inputs like seeds, fertilisers and the degraded quality of soil. As a result of the government's policy of heavily subsidising urea, there have been problems of soil erosion and even groundwater poisoning. Too much urea use can lead to an imbalance in the soil nutrients. For best results, a balance of all three nutrients (Nitrogen Phosphate Potassium—NPK) is needed. Pottassic fertilisers are mostly imported and therefore costly for farmers. After years of neglect, the government is now encouraging the use of more pottassic fertilisers and less urea. The price of urea has been raised to discourage excessive use.

One big problem in recent years has been pest attacks that have led to the destruction of entire crops. The use of pesticides has not always been successful. There have been many suicides among farmers because of spurious pesticides which led to crop failures and indebtedness. A comprehensive and easily accessible crop insurance system has not been developed though it has been talked about for a long time. Often the poorer farmers resort to low value agriculture which means growing produce that has very little market value but is easy to grow. The persistence of poverty in many cases is due to the fact that many small farmers continue to produce low value agriculture from which they earn very little.

Proper inputs like fertilisers that have balanced nutrients required for the soil (NPK), high quality seeds and regular watering can bring about a great change in the productivity of land. Rural infrastructure like a network of roads is also of importance because farmers can then take their produce to bigger towns and if they can hold on to their produce through proper storage facilities, they can get better prices. But, instead of providing better infrastructure through fresh investment, more subsidies have been provided by the government to poor farmers in the form of cheap food and fertilisers that, in any case, never reach them fully.

Rising input subsidies is a problem for the government and it is essential to involve panchayati raj institutions to charge and collect water and electricity charges from farmers on the basis of actual consumption. Where it is not possible to use volumetric pricing, farmers could be charged a flat rate, though care has to be taken that there is no misuse.

On account of various problems related to higher costs of production and low price realisation, more and more farmers have had to sell their land in recent years and join the ranks of casual farm labour. Some have become labourers doing odd jobs to eke out a living. Unfortunately, even the wages of farm labour have been declining. The government has tried to help such farm and non-farm labour by imparting skills through various employment generation schemes so that they could become self-employed. But many loopholes have surfaced over time that have allowed the non-poor to take advantage of the programmes and to collect assets like buffaloes and sewing machines which they later sell for cash. The failure of the government's centrally sponsored schemes has been due to the fact that it did not involve the local people and officials who are familiar with the local conditions and could take decisions about what jobs could be created. Little effort was made at involving key people who would know the needs, resources and skills of the local population.

Though different governments have been in power at the Centre over the last five decades, no government has felt secure enough to introduce drastic changes in agriculture and take tough decisions because the agricultural lobby comprising rich farmers is very strong. The government was expected to be a provider of a social safety net for poor farmers and, more importantly, was to make access to credit easier.

The Congress government, which remained in power for years, played a paternalistic role instead of providing leadership and encouraging people's own initiative in promoting rural development. What is required is a participatory approach that takes the help of local NGOs and the private sector to organise change in the rural structure in order to make it more efficient.

The main problem continues to be the fall in public investment in agriculture in the post-economic reform period (after 1991) that has prevented the government from undertaking a thorough modernisation and upgradation of rural infrastructure. Private investment did rise but could not fill the gap created by the massive cut in public investment, especially in the area of irrigation. As a result, the gross irrigated area that increased at the rate of 2.5 million hectares per annum during the 1970s and the 1980s, came down to less than a million hectares per annum. Since 1991, on the whole, it has impacted on long-term agricultural growth which rose only by 1.6 per cent between 1970 to 2000.

Even so, in absolute numbers, more people are involved in agriculture than before (235 million in 2001) though as a percentage the workforce dependent on it has declined. A fall in government investment has meant that the basic maintenance of rural infrastructure—canals and roads—has not been properly carried out. More investment in rural roads, canals, market and storage spaces, would have raised agricultural productivity in the 1990s.

Regular jobs in road building and other infrastructural activity as well as village industries would have benefited the rural poor. Building of roads was neglected for years. Even when various projects were started, many hurdles cropped up regarding acquisition of land on which the roads would be built. Bureaucratic red tape and corruption have taken their own toll on the progress of road projects as a result of which the roads to the interiors have not been constructed; or where they exist, they are poorly maintained.

There are other reasons for low realisation of prices by farmers. These are due to various internal controls on commodity movement within the country. A number of restrictions exist on processing of commodities and their movement and there are legal impediments to the entry of big private sector companies in agricultural marketing and agro-processing, including the processing of groundnuts and mustard oilseeds which are reserved for the small-scale sector.

Liberalisation of these sectors could lead to major private and foreign investment initiatives that would facilitate high value addition in agriculture and vertical integration between farmers, processors and retailers. Contract farming in which the farmers enter into a contract with a food processing company to produce a specified crop, would also lead to higher value from the produce being realised by farmers. Indian agriculture needs diversification but farmers are afraid of taking new type of risks. The private sector's involvement in agro-processing and contract farming would open up opportunities for sharing risks with farmers. The huge potential of increasing agricultural exports could be exploited and large-scale processing would help farmers abide by the WTO food hygiene norms more easily. Cold storage facilities and refrigerated trucks could save a lot of the perishable products produced in the farms.

Private sector research in horticultural products is also needed in the face of a very low (0.3 per cent of agricultural GDP) amount being spent by the government on research and education. There is also a need for extensive research in post-harvest technology which is essential for promoting value-addition to products. Thus, there is an urgent need for enhancing public investment that would facilitate more private sector investment required for raising the incomes of small and medium farmers.

Food Subsidy

The Government of India decided to subsidise food for the poor right from the time of Independence. The 'socialist pattern' of society was the cornerstone of India's chosen path for economic development and helping the poor by providing cheap foodgrains was part of the Nehruvian idea of the state's role. But over the years, increasingly, it has been realised that the poor do not necessarily get all the food that is directed to them by the Central authorities and so 50 years after Independence, the government set up a targeted public distribution system (TPDS). Under the new scheme, the below poverty line population (BPL) are allowed a fixed quota of grains per month. The BPL population has been issued identity cards on the basis of which they have been allowed to draw 10 kgs of wheat per month. This scheme has been successful in some states but due to various lacunae in the public distribution system, it has resulted in a huge pile up of foodgrains.

This is because many of the very poor were not keen on lifting their quota of foodgrains from ration shops. Because for low income people, availability of food grains at an appropriate time and place (close to their homes), is most important. If they have to travel miles to reach ration shops only to discover that they are closed or that stocks have not come, or that they have run out—they will buy next time from the open market, at a higher price.

The price of ration shop foodgrains has veered closer to the open market price because under pressure from the certain lobbies that pressed for a reduction of subsidies, the government has had to raise the price of foodgrains in ration shops (the issue price) under Public Distribution System (PDS) for those above the poverty line. People who are poor but not very poor do not have much incentive to buy from ration shops because there is not much difference between the issue price and the open market price, as a result of which foodgrains pile up in such shops. And if foodgrains are not lifted by the poor, then the states buy less the next time and the food stocks of the country, with the Food Corporation of India (FCI), mount and cross the required norms for keeping such stocks.

The pile up was also due to the state governments' reluctance to lift grain because many were bankrupt. The Food Corporation of India went on buying foodgrains for the PDS at prices announced at the beginning of the agricultural sowing season from farmers and the Minimum Support Prices (MSP) were set by the Central government. In addition, the government has had to store foodgrains in godowns under the auspices of the FCI which also could not manage the stocks in the most economical manner. It has been faced with escalating storage and maintenance costs. Huge losses have occurred due to destruction from rats, fungus and insects. Finally, in 2006, the stock pile has been depleted through exports and distribution to the poor and the government of India has turned into a net importer of wheat for building fresh food stocks. Thus, the whole system of subsidies for the poor had resulted in a pile up of foodgrains which did not benefit the poor much.

The government has placed too much emphasis on feeding the poor through subsidies—which have actually not helped the poor—rather than by giving them employment that would give them incomes with which they would be able to buy from the market. The huge network of the food distribution system has resulted in a network of corrupt practices.

There are agents and middlemen who divert a huge proportion of the food, sugar and kerosene, meant for the poor, to the open market every season. The diversion ranges between 10 to 30 per cent. The food subsidy bill was Rs. 2,850 crore in 1991-92 and mounted to Rs. 13,670 crore in 2000-01; Rs. 25,160 crore in 2003-04 and Rs. 25,800 crore in 2004-05.

Basically, as pointed out before, the food stocks have been built up because farmers have been keen to produce wheat and rice and not enough pulses, oilseeds and coarser foodgrains which are consumed by the poor. Many are just small farmers who do not want to grow other crops because they feel insecure about their ability to sell them in the market. Year after year, they grow the same crop and sell it for their subsistence. They are not also investing in infrastructure, like minor irrigation works, adequately nor buying better seeds, or undertaking processing activities for better value realisation. In the ultimate analysis, the size of the crop and its quality is determined by the monsoons and the farmers do not seem to have any device of averting a crisis in case the monsoons fail.

Despite uncertainties of agriculture, it is strange that 68 per cent of the workforce is still dependent on it for their livelihood. It is due to the slow growth of jobs in the industrial sector and the non-farm sector in villages, that so many people are still dependent on agriculture for their livelihood. In western agricultural countries, the proportion of population dependent on agriculture is minuscule as compared to India but their productivity is so high that they are responsible for a large share of world's export output. Many changes thus are needed to make Indian farmers prosperous and reduce their dependency on the monsoons. If they have higher spending power through higher incomes, industry too will prosper. A healthy growth, however, in the sub-sectors of agriculture has taken place in some states, especially in livestock, fisheries, poultry and dairy products. India is the biggest milk producer in the world. But there has been a decrease in the importance of forestry. On the whole, non-agricultural sectors have not expanded commensurate to the increase in the workforce. A large number of workers earning low incomes are forever trapped in agriculture.

Given the large variation in the climate and soil conditions, India is capable of producing a wide range of high value horticultural products which can enrich farmers. Only 1 per cent of the 140 tonnes of fruits and vegetables produced in the country goes through any kind of processing. There is a big possibility in floriculture and export of flowers. But what it requires is modern infrastructure like cold storage facilities and refrigerated transportation from growers till the cargo's shipment. Grading and quality control would also be needed for these emerging sectors.

Land Reforms

Despite all the efforts at modernising agriculture, millions of farmers have remained small (and poor) producers because of the tiny size of holdings. This is a problem which has not been corrected through vigorous and continuous land reforms. Land tenancy rights remain a fuzzy area and many small farmers do not have guaranteed rights for staying on the land as sharecroppers. Redistribution of land which started with great fanfare, petered out after a few years after Independence.

Intermediaries (*zamindars* and *jagirdars*) were abolished within a few years of Independence and land was given to the actual tillers of the soil and this redistribution accounted for 40 per cent of the cultivated area. Ceilings on landholdings were imposed and the surplus land was to be distributed among the landless poor. Two rounds of land reform legislations took place, one in the 1950s and the other in the early 1970s. But the objective of land reforms was only partially fulfilled. The idea behind land ceiling was to discourage concentration of land ownership beyond the ceiling level because it presented the possibility of dispossession of numerous small and marginal holders of land through the flourishing land market dominated by big farmers. But exemptions for plantations and the political clout of big land-owners prevented the Land Ceiling Act from having a wider impact. Only two per cent of the land which was under cultivation, was acquired by the government for distribution among the landless. Thus, inequalities in the distribution of land persisted. As always, big farmers continue to dominate and dictate agricultural policies and get the maximum benefit from government's subsidised inputs and credit schemes.

It is because of the small size of holdings that farmers have not been able to produce commercially for the market. Small holdings do not allow for mechanised farm implements and other improvements that could increase the yield of farming. That is why it is so important to have farms of economically viable size; only in some states land reforms have been carried out (like in West Bengal) so that agricultural productivity has increased due to innovations and better inputs.

Ideally, land reforms involve redistribution of land—from big landowners to smaller ones; better tenancy rights through law enforcement and consolidation of small and scattered landholdings. The latter is one of the main reasons why mechanisation and other farm improvements have not been carried out in many farms.

Some states have enacted laws that guarantee better tenancy rights for the tillers but consolidation of farms also has had rather slow progress. Land reforms thus remain more or less undelivered and their absence is the root cause for lack of progress in certain poor states like Bihar.

So far, mechanisation has been carried out only in a few states like Haryana and Punjab and these states have shown the benefits of using tractors, threshers and other mechanised farm implements. Mechanisation enables the farmers to till the land more effectively and efficiently as a result of which productivity rises. It is quicker and it reduces costs if the land is big enough. Around 59 per cent of farmers are marginal farmers, holding less that one hectare of land The ceilings on landholdings are still in place and according to some noted agricultural economists, there is no case on grounds of efficiency for doing away with the ceilings and encouraging large-scale corporate farming. Some noted economists have argued that this would lead to an exodus of rural poor into cities. Hence, effective implementation of existing ceiling on landholdings is probably necessary for ensuring adequate employment and for protecting small and marginal farmers. They argue that removing restrictions on leasing of agricultural land is important as it would help in augmenting the operational holdings of the small and marginal farmers.

Agricultural Credit

Even small farmers could use some form of mechanisation and better inputs if they had access to credit. Rural credit is still not easily available to the average farmer because of the bureaucracy of the public sector banks which are operating in rural areas. Despite years of having the policy of giving cheap credit directed to farm sector, bankers have been very reluctant to lend to small and medium farmers. They blame it on the non-repayment of loans by farmers.

The marginal farmers with less than two hectares, including tenants, account for 80 per cent of all holdings and roughly one-third of the farming community depends on 'informal' sources for meeting their credit requirements. Commercial banks do play a major role and dispense 50 per cent of the credit to farmers. About 43 per cent of the credit requirement of farmers is met through the cooperative banks and the regional rural banks give seven per cent of the credit needed. In the post-reform period, direct agricultural advances by commercial banks to farmers declined to 12 per cent of their total advances against the target of 18 per cent. This is because the government no longer insists that the banks adhere to targets of agricultural credit.

Also, because regional rural banks (RRBs) were created to cater, especially to small farmers, shopkeepers and landless labour, there is less emphasis on the commercial banks' activities in the rural sector. They also monitor the projects of the borrowers and 90 per cent of their loans are given to the poor in rural areas. Cooperative credit societies have been very active in some states and, in some others, have been embroiled in scandal. After the nationalisation of banks (1969), commercial banks have been a major source of agricultural finance. But because of various real or perceived difficulties in obtaining loans, small farmers have been taking recourse to borrowing money from moneylenders, landlords and traders at high rates of interest. Farmers could borrow from cooperative banks but cooperative banks have to be recapitalised and refinanced and they need to be restructured in order to become more professional and transparent in their lending activities.

The *kisan* credit scheme that was devised to give timely support to farmers from the banking system in a flexible and cost effective manner, is not very successful because of various stipulations and restrictions. Its operation seems limited only to obtaining fertilisers from 'fixed' shops.

SHGs and microcredit have been very successful in some states in dispensing credit to small borrowers, especially to women. These have to be encouraged and their operations have to be extended to the poorer states in order to give full benefits to farmers through group collateral. Women are using credit for land preservation and related activities like animal husbandry, dairying, horticulture, and agroforestry, provided that they have contractual arrangements with dealers and processors for the provision of inputs and services for marketing. They can be linked with banks and National Bank for Agriculture and Rural Development (NABARD)—the government agency for rural credit and development.

High value agriculture needs higher working capital and also entails higher risks. Credit for high value agriculture can be facilitated through processors, input dealers and NGOs that are vertically integrated with farmers, including those engaged in contract farming. These could provide critical inputs or processing facilities to farmers. If such a system of financing is encouraged, it would increase the credit flow significantly. In fact, these dealers/processors can act as non-banking financial intermediaries who can get refinance from the banking sector to give loans to agriculture and also bear the risk of default. Such arrangements would help to reduce the transaction costs and ensure recovery of loans.

Educating Farmers

Basically, in all developing countries that are today ahead of India in agriculture like Brazil and Thailand, an agrarian revolution has been carried out through audio-visual methods and efficient extension work. Lack of adequate literacy among farmers has been a serious handicap and has led to their being ignorant of warnings and advice from experts. Hence, human development must be a priority area in rural development. Use of information technology and communications (ICT) can educate semiliterate farmers about crop outcomes and the price and demand situation in the market. Otherwise, farmers remain fatalistic and tradition-bound and when they are uninsured, they are vulnerable to pressure from local moneylenders and end their lives when faced with heavy loan repayment. If there is proper extension work in the villages where knowledgeable persons (who have undergone training) come and demonstrate the new methods and benefits of good storage and biotechnology research, farmers would learn faster and invest in the right kind of technology. Farmers' wives have to be taught rudimentary food processing and fruit and vegetable preservation that would yield them additional income.

Competitiveness against Foreign Imports

Low productivity in India means that not only is there less output per acre but also that the cost of producing a kilo of agricultural output is higher as compared to more advanced countries. High costs mean losing out against competitors. With removal of quantitative restriction or quotas on all imports that were in place for many years and the phasing out of duties in the near future, there is every likelihood that there would be a flooding of better quality farm goods in the markets which people would buy because of lower prices. That is when the farmers will be hardest hit and the long neglect of agriculture will begin to surface. Competition will be strong in the area of fruits, vegetables, grains and commercial crops. In each area, if agricultural productivity and efficiency improves, farmers need not fear the dumping of goods from outside because people are basically still very price sensitive.

India has responded to the tough competition by raising tariffs in some of the commodities. This cannot be the solution in the long-term because not only will it lead to others raising retaliatory tariff walls; it will also mean denying Indian citizens access to better quality, cheaper food products.

Unless there is overall rural development with focus on agriculture, problems will remain because three-fourths of the population will not be able to participate, on account of their various inadequacies, in the global economy. As pointed out above, infrastructure is important because very often the roads connecting rural areas to towns are badly affected during the rainy season. Rural produce cannot be taken to the markets on time leading to losses. It is basically the lack of ancillary and support services that prevent the farm population from realising better returns for their hard labour. Processed food like cottage cheese is often sold in nearby village markets at low prices and not sent to big towns because of the unavailability of refrigerated trucks. Unless agricultural productivity improves, the lives of millions of people will remain below potential and their demand for industrial goods would be low with the result that industrial growth will suffer. Low incomes would mean lower capital formation in agriculture as it became evident in the 1980s.

Agriculture has to be drastically modernised in order to keep pace with the developments taking place in competing countries; public and private investments, which are critical for improving productivity, have to rise. The people dependent on agriculture have to be reduced and this can only be done through better infrastructure and human development. They can then be moved out to other jobs and occupations.

For sustainable development of agriculture, soil conservation and watershed programmes have to be adopted across the country because already, three-fourths of arable land has been brought under cultivation. Increase in production can only be achieved through more intensive cropping. For conserving precious water resources, every possible means of preserving water bodies will have to be made because agriculture uses 85 per cent of fresh water. Irrigation systems have to be maintained properly and there has to be proper cost recovery from water usage. Giving free water for reasons of political populism is going to lead to misuse of water, like growing water intensive crops like rice and sugarcane in areas like Punjab that traditionally have grown only wheat.

All restrictions on the movement of foodgrains and other agricultural commodities introduced during times when agricultural prices kept rising, because black marketing and hoarding were suspected, ought to be removed because such impediments restrict the size of the market within the country.

Futures trading in agricultural commodities has been re-introduced and such trading in which the farmers can have contracts with buyers, and the delivery is in the future at fixed prices, would help them get better and stable prices. But futures trading requires proper infrastructure like storage facilities and market information available to all. Without proper regulations speculators can enter futures trading that can lead to high prices of foodgrains.

7

Indian Planning

India's entire industrialising experience is encapsulated in the Five Year Plans. Pandit Nehru wanted to make India an industrial nation and reduce the dependence on agriculture. India went for huge Five Year Plans like the Soviet Union. Many people wonder why India chose to have such centralised planning soon after Independence. The government could have opted for export led growth or could have gone for a market-led economy with a small role for the government. It could not do so because, even before Independence, the National Planning Committee was set up in 1938 by leaders of the Independence Movement, the founding fathers. The members visualised an India in which the government would have control on basic industries like steel, coal, iron, railways, shipping, waterways—all natural monopolies. The 'Bombay Plan' followed and it too emphasised the importance of planning for development. Nehru set up the Planning Commission in 1950 to make an assessment of the country's basic needs, the stock of human and material capital. The Five Year Plans were envisaged to utilise effectively the nation's resources. Nehru felt the need for rapid industrialisation in order to pull the country out of poverty and deprivation that had existed under the British rule. For a model he looked to Russia that had succeeded in a few years' time in becoming a major power.

The Soviet Union had launched successfully a number of Five Year Plans that had undertaken a detailed mapping of the requirements of each region and each state, and each sector like agriculture and industry. In a few years' time, it had made rapid strides in the field of science and technology and had given employment to all its people.

Emulating the Soviet experience, India's financial resources were to be divided between the various sectors according to a detailed national plan that proposed financial outlays and the means for implementing the Plans.

Prof. P.C. Mahalanobis, a famous Physicist and Statistician, was asked to draw up a blueprint for rapid economic growth based on a detailed plan of resource mobilisation. It was thought that such a national plan would take care of all the problems in the remote states also. The First Five-year Plan drew its blueprint from the famous model of growth by two internationally famous economists, R.F. Harrod and E. Domar. It basically underscored the importance of investment and its relationship to growth through an 'accelerator-multiplier' effect—in which investment created demand for goods and services in different sectors and spurred growth in the industries producing those goods and services. This led to an increase in incomes that led to job creation.

The First Five-year Plan emphasised agriculture because the national leaders realised its importance as being the biggest provider of jobs and incomes. India had remained poor because of backwardness in agriculture and its poor returns. The Plan was to be a rehabilitation programme for the economy hit by war and partition. The main increase in output came from a better utilisation of existing capacity and not just from an increase in the capacity of production.

The Second Plan emphasised industrial growth by building up the capital base of the capital goods sector so that rapid economic growth could be achieved. First, India lacked the basic industries (that included heavy industry) and this had to be tackled by starting a series of heavy industries. If a basic infrastructure was available for production of heavy or capital goods, other goods could be produced easily. If machines could be produced, they would be available for the production of consumer goods. But because it required a huge investment, capital goods production was to be left in the government's hands. This was also the model for development followed by Japan and later by South Korea.

Since foreign exchange was valuable for the import of capital goods and heavy machinery, it had to be conserved and rationed out for less important purposes. Thus there came about rationing and control of foreign exchange. Basically, emphasis was laid on self-sufficiency or self-reliant development and rapid economic growth in order to undo the damage done throughout the period of British colonisation.

It was decided that India was to have a 'mixed economy' with a large private sector—the entire agricultural production was in private hands, and a large public sector that would have full control of the 'commanding heights'.

India had an inherent advantage in setting up a machine building industry as it was in a position to produce the cheapest steel. And in the first decade of industrial planning there was a significant increase in the output of heavy industry. Industrial growth went up to seven per cent per annum.

Emphasis on heavy industry cleared the way for the future important role of the public sector. All projects requiring large investment, and a long gestation period were to be in the public sector's domain and balanced regional growth was to be a key goal.

The Third Plan was essentially a continuation of the Second Five-year Plan in terms of the basic strategy except that targets and sights were raised and output was expected to grow faster so that the annual rise in national income was to be more than five per cent. It was also aimed at achieving self-sufficiency in foodgrain production to meet the requirements of industry and exports. Stagnation in foodgrain output in the first three years of the Third Plan due to a severe drought was a big set back. There was a Plan Holiday after the food crisis and the Pakistan War; the Fourth Plan was started after a gap of three years in 1969.

From the First Plan, we have completed the Tenth Plan (2002-2007) and launched the Eleventh Plan (2007-2012). During the last five decades, various problems have been identified regarding the planning process and its overemphasis on centralised control. Many key parameters of central planning have been changed and today, planning is no longer what it used to be—by command and control and detailed mapping of resources and needs. It is no longer centralised and output targets are not given as fixed and inflexible entities to be met each year.

Many types of inefficiencies were identified during the course of India's experience with planning. The public sector enterprises faced losses and high costs. The mistakes have somewhat got corrected over the last few decades. Today planning is more through incentives and inducements and is much more decentralised than before.

Planning today also involves the states, districts, blocks and *panchayats*. India being a vibrant democracy, through the election process, the entire population is involved in planning. The planning process is dispersed over a large number of states, districts and local governments and bodies like the village *panchayats* and urban municipalities are involved. But decision making in respect of the contents of the plans and the methods of executing them remain with the Central government.

Planned development did have its positive outcomes and India transformed, albeit slowly, to one of the four largest economies in the world. In capital goods production, much was achieved and India can today produce its own machinery, transport and sophisticated defence equipment. The emphasis on higher education has yielded a crop of mechanical, electrical and civil engineers. Software engineers have emerged from India's several Institutes of Technology and Electronic Engineering, established with foreign collaboration.

Agriculture, which was left entirely to the private sector, unlike in the Soviet model, grew at a varied pace over the years and India has reached self-sufficiency in food. India, until recently, had a huge stock of foodgrains. It no longer imports foreign food in bulk. India had been growing at a steady rate of three to four per cent on an average for three decades (1950-1980) though this rate was lower than the high rate of growth achieved by developing countries like South Korea which started out its development programme around the same time

There have been many failures in the Planning process, especially in the way some of the public enterprises were run and the proliferation of controls that took a toll on the growth of private enterprise. The licence–permit *raj* led to many shortages and the emergence of black markets, nepotism, as well as petty corruption. There was a good amount of cost overrun and misallocation of resources in the public sector enterprises as well as overstaffing, favouritism, and interference in internal management. This was largely due to the absence of healthy and fierce competition from outside the country and also from within. Many civil servants developed a vested interest in inflating the public sector's costs and its scope as they derived numerous benefits and they actively promoted State intervention because it opened up more job opportunities and new areas in which they could exercise power.

A lot of distortions thus cropped up in the way the allocation of resources took place and the inflexible ways in which the plans were managed. But there is little doubt that, given the circumstances under which India gained Independence, planned development was the only option open for the leaders.

Looking back, the first Congress government after Independence under Nehru wanted to correct the retarded and unbalanced growth under the British in which industrial expansion took place only in the finished consumer goods industry. In fact, the Indian textile industry gained by the protection granted to it after World War I and this enabled it to become one of the largest in the world. But Nehru wanted rapid industrial growth all round that seemed achievable only through national planning. The government and its advisors took a poor view of export-led growth because—in the circumstances surrounding 1947, there were few possibilities for export expansion as the economy was in shambles. The need for essential imports in the form of oil, non-ferrous metals and chemicals meant a high foreign exchange requirement which could not be accessed through export growth alone. Import compression of consumer goods was thus resorted to so as to make foreign exchange available for starting industrialisation.

According to the import control strategy, industrial output growth was expected to accelerate once the capital goods industry was in place through the import of essential machinery and technology. It was hoped that the country would then reach the 'take off' stage and achieve a high rate of industrialisation and per capita income growth.

But, in fact, after rising briefly over a short period, industrial growth decelerated. This was due to various quantitative restrictions imposed on production in the private sector and the import trade. It resulted in the emergence of a high cost industrial structure which was not efficient as the latest innovations and technology could not be incorporated. Such import substitution policies ignored important factors like economies of scale and the need for speeding up technological change through vigorous imports.

After the First Five-year Plan, agriculture was not the main focus and the resultant stagnation of agricultural output in the first three years of the Third Plan alerted the Planners and moved them to act.

It led to the Green Revolution in the 1970s with High Yielding Varieties (HYVs) of wheat and rice being introduced in some regions and the application of other inputs like fertilisers and irrigation facilities that were enhanced. It made a difference to Indian agriculture for years to come.

After the 1991 economic reforms, around the Eighth Five-year Plan (1992-1997), a clear change of direction was visible and there was evidence of 'indicative planning' that was distinctly more market friendly than before.

The Planning system was to be more flexible and have a clear role for the private sector. Outlines and general directions for growth were indicated for various sectors of the economy and the incentives for achieving the indicated growth rates were given to bankers, exporters and industrialists. Desirable objectives were thus given to the economic sectors and the means of achieving them were to be found through inducement rather than centralised direction and control. The policies used were tax incentives, low rates of interest, easing the rules for foreign investment and lowering of import duties.

Plans

The Plans deal with the public sector mainly and include various schemes, institutional changes and measures for fulfilling certain objectives. Most require the construction of projects and investment by the government. These come under 'investment or capital expenditure' in the Budget. The Plans also provide various sources of financing these outlays or projected expenditures like tax revenue, borrowing and external assistance. The private sector is also associated in the financing and execution of the Plans—more so since the liberalisation of the economy in 1991.

In recent years, greater emphasis has been given to decentralised planning and greater participation of people from all walks of life. State planning boards, municipalities, *panchayats* and NGOs prepare their plans incorporating their aims and means for achieving their goals. The National Development Council, which has representatives from the Centre and the states, discusses these plans and takes decisions about what to include and what to exclude.

On the whole, the First Five-year Plan (1951-1956) was a great success with industrial growth picking up. The Third Five-year Plan and the Fourth Plan (1969-1974) were marked by lack of success and underperformance. During the Third Five-year Plan there was a severe drought and two wars with neighbours—China and Pakistan. It called for a three year postponement in the fulfillment of the planned targets and a Plan Holiday was declared. The Fourth Plan (1969-1974) at first witnessed record food and industrial production but due to the failure of monsoons, the price situation deteriorated. From mid-1972, there was a huge influx of refugees from Bangladesh creating a number of problems. During the Fifth Plan (1974-1979), Emergency was declared and the Janata government terminated the Fifth Plan in 1978.

During the Sixth Plan (1978-1983), later replaced by a different period (1980-1985), there was a drought situation in many parts of the country and this affected the agricultural production. But on the whole it was a success. The Seventh Plan (1985-1990) aimed at increasing food, work and productivity and was considered a great success because it achieved a growth rate of 6 per cent for the first time as against a target of 5 per cent GDP growth. The decade of the 1980s achieved an average growth rate of 5.8 per cent as against the average of 3.5 per cent in the previous five plans.

The Eighth Plan was postponed by two years due to a number of political changes at the Centre (1992-1997), but the rate of GDP growth touched 6.8 per cent. Private investment became very important. The Ninth Plan viewed growth, social justice and equity as important goals. During the Ninth Plan, the growth rate of agriculture declined to about 2.1 per cent from 4.7 per cent achieved during the Eighth Plan. Similarly the growth of the manufacturing sector also declined to 4.5 per cent from 7.6 per cent during the Eighth Plan. The decline was due to the 'Asian Crisis' that had occurred in 1997 which led to a decline in demand from other parts of the world for industrial goods and which affected the growth of the Indian economy adversely. There were also disasters within the country—an earthquake in Gujarat, a cyclone in Orissa and the Kargil War. The GDP growth declined to 5.3 per cent. The Tenth Plan targeted a growth rate of 8 per cent.

The Tenth Plan has addressed the weaknesses in India's poverty reduction programmes and aims at equity and social justice. The main thrust of planning has gone back to agriculture once again and it is no longer being treated as residual. The Eleventh Five Year Plan has been launched with focus on faster and more inclusive growth.

Annual reviews are carried out with respect to the central assistance for the state plans by the Planning Commission. The Annual Plan exercises have become very important because while the broad policies and the sector-wise plans are oriented towards a Five Year perspective, they are revised mid-term every third year.

In general, it has been found by the Planners that a multiplicity of government agencies has been wasteful and 'downsizing' the government has been favoured. Instead of centralised planning with a rigid structure, a diffusion of authority has been followed in recent years. More emphasis has been given to the efficiency of the economic system and reducing the Incremental Capital Output Ratio (ICOR), than on increasing plan allocation every year. The idea behind this move is to raise the efficiency of capital and adopt labour-intensive techniques for more job creation.

National Income and GDP Growth

India's national income is calculated by various methods. According to Dr. V.K.R.V. Rao, one of the first to calculate India's national income: "National Income is nothing more than a simple linear aggregation of incomes accruing to the factors of production supplied by the normal residents of the country in question." Basically, national income is the money value of the goods and services transacted within the country each year. It is a measure of the overall level of economic activity.

We can measure the total amount of economic activity or national product which is the value of all goods and services crossing within the country's boundaries by:

(i) adding up all the incomes earned in different economic activities like wages, rents and profits;

(ii) product or output method which adds up all the output produced in the country by each firm and each industry in terms of its value added—the less the value of its output, the less the value of intermediate purchases from the firm; and

(iii) the Expenditure method, which totals all the items of final expenditure incurred by individuals and the government on current consumption plus industries' and government's purchases of capital equipment within the country. Payments by one firm to another for raw materials, components or other inputs must be excluded.

Gross Domestic Product relates to all economic activity taking place within the geographical limits of the economy and if the income method is used, it is called GDP at factor cost. If we add net property incomes from abroad and net indirect taxes, then it would give the Gross National Income (GNP).

All transactions are measured in money terms and give the national income in current prices but it is necessary to allow for price changes when making comparisons between years. Values at current prices have to be adjusted by an appropriate index of prices in order to obtain estimates at constant prices. Any observed changes will then reflect the changes in quantity and not in prices. Thus, GDP has to be deflated by the prices of the base year chosen in order to obtain a series of national income at constant prices.

GNP makes no allowance for depreciation or wear and tear of capital equipment. Net National Product (NNP) takes into account depreciation from the gross measure. The Central Statistical Organisation produces the data for all the national income accounting. A new series of figures have been generated with the base year of 1993-1994 prices.

There are various national surveys that generate employment and industrial production figures. There can be and there is a good amount of underreporting, especially in the services sector. In general, India has quite a large non-monetised sector in which barter takes place instead of monetary transactions. There is also a big amount of 'black money' in the economy which is unaccounted for. In agriculture, though most of the crops and their value are covered, fruits and vegetable production statistics are inadequate. About 40 per cent of the geographical area under agriculture is without the benefit of reliable statistics on crop acreage by crop season.

Agriculture's share in the GDP has declined continuously over the years. The Services sector has become important and the manufacturing sector's contribution has remained rather stagnant, increasing only a little. In 2003, agriculture contributed 22 per cent to the GDP, industry 27 per cent and services 51 per cent. In USA, agriculture contributed only 2 per cent of the GDP while industry's share 23 per cent and services sector contributed 75 per cent.

The per capita income is the average level of national income for each member of the population. India's per capita income has trebled during the last two decades. The projected per capita income for 2050 was $1,700 in 2005, but the actual per capita income in 2004 was $620 only.

In 2004, India's gross national income was $675 billion. In 2004-2005, India's GDP (at factor cost) at current prices was Rs. 2,830,465 crore and at 1993-94 prices was Rs. 1,529,408 crore. The net national product (at factor cost) at current prices was Rs. 2,535,627 crore and at 1993-94 prices was Rs. 1,354,599 crore (*Statistical Outline of India 2005-06*, Tata Services Ltd.).

8

Industrial Growth

Pattern of Industrialisation

Much of the industrialisation strategy that was adopted by the government after Independence was determined by the neglect of industry for 200 years under British rule. India was famed for her manufactured products—textiles, luxury handcrafted wooden and ivory items and metalwork during Moghul times and their quality and workmanship were indisputably high. During the British rule, India was treated mainly as a supplier of raw materials for British industries. Instead of encouraging industrialisation by starting new industries, India was forced to specialise in the production of coffee, jute, cotton, rubber, and indigo which were transported from India and consumer goods made in Britain were transported for sale back to the colonies including India. Free trade was imposed on India so that Indian industries could not grow during the first part of the 19th century as they could not compete with cheap imports of a whole range of manufactured goods, from biscuits to cotton textiles.

The first indigenous manufacturing industry was the cotton textile industry which was started by an Indian in Bombay soon after World War I. Protection was given selectively to indigenous industry to encourage fast growth because of a big and contentious debate that took place in Britain. British industry was facing a slow down also and many industrialists wanted to set up factories in India with the help of a projective tariff wall. Somehow, the protection that was offered through high tariffs benefited the Indian entrepreneurs also. Other industries were also started in jute and steel—these were the most important so British agents managed them.

Yet, a real industrial revolution with a series of inventions and innovations did not take place in India as it did in Britain. India remained technologically backward as hardly any machinery was produced in India during British times and all Indian industrialists had to import machines from abroad.

After Independence, the task before the government was enormous because India had a weak production base. There was no capital goods industry and the government was determined to set up steel and power plants which required heavy investment and were crucial for achieving rapid industrialisation. Pandit Jawaharlal Nehru, India's first Prime Minister, was interested in production of heavy machinery that would help to produce other machines. His vision was to make India self-reliant and powerful. To set up industries that produced basic goods, that would be used by other industries, was the driving force behind the strategy that determined the pattern of industrialisation. The government decided that heavy industries were going to be reserved for the public sector (the commanding heights) and India soon established a big production base comprising public enterprises that were engaged in the production of basic industrial goods like oil, iron and steel and cement. Nehru also insisted on the growth of science and technology and the establishment of agricultural research institutes. These had been lacking during British times.

The role of the State had been important in the industrialisation of the Soviet Union and Japan. The pattern of development in India was modelled after these countries, especially the Soviet Five Year Plans in which the State would build the infrastructure and heavy industries. The importance of the public sector in industrialisation was most fashionable at that time, especially in the newly independent colonies.

Foreign capital was allowed but only to help fill the gap in India's technological needs, and the main emphasis was on India's self-reliance. With technological assistance from USSR, US and UK, various heavy industries had been started through joint ventures, specially in the iron and steel industry. To create a pool of future engineers and technical and scientific personnel, Indian Institutes of Technology (IITs) were started in major states.

Most consumer goods manufacturing industries were left to the private sector. The policy makers, however, believed that the private sector should not be allowed to waste precious resources by starting the manufacture of many consumer goods. Their expansion was therefore controlled and their activities curbed through licensing and regulations. The idea was to have a set of competitive industries and any tendency of big players gobbling up smaller ones, was to be curbed. Side by side, small-scale industries were encouraged to absorb the growing population, especially those people who were not able to find work in the rural areas. Private monopolies were discouraged through law. As per the socialist pattern that was adopted, small enterprises were given importance and equity in income distribution as well as a regional balance were goals to be achieved.

Protection was granted to the capital goods industry in order to nurture it as an 'infant' industry. Import substitution formed another plank of the industrial strategy. This was not unusual for developing countries at that time because, otherwise, huge amounts of money would be needed to import essential inputs. Though the country could have paid for them through exports, at that time, soon after World War II, the prospect of rapid export growth did not seem too bright.

Many people wonder why India chose a pattern of industrialisation that put so much emphasis on regulation and controls. It is perhaps because at the time of Independence, India had limited resources and the founding fathers aimed at rapid industrialisation. They chose the Soviet model of development because of the success that the Soviet Union displayed in terms of scientific and technological advance. India thus modelled the entire industrialisation pattern after the Soviet Five Year Plans. The framework for the future course of industrialisation was set up through the Industrial Policy Resolution 1956. The Industries (Development and Regulation) Act 1951, provided the legal basis for the industrial licensing policy which was revised on July 24, 1991. In the revised version, after nearly four decades, industrial licensing was finally abandoned and the government announced measures facilitating foreign investment and technology transfers. For the first time new areas, hitherto reserved for the public sector, were thrown open. The private sector could operate in all areas, except defence, railway transport and atomic energy. Industrial license for manufacturing activity was limited to industries reserved for the public sector; 16 industries of strategic, social or environmental concern; and for those industries that were reserved for the small-scale sector. Industrial licensing had earlier been required for the creation of industrial capacities and expansion of existing units. During the decades following Independence many revisions in industrial policy did take place so as to give a thrust to industrial growth but the dismantling of the control and licence-permit *raj* was not fast enough.

Gradual reforms had already started in the 1980s, but the impact in terms of leading to higher industrial growth was not very spectacular.

Looking back, one can see where the policies went wrong. But one cannot question the reason why Nehru opted for a faster rate of industrialisation because, apart from making India self-reliant and powerful, a fast rate of industrial growth was important for absorbing people from the countryside, those who could not be gainfully employed in farms and were in effect 'surplus' labour.

The 'mixed economy' model in which both the private and the public sectors played important roles was adopted. Today, of course, the private sector is much more important than the public sector in manufacturing activities (around 75 per cent of all economic activities are in private hands). The mixed economy model worked for some years but the employment growth was not fast enough to absorb the surplus agricultural labour. Industrial growth remained slow with an average rate of about five per cent over the last four decades.

India has not been able to achieve a high rate of industrial growth because of various structural problems and also because some of the government's economic policies did not encourage rapid industrial expansion. Even when the liberalisation of the industrial sector did take place, industrial growth did not surge forward as expected. There has been sporadic high growth followed by recession and slowdown. The main problem of inadequate infrastructure responsible for thwarting industrial growth has remained.

The experience in India was very different from that of UK and unlike the spate of inventions and discoveries that preceded the Industrial Revolution, industrialisation in India was fragmented and incomplete. The challenge lay in acquiring all the latest machinery and equipment to start the process but the main constraint was capital. The heavy industries absorbed a lot of capital instead of labour and became capital intensive rather than labour intensive. The import substitution regime did not allow for rapid change in technology.

From the beginning, the government was concerned with conserving the limited foreign exchange it had at its disposal which was earmarked to be spent on the import of essential items (capital goods) to start big industries. The Government of India had a paranoia about the drain on foreign exchange for imports of consumer and luxury goods. A lot of harassment accompanied the restricted import policy and it led to a crop of corrupt customs officials. Unfortunately, curbing the growth of industries in the private sector later hurt India's competitiveness abroad.

Yet, India's industrialisation process started quite well. Between 1951-1965, industrial growth was rather high at eight per cent. But the balance of payments crisis in 1966 caused stagnation in industrial growth. The rupee was devalued and more restrictions were imposed on imports and foreign exchange outgo. India's industrial progress got cut short by the severe drought of 1965-66 and the two wars with China and Pakistan in the 1960s. India's food import and defence bill caused the foreign exchange crisis. Moreover, due to slow growth in demand for industrial goods from the agricultural sector the necessary boost for industrial growth was missing.

India became virtually a protected country where foreign goods were not allowed. All the scarce foreign exchange was going to be used to buy important (essential) commodities like crude oil and defence equipment. It was believed that consumer goods could be produced at home and as such, were not given high priority. Consumer goods industries as a result did not get a boost and quality suffered.

Whatever was produced was, however, quickly snapped up by the fast growing population because there were no alternatives available. It was a seller's market and as a result producers paid little attention to improving their products. There was no competition from foreign goods and therefore no improvement in style or design, but people did buy abroad with a frenzied zeal just because nothing of quality seemed to be available in India. But consumers living in India had to make do with what was available locally as they could not compare the quality with imported goods. This absence of quality consciousness appeared in Indian exports in the 1970s and 1980s.

Indian made goods stood out for their lack of finish, design and finer embellishments in the international market.

Thus, exports suffered because components and embellishments were not easily importable and they lent a poor appearance to Indian products. As Southeast Asia became developed, goods from Bangkok and Hong Kong started capturing the markets abroad. Their products were cheaper and better in quality and design. Even simple gadgets could not be bought in India and people purchased 'gadgets and appliances' on trips abroad. Even proper toasters could not be bought in the Indian market. New York stores specialised in gadgets for Indians to take home.

For many other reasons related to lack of administrative and infrastructural support, exports suffered and industrial growth too could not get the requisite boost from the rapid export growth of consumer goods.

But even so, between 1950-1990, both the factory and non-factory branches of manufacturing displayed a higher growth rate of value addition than the agricultural sector. Between 1971-1980 the average industrial growth was 4 per cent and between 1980-1985 it was 5.5 per cent—rather moderate on the whole but not too bad. (The Index of Industrial Production measures the rate of industrial growth and is composed of the production output of many industries). But the growth performance of the industrial/manufacturing sector cannot be regarded as satisfactory in comparison with China, Thailand, South Korea and Malaysia. Besides, industrial growth fell short of the targets of the successive Five-year Plans. Only during the First and the Seventh Plans, the performance was comparatively better in terms of targeted growth.

Thus, there were three phases of industrial growth, the first phase was of rapid growth which ended in 1964-65. The second phase of deceleration and at best moderate growth which extended from 1965-1966 to 1979-80. The decade of the 1980s was characterised by recovery and revival of industrial growth. The deceleration was largely confined to heavy industry and basic and capital goods.

Many reasons can be seen as responsible for this pattern—slowdown in public investment, inadequate infrastructure and poor management of existing infrastructure that was mainly in the hands of the public sector.

While the aim of establishing a capital goods industrial sector was more or less fulfilled by the 1970s, it was soon realised that India was falling behind in technological advance, innovations and latest know-how. Partial relaxation of the import policy was followed in the 1980s and import of components and spare parts was allowed under special licenses. There was much debate about the restrictive practices of the government and under Mrs. Indira Gandhi, certain reforms were started that aimed to make India more competitive at least *vis-à-vis* its neighbours, who as the Newly Industrialising Countries (NICs) were showing much faster rate of growth in exports, experiencing a fast reduction in poverty and had captured the export boom just after the Vietnam War.

While huge amounts were spent during the first three Five Year Plans for developing capital goods industries and making India self-reliant in steel, cement and heavy machinery, gaps surfaced in the management of the public sector undertakings that prevented efficient production and a rise in productivity. This was especially apparent in the infrastructural industries like power, road transportation and steel. If the Plans had been efficiently executed, India would have had a good infrastructure base. Even in basic and heavy industries, progress was not spectacular. Gradually efficiency was sacrificed in order to keep the public sector undertakings (PSUs) running even at losses, as they were important for political patronage.

Since the emphasis was not on enhancing productivity or competitiveness, many PSUs were run by bureaucrats specially on the management side. Cost overruns and losses mounted as there was little accountability and PSUs were often treated as fiefdoms of ministries. Yet, despite political interference, some PSUs gradually emerged to be forerunners in industrial production, generating profits—the *navaratnas*.

On the other side, since the private sector was burdened with restrictions of all kinds, the growth of private firms was curbed. Big industries like textiles were controlled in many ways and there was a compulsory levy on textile mills for producing cheap cloth for the masses. Many mills required drastic modernisation and expansion of their weaving capacity but these also were curbed because priority was given to the decentralised (small-scale) sector for making handloom cloth in order to generate jobs in rural areas. Though a number of small-scale industries sprang up, due to the lack of capital and infrastructure, they never achieved the high productivity of the Southeast Asian countries' small enterprises.

The import substitution strategy that was followed did offer protection to indigenous industries but, as pointed out above, it soon led to technological backwardness due to restrictions on imports of 'state of the art machinery' and equipment. The licence-permit *raj* led to severe restrictions on industrial expansion and innovations in many of the big industries. The licensing policies also led to corruption and high-handedness as well as favouritism. Industrialists spent a good amount of time flying between Bombay (and other major cities) and Delhi, trying to cajole bureaucrats and their underlings to grant them licences. They had to convince them that their need for certain imports or expansion of manufacturing capacity was genuine.

Meanwhile, the bureaucracy became all powerful and bureaucrats had unlimited power to undermine the efforts of industrialists to increase production or expand the capacity of their industrial units. In 1971, the phobia against the expansion and monopolistic practices of big companies led to the MRTP (Monopoly and Restricted Trade Practices) Act that thwarted the growth of large business houses. The government was most concerned to prevent the concentration of economic power in the hands of a few. Similarly, the suspicion against foreign investment, a legacy of the past, led to the passing of FERA (Foreign Exchange Regulation Act) in 1973. It led to a severe curb on the investment and functioning of foreign companies in India and made India less attractive as compared to other developing countries as a destination of foreign direct investment. Foreign investment instead went to Southeast Asia and to China where it was invited with great open economic policies.

Finally, the reservation of certain industries for the small-scale led to a perverse trend. Small-scale sector units kept multiplying their manufacturing operations in order to avail of the concessions inherent in the policies of the government instead of trying to raise efficiency and undertake innovations. Their productivity suffered and the prime aim of encouraging the small-scale sector, which was employment, did not materialise.

Industrial expansion being slow failed to take labour off the farms and thus offer some relief to the farm sector, and possibly raise agricultural productivity.

Industrial growth has remained lacklustre even in the 21st century. Indian industry is not growing fast enough to offer jobs to the millions of job seekers; it is also not fast enough to give the economic growth of the country a boost. Instead, in recent years it has been gripped with significant slowdowns and downturns.

The downturn which began in 1999 was due to the excess capacity in some industries and it resulted in the postponement of fresh investment as the demand for industrial goods had also not grown sufficiently. As pointed out above, demand comes from the agricultural sector and from the export sector. When these two sectors grow slowly, industrial growth also suffers. Lack of sufficient investment and the prevarication of industrialists about their future plans for investment in plant and machinery has also been caused by an increase in the flow of imports. Many are uncertain whether they would be able to survive in the face of increased competition and, in fact, some industries have even shut down. After 2004, industrial revival began and has been due to lower interest rates and the consumer boom in the automobile and the consumer durables sectors.

India and South Korea

Prime Minister Rajiv Gandhi was very fond of quoting South Korea's example of rapid economic growth in the 1980s. India's slow private sector growth contrasted sharply with South Korea's, especially in the area of manufacturing capabilities. South Korea received huge amounts of direct foreign investment (DFI) and increased its productivity growth rapidly. In India, on the other hand, instead of raising productivity, various constraining factors led to an increase in the incremental capital output ratio (ICOR)—the number of additional units of capital that are required to produce an additional unit of output, which clearly showed that more capital was required for producing a unit of output. All countries that use more efficient techniques have experienced a decline in ICOR. The productivity of a particular unit of capital depends on the efficiency of the workforce. Productivity is greater when there is an uninterrupted flow of materials to the workplace and the ICOR is lower. But if there are restrictive practices on the part of the workforce, it results in lower output and higher ICOR. In India, trade union activity and lockouts contributed to higher ICOR in the 1970s and 80s.

In the 1980s, when Southeast Asia was making important and significant strides, Indian industrial growth was languishing and failed to keep pace with the other newly industrialising countries (NICs). Exports were not encouraged in an aggressive fashion and, unlike South Korea, there was no culture for export production through strict quality control, close monitoring of export orders and their timely delivery. In fact, there was an 'export-pessimism' that de-emphasised the role of exports in India during the 1970s. India thus missed out on the great export boom that took place in the Southeast Asian region.

There was a rapid rise in third world industrial exports from 1970 to 1983 when it doubled from 5 per cent of the world trade to 10 per cent. Korea exported four times more than India by 1980 and in 1990, its exports to the Organisation for Economic Co-operation and Development (OECD) countries were valued at $41 billion where as India's were only $9 billion.

The import substitution regime had a far-reaching impact as exports were not considered important and crucial for growth. In general, exporters lacked information about the trends in demand and styles prevalent in the export markets and they could not find proper marketing links abroad that would assure them continuous orders. There were problems of transportation also. South Korea had cheaper means of transportation through bulk handling by various special export oriented companies. All these problems led to India's minuscule presence in markets abroad. Indian exports were 2.5 per cent of the world trade in 1947, but fell to 1 per cent in 1965 and to 0.7 per cent in the 1980s.

Indian exporters also did not care for a high rate of growth because they could always sell at home. When large consignments of export goods were rejected by buyers abroad due to lack of quality control, it could be sold at home. With shoddy goods and poor finish, Indian goods began earning a bad name in the international markets and gradually they were pushed over to the lower and cheaper end of the market. Rarely did posh stores in America, UK or France keep Indian merchandise and, in general, they were sold in the street markets at cheap rates.

Perhaps one can blame the licence-permit *raj* and excessive state control for the slow industrial growth but India did manage to establish a huge capital goods industrial base. The dominance of the public sector was significant in the production of steel, cement and petroleum products. Looking back, the insecurity about being dependent on industrialised countries for basic industrial goods in the initial years after Independence has gone, and the sentiment that promoted such a strategy can be understood. But there is little doubt that the initial thrust towards promoting a prominent public sector and a bias against the private sector can be held responsible for much that ails the industrial sector today, like lack of quality control and industrial efficiency or high productivity growth.

With many of the restrictions gone since 1991, the ball is in the court of the corporate sector which now controls most of the manufacturing sector. Yet it is facing a new set of difficulties and is still not able to achieve double digit growth in a sustained manner.

In the post-1991 period, in 1995-96, there was a surge in industrial growth but it did not last long. In recent times, the main constraint on industrial growth is, like before, in infrastructure. Costly power, slow and inefficient transportation system and high cost of finance and even availability of skilled labour remain the main areas in which India is lagging behind its competitors, mainly China. High transaction costs that include bureaucratic hassles, bribes, and unnecessary paper work which the Indian industrial producers have to undertake in order to export—from factory gate to the foreign market—remain the main hurdles in India's becoming a big exporter of manufactured goods.

China's Emergence

China's emergence as the world's manufacturing hub has thwarted the growth prospects of all Asian countries in manufactured exports. India till recently was selling huge quantities of raw materials to China much like its other neighbouring countries. China is using imported inputs to increase its manufacturing and export growth.

India's Special Economic Zones (SEZs) are also not as effective as in China in churning out quantities of cheap exports. Most people blame Indian labour laws which are not as flexible as China's. India is also unable to compete because it is still difficult to reduce and expand the size of the firm to remain efficient. But recently, many states have modified labour laws for the SEZs in order to enable producers a greater leeway regarding hiring and firing of labour. It is, however, the quality of Chinese labour that gives them the edge over other producers. Its labour force is educated and disciplined and has contributed immensely to China's manufacturing success.

After the dismantling of the Multi Fibre Agreement, competition in textiles has also become acute but India has secured niche markets in certain woven textiles and hosiery items. Indian textiles, much more varied and rich in design with complex weaving techniques, especially from the handloom sector, are still catering to specialised, smaller markets but China is surging ahead in mass markets.

It is only in recent years that Indian companies have been allowed to borrow abroad at cheaper rates and to establish subsidiaries in industrial and developing countries. In fact, many industrialists have successfully established bases in different countries. At one level, Indian industrialists have made a big mark in some areas but some of the old traditional industries are languishing. Most successful ventures have been based on using the latest technology and on using more capital than labour. Over the last five decades, a large number of new industries have come up and it is natural that some older industries would die a natural death. With a better infrastructure many would survive the competition from neighbouring countries.

India's industrial base is huge despite all the problems and the moderately high industrial growth that has been achieved over the years. Over the last 50 years industrial production went up about five times and India is the 10th most industrialised nation in the world. India's engineering exports have grown manifold since the 1980s and there has been a marked improvement in technological and managerial skills in some industries. There has been a big increase in the production of metallurgical industries like iron and steel, chemicals, petrochemicals, fertilisers, capital goods, captive power plants and construction industries. India has an impressive R&D capability, especially in pharmaceuticals and Indian engineers are providing consulting services, design and project management expertise to governments and private businesses in various countries.

Where slow industrial growth has hit the most, however, is in the area of job creation for the expanding labour force and in not being able to give a bigger boost to the country's economic growth.

MNCs and Indian Industry

A number of multinational corporations (MNCs) entered into joint ventures with Indian companies after 1991 and much was expected of them in terms of imparting better technology, management style and new products. Indeed, the domestic market has been flooded with international brands of consumer goods and consumer durables like refrigerators, washing machines, cars, and TV sets. Big brand names have captured the market and many Indian brands that were well-known before the liberalisation phase have been edged out. Even in kitchenware and ceramics, cosmetics and popular snacks, foreign brands are dominating. There are a few survivors who have greatly improved their quality and are able to offer tough price competition to imported goods and locally produced branded goods. As pointed out above, Indians are very price sensitive and this has meant the survival of many indigenous producers and manufacturers and the exit of many foreign manufacturers who tried to set up base in India. Yet, the difference between China and India is that the MNCs have mainly concentrated on India's domestic market and not on exports to neighbouring countries. China's MNCs have boosted its exports and industrial growth. Even in the retail trade, China has benefited enormously from the presence of giant retailers like Wal-Mart which sources its products from China in big quantities.

In recent years, many companies who were disillusioned with their Indian partners left and many others are setting up subsidiaries rather than remain in joint ventures. Indian industrial goods have no doubt benefited from the inflow of technology and know-how from these foreign investors.

But employment in these foreign companies has been growing slowly because they require highly qualified personnel and only a handful are able to gain entry. While the manufacturing base has been expanding, it has been through greater use of technology rather than by hiring more people. Employees of MNCs are considered the privileged lot today.

The Informal and Small-Scale Sector

The organised sector or the factory sector is the one in which a unit employs 10 or more persons and uses power; or 20 workers without the use of power. The formal or organised sector where people have permanent jobs, and the national labour laws are applicable, employs eight per cent of the labour force. Hiring and firing is difficult in the organised sector because of the old laws which aim at protecting labour from exploitation and low wages. The production units are formally registered and unionised.

The need for flexible laws has been pointed out by the World Bank and IMF and many industrialists have asked for an amendment of the Industrial Disputes Act 1947, which would enable the employers to reduce the size of their units when necessary and thereby cut costs and become competitive. Many industries, like textile mills, need to shed labour because production processes have become computerised and for the right finish and quality, more sophisticated machinery rather than more labour is needed. Many industries however are able to remain flexible despite the labour laws because they hire all managerial personnel on a contract basis whom they can hire and fire with ease. They are also able to break trade unions by hiring workers on contractual basis. Actually, the impact of labour laws has been diluted by various means devised by organised sector. This flexibility has affected job creation in the organised sector.

In India, the productivity of an average worker is not as high as in China and, therefore, factory owners are tempted to use more capital than labour. The productivity of the average manufacturing worker is higher by 50 per cent in China as compared to India though it is 25 per cent more expensive. The rise in capital intensive production in India is responsible for the slow growth in jobs in the organised sector.

The informal or unorganised sector that encompasses all other production units, produces many goods and services. But it lacks amenities and job security for workers. Infrastructural problems affect its productivity and other factors like the small size of units affect the cost of production which is higher than in the formal sector. The informal sector also includes services like domestic service, drivers, couriers and self-employed construction workers and other services in which there is no social safety net and people are hired and fired constantly. The informal sector badly needs reform and a social insurance scheme. Women workers especially need protection from exploitation against low wages and long hours of work. Since millions of workers are involved in the informal sector, this sector needs technical upgradation, regular and cheap raw material supply, credit, marketing facilities and skill development.

The Small-Scale Sector

The small-scale sector, with its small sized units, also falls under the informal sector. It includes tiny household enterprises as well as small-scale industries that are quite modern and often have the latest machinery. The definition of a small-scale unit is through the threshold level of its investment in plant and machinery. For Gandhiji, village small-scale industries were important for the economy because they provided employment to many and required very little capital. The small-scale sector has flourished since Independence despite the rather serious problems that threaten the survival of many units. Since Independence, small enterprises have been encouraged through differential taxation and other incentives like easy acquisition of land, subsidised inputs and easier terms of credit. The protection of small-scale units was begun by reserving the production of certain items exclusively for them in 1967. At first only 67 items were reserved for the Small-Scale Industries (SSI) sector but by 1984, the total number of items reserved went up to 873. Though the reserved list has been reduced every year, in 2005 there were 605 items still reserved for the sector. The development of the small-scale sector was aimed at meeting the growing demand for consumer goods that required little investment. Large-scale industries have been allowed to enter into production of many of the items reserved for the SSI sector except that they have to agree to export 50 per cent of their production. In recent years, many products that require sophisticated machinery and larger-scale of production like leather products, plastics and chemicals have been 'de-reserved'.

Encouragement to the small-scale often meant curbs on the expansion of capacity of the large-scale units. As discussed above, the textile industry was controlled in order to allow for the small-scale sector to produce handloom cloth. Certain categories of cloth were reserved for handlooms and a certain fixed proportion of yarn output of spinning mills had to be in hank form for handloom production. Similarly for footwear, small-scale industries were favoured against large-scale production units.

There are around 120 lakh small-scale units in the country (unregistered as well as registered) and the small-scale sector accounts for 40 per cent of the manufacturing output and 50 per cent of the employment in the industrial sector. It also accounts for 33 per cent of the exports. The number of small-scale units in the country is growing at the rate of 4.7 per cent annually. The production is growing at 7.5 per cent. Since they employ around 250 lakh persons, it is an important sector of the economy and provides jobs for many of those who are without much formal education or capital. The investment limits in plant and machinery have been raised from Rs. 1 crore to Rs. 5 crore recently in order to enable small-scale units to modernise and become competitive.

There are two major problems that most small-scale units are facing—finding working capital and appropriate marketing channels. Another problem is skill development and training. All small-scale units are faced with the problem of getting adequate and timely credit. About 95 per cent of the small-scale units (accounting for 33 per cent of the employment in the factory sector), are not getting more than 3 per cent of their credit requirements. In 2005, interest rate concessions were granted to them but the total credit covered only 6.5 per cent of their production. Banks, when approached by the small and tiny units, show them a lot of rules and regulations and ask for collateral security and third party guarantee. These create problems and delays in credit dispensation. Village based units are even less fortunate even though priority area credit should go to village industries. Specialised branches for SSI units have been opened in some villages. The government has made many provisions for credit to the small-scale sector but their impact has not been very satisfactory. In 2004, Small Industries Development Bank of India set up a fund of Rs. 10,000 crore and the Laghu Udyan Credit Card Scheme was also started.

The small-scale sector also has problems in finding proper marketing channels because they are without brand names and though the investment limit in plants and machinery has been raised, not all units are in a position to invest. More and more, most units are not able to make quality products. Better machinery and equipment will guarantee flawless, better quality products and help in reducing the cost of production. Excise duty exemptions would make a difference to their pricing and would make them more competitive.

Somehow, despite much active encouragement, the small-scale sector did not become competitive over the years. It has remained poorly equipped and has continued to produce mainly for the domestic market. India being such a huge country has always been a more attractive market for domestic producers than distant export markets with their uncertainties. Some small-scale units, however, are not very labour intensive and use more capital than labour.

In case of neighbouring Southeast Asian countries, from the beginning, there was a big emphasis on export growth that made the small and medium enterprises compete fiercely to corner the growing market. As a result their quality improved rapidly compared to Indian small-scale units.

The policy of protecting and nurturing the small-scale sector has been reviewed and many of the negative points have surfaced. Every year, more and more items that were reserved for the small-scale sector are being 'de-reserved' as it has been found that the restrictions on expansion of units and ceilings on investment for them to qualify as the small-scale unit have been responsible for low efficiency and high cost of production.

There is a strong pressure for more 'de-reservation'. It has been felt that the products reserved for small-scale units can be freely imported, especially with the quota system for imports gone. It seems meaningless that Indian large-scale units are not allowed to produce the same items.

Basically, even though various governments at the Centre have remained interested in promoting the small-scale sector, and as a result the small units have grown in number, employing more labour every year, huge constraints remain in their infrastructure, financing and marketing. They can become viable and profitable, like some very successful textile and jewellery units, only when infrastructure improves as in clusters.

From 1991, the industrial policy has been directed at making the small units integrate with the large-scale units and has allowed that 24 per cent of a small units' equity capital can be owned by large industries. Cheap land for setting up small-scale units, power and access to latest technology have been encouraged in the case of tiny units. Institutional finance too has been made easier. But it remains to be seen how they would be able to withstand the forces of competition unleashed in the country through further tariff reduction measures. They will continue to need help from the government for infrastructure and marketing of products.

Clusters of small-scale units with common infrastructural facilities are gaining popularity. There are many cluster-based industries in India today and with common sources of power and transportation when serviced by proper highways, these clusters may show the way for future development of small-scale industries. Sixty clusters were focused on for development in 2003 by equipping them with the latest technology. Training facilities are also available in these clusters.

Some effort has also been made to provide small-scale weavers with designs and fashion trends. The handloom sector will have to be upgraded and widely modernised in order to increase the number of jobs and raise labour productivity so that wages and incomes improve. The marketability of the products has to be undertaken carefully in targeted markets for best results.

Public Sector and its Decline

At the time of Independence, the private sector was rather small and it did not possess the capability or means for starting vigorous and rapid industrialisation. Before, the Indian leaders looked upto the models of countries in which the public sector had played an important part like Japan, South Korea and the Soviet Union. India was set on the path of public sector-led industrialisation in which capital goods production was given emphasis. All key and strategic industries were to be in the public sector and it became the main employer of labour force in the organised sector. The government set up several key industries which at that time absorbed huge amounts of funds. The private sector was allowed in other industries like consumer goods and of course, agriculture that was almost wholly controlled by the private sector. Since the public sector became important as an employer, even today, about three-fourths of the people working in the organised sector are working in the public sector.

Emphasis on public sector has led India to build a huge capital goods base. Some of the biggest and most profitable companies in India are public sector companies. Public sector companies are owned by the government and are run by government officials. Lack of professional managers and general lack of accountability has led to the emergence of a large number of loss-making companies also. To sustain them, the government has to siphon off money from the exchequer every year which in turn adds to the government's fiscal deficit. In any case, the public sector ceased to be confined to heavy industries but went into airlines, hotels, consumer goods production like watches, areas in which it hardly had any advantage in terms of expertise.

Public sector savings kept declining over the years and though some PSUs were doing well, many needed heavy bailouts for which the government had to borrow heavily from the market.

Since the economic reforms began in 1991, there has been a lot of stocktaking about the performance of public sector companies and it was decided to disinvest (divest) them and the government would reduce its stake in them by selling off shares. Those which could not be revived at all could be sold off and for those which could be saved through restructuring, it was proposed that a package would be made out for their revival. Over the years, not many of the public sector companies have been disinvested mainly because of the fierce opposition to disinvestments.

The main fear of disinvestment is from the labour unions. On the one hand, the government needs to get out of many loss-making public sector concerns, on the other, it cannot wind up these units easily because of the resistance from a body of public sector employees who have got used to many perks and comforts. They are reluctant to leave even when tempted with VRS because to them working in a PSU means a certain amount of prestige, an official address (so important for everything) and security which they are reluctant to give up.

The performance of most of the public sector enterprises, on the whole, has not been extraordinary though some have shone and made huge profits. Bureaucrats without having any special expertise in the field of certain industries have been appointed to manage and run these enterprises. They have been overstaffed and their efficiency in many cases has been very poor. There are still 240 central PSUs and 1,000 state level PSUs. They not only produce goods but also services like power generation, banking, insurance, and road transport. The procedure to be followed in disinvesting or privatising public enterprises has been looked into deeply by the Disinvestment Commission that was appointed in 1996. But even after 13 reports no progress was made except that from 1999-2000 to 2004, when many PSUs came up for disinvestment with a focus on strategic sales of equities.

There have also been allegations of selling stakes in PSUs cheap, a process that has been christened 'selling the family silver'. Yet the government went ahead and disinvested in some important PSUs.

As pointed out above, some public sector units have done extremely well and their profits have multiplied over the years. It only goes to show that if the units are professionally managed they perform at par with the best of private sector undertakings. The PSUs that have succeeded have had professional directors and CEOs and have probably not faced much political interference. But many of the state run PSUs have gone into the red due to local politics.

It is these loss-making PSUs that have to be disinvested first, but the task is not easy. It is much easier to sell the government's stake in profit making PSU like BHEL.

The main stumbling block, which is of finding an acceptable solution to the threat of the retrenchment of thousands of employees, has to be sorted out first. Disinvestment will reduce the pressure on the exchequer of frequent bailouts and money for the life support of the loss-making enterprises. Even when everyone agrees that a certain enterprise like Air India is in need of disinvestment in order to make it more competitive, when it comes to the actual nitty-gritty of sale, many hurdles arise and the whole exercise is postponed.

Again, the problem of disinvestment is related to lack of alternative job opportunities for the staff that is likely to be retrenched after the sale of equity to a private enterprise. If the country had been growing at a higher rate, there would have been more diversification of production and many more jobs in the market. Unfortunately, the employment growth in the organised sector has been very slow and PSU staff resist any change.

The disinvestments issue has been highly politicised in recent times because the current UPA government has chalked out its policy towards Disinvestment in its Common Minimum Programme and clearly stated that profit making PSUs would not be disinvested. With problems of raising finance for funding various ambitious rural and infrastructure projects, there have been attempts to sell off shares of profit making PSUs as well. They would immediately garner enough resources but the Left parties which are in the coalition at the Centre, have been very vocal about their objections. The entire Disinvestment Programme, which many feel is the cornerstone of the economic reforms, has therefore been stalled for sometime.

9

Infrastructure

It is the lack of an efficient infrastructure in India which stands out when one travels across China, Thailand or Malaysia. The most marked difference is between India and China today. Without modern and efficient infrastructure, higher growth prospects in industries and agriculture are not possible. Infrastructure includes roads, power, ports, railways, telecommunications and airports. Because of the inadequacies in infrastructure, most big enterprises have made their own arrangements for power and water but have to depend on government maintained roads and railways. India is among the last when ranked according to the quality, price and reliability of infrastructure services. It is a major constraint that India is facing today in raising the rate of economic growth. Over $320 billion would be required for upgrading the infrastructure over the Eleventh Five Year Plan, according to Economic Survey 2006-07. But in 2003, India's spending on infrastructure as a proportion of the GDP was only 3.5 per cent ($21 billion) as compared to China's 10.6 per cent of GDP or ($150 billion) (Mid-Year Review, December 2005, Ministry of Finance). The role of the public sector in building India's infrastructure was very important from the beginning but after 1991 it was realised by the government that the needs are too great and private sector has to be involved in building infrastructure. The private sector has been given incentives to invest but since the gestation period of most projects is long, the private sector's interest has not been very great. But in telecommunications, the entire development has been through the private sector.

Power

Indian industries, big and small, require power for their daily functioning and without adequate power, productivity is likely to suffer. The power situation in India is quite dismal even though the per capita consumption of power remains very small as compared to the industrialised countries. The power supply has not matched the demand for power and in big metro cities there are frequent power cuts which make life difficult. Industry too has to pay a higher per unit cost of power than India's competitors and the quality of power is variable and erratic. Many industrial units across the country have their own captive power plants and are no longer dependent on the state's supply. Every urban middle income household has some sort of an inverter because in the summer months when power cuts are most frequent, the inverter can at least make a fan and a few lights work.

When the economic reforms began, the government went ahead and invited foreign investors and they came to the power sector. But by 2001, many had left and one after another, there were problems with investors and the tariffs they wanted to charge. The US Multinational company Enron entered the Dabhol project in Maharashtra for power generation. It was one of the biggest companies from the US that entered the power sector. This was part of the private sector power policy that was introduced by the government in 1992.

With great fanfare they started the project which was preceded by a lot of controversy. The details were worked out in secrecy and the tariff was fixed in dollars. To reassure the investors that their money was safely invested, the Centre and the state, both gave guarantees of adequate returns so that in case of default or any problems, these could be invoked and the power company would be protected.

Enron succumbed to the pressure of pleasing various government officials and when the government changed, they could not recover the money which was due to them according to the terms of the contract from the main buyers of power like the Maharashtra State Electricity Board.

The Enron controversy and the Maharashtra government's defaulting in payment has done a lot of damage to the country's image as a suitable destination for foreign investment. The company went for arbitration abroad because there was little chance of recovery of dues. The revival of Dabhol project, closed since June 2001, was initiated in 2005.

Recently, the Electricity Bill was passed (Electricity Act, 2003) and reforms, long awaited, were introduced. Generation of power has been privatised and in many states, including Delhi, the distribution has been privatised. Different power companies like Tata Power, BSES and others have been given charge of distribution. In time, there would be a choice available to consumers as a result of the Electricity Act to choose from the different distributors of power.

The government has also encouraged various industries to set up captive power plants that cater only to their demand. Because though demand has been rising by around 9 to 10 per cent since the 1980s, there has been a consistent shortfall in the supply of power. Around 61 per cent of the manufacturing units have their own generators compared to 27 per cent in China, where the cost of power is 39 per cent lower than in India.

The targets set by the Five Year Plans have not been met mainly because hydroelectric power has not been growing at a fast and even pace and thermal units have faced several problems that have led to their underperformance.

The slow pace of reforms in the power sector has also been due to political interference because politicians have been generous in doling out free power to the farmers and have turned a blind eye to the thefts that have affected the regularity of power supply.

In fact, the farmers have been cross subsidised by commercial and industrial users of power who have been paying uneconomical tariff rates. Actually the electricity tariff charged from industry and commerce users is higher than the average cost of supply and the costs have risen faster than the rise in the price of the manufactured products. High price of per unit of power has been a disadvantage for Indian industry in gaining competitiveness abroad.

Beside, the slow growth in power supply is also due to the poor state of finances of the State Electricity Boards (SEBs). Most have been in the red and their perpetual losses have resulted in the poor state of their machinery and equipment. The financial losses have been due to heavy transmission and distribution (T&D) losses that are basically due to inefficiencies and rampant power thefts. The lack of modernisation has led to frequent breakdowns and power cuts—a recurrent feature in summer in major cities and towns. The refurbishment and modernisation of SEBs is essential for improving the state of power distribution through them.

The T&D losses have to be cut down because they are also responsible for their bankruptcy of SEBs. These losses are also due to the sparsely distributed loads over a large area, particularly the rural sector. Being saddled with losses, there is underinvestment in transmission systems. T&D losses have been 20 to 22 per cent against the international average of 9 per cent. The power tariff has also not been fixed appropriately and has remained below the economic charge.

Frequent breakdowns in machinery lead to the poor and uneven quality of power generated. Not only is there a problem with power cuts but frequently changing voltage is another problem facing all consumers.

The electrification of village India is also moving at a slow speed with 1,25,000 villages remaining without electricity. Even though India has a very low per capita consumption of energy, having no power leads to the use of biomass for cooking and heating. Having electricity in villages is important for reducing infant mortality because respiratory infections arise from the use of other types of lighting and heating, specially biomass.

Oil

For India, crude oil is a very important source of energy as most of the industries are fuelled by hydrocarbons. India imports about 70 per cent of its oil needs from abroad. Finding alternative sources of energy and increasing the supply of domestically produced oil has been rather slow. The government heavily subsidises oil consumption in the form of LPG, kerosene and diesel. The oil companies are compensated for supplying products to the public at subsidised prices and the difference between the market price and the selling price which used to be deposited in the oil pool account has now been dismantled. Today petrol prices are linked with international prices and it is the petrol prices which rise first when there are international price hikes, and cause inflationary pressure. Alternate forms of energy and energy conservation measures are urgently needed in India not only to reduce the dependence on imported oil but also because, as the number of vehicles increase, the pollution levels are likely to go up in all metro cities.

There were large investments in oil exploration in the 1980s and these were financed through borrowings, mostly from international capital markets. The government has also financed oil exploration at the rate of 0.5 per cent of the GDP, annually, since 1980-81. But despite the investment, India's oil potential has remained under-explored. The momentum to develop the known fields has also slowed down and production of oil has not been adequate. Many reasons can be given—delays in the implementation of projects to maintain reservoir pressure, strikes and the advanced age of oilfields that led to large quantities of gas being flared in the second half of 1980s at a cost of $2 billion. Similar factors and overexploitation has rendered unproductive more than 700 wells in the Gujarat and Bombay High Offshore regions with an annual production of only 5 millions tonnes in the 1980s.

Earlier, until the reforms in 1991, the government had decided to limit the use of private capital in exploration, development of discoveries and production, but from 1992 the government decided to allow private investment in the oil sector.

Nevertheless, crude production has been going down and mainly public sector enterprises like Oil and Natural Gas Corporation and Oil India Ltd., are involved in upstream activities such as exploration and production. In 2003-04, (both public and private joint venture) onshore production of oil was 11.4 million tonnes and offshore production was 17.7 million tonnes. Downstream activities like refining, marketing and distribution are confined to Indian Oil Corporation, Bharat Petroleum and Hindustan Petroleum Corporation Ltd.

The transport sector is the biggest consumer of petroleum. Kerosene and LPG consumed by the domestic sector, are heavily subsidised. LPG is released through the public sector oil corporations and kerosene is sold through the PDS's ration shops. Some decanalisation has taken place in recent years and the private sector is also involved in the sale of kerosene and LPG. For transporting petroleum, the most efficient method is underground pipelines as it is much cheaper than railway transportation. Petronet, a holding company, has the responsibility of raising the finance for planned projects in the sector.

Roads

China has 19,000 miles or 30,000 km of expressways which is 10 times more than in India. As everyone knows roads are the arteries of a nation and the better the roads the better the transportation of people and goods across the country. Unfortunately, in India the condition of most roads leave much to be desired. Some beautiful highways have been built recently but even in the 21st century, many villages remain unconnected with the main roads of neighbouring towns. From lack of good road network arise a million other problems like lack of access for villages to markets.

To establish a good network of roads heavy investment is required and it can't be done piecemeal. China's rapid advance in recent years is due to the road network that has been installed within a short period.

The responsibility for managing India's national highways is shared by two central agencies, the Ministry of Surface Transport and the National Highway Authority of India (NHAI) along with the public works departments of various states. India has a total road network of about 3 million km. Around 60 per cent of the country's total freight is carried by trucks along highway routes. The national highways carry 40 per cent of India's road traffic though, as arterial roads, they have received only 20 per cent of the total road expenditure of the government. The aggregate length of roadways has increased eight-fold but the traffic has increased almost twenty-fold. India has a problem of road efficiency because national highways have increased only 1 per cent a year and the length of state highways has increased by 1.8 per cent a year.

Of the total 66,590 km national highway network (2006), 12 per cent is four lanes, 50 per cent is two lanes and 32 per cent is one lane. Expenditure on national highways declined from 1.4 per cent of the total plan during the 1950s to 0.6 per cent in 2000. (World Bank: India Country Framework Report for Private Participation in Infrastructure.)

Indian roads carry 85 per cent of the passenger and 70 per cent of the freight traffic. The highways, though they comprise only 2 per cent of the road network by length, carry 40 per cent of the traffic. A revenue model has been devised for financing the building of roads and its components are tolls and fuel cess.

Even though the government has been inviting private investment in roads, the attractiveness would depend on whether the investors would be able to get adequate returns on their investment. Private initiative in developing toll roads has been small because it is a rather new initiative. The Ministry of Surface Transport and NHAI have signed contracts with the private sector for nearly 20 bridges and bypass projects in the recent past. Several such projects have become operational. Some projects have been given by NHAI to the private sector for developing four to six lane stretches on certain national highways.

The Ministry of Finance determines the allocations for the road sector and, quite a few times, the Annual Budget of the central government has introduced levies on petrol for NHAI and the development of national highways. The private sector has been involved in constructing national highways and expressways on a build operate transfer (BOT) basis. Real estate rights have been granted in the case of Bangalore-Mysore Expressway Project. A special purpose contract vehicle has been established for the execution of many projects. The Golden Quadrilateral has more or less been successfully completed with 846 km of roads connecting the major cities of Mumbai, Delhi, Kolkata and Chennai.

Most of the projects in India have had extensive public sector support. Although bridges and bypasses can be financed by toll facilities, there is very little experience with highway tolls. Much higher levels of public support is to be expected during the development of a road programme. Each project will have its own commercial financing and policy risks.

The main challenge is giving connectivity to all villages with towns and cities. There are 1.70 lakh unconnected habitations in India which require 3.69 lakh km of new construction and 3.68 km of upgradation through reconstruction and repair.

Railways

Indian Railways is one of the oldest in the world and many of the problems that have surfaced today are due to the fact that it's rolling stock and equipment are very old. The use of railways as a mode of transportation is increasingly being replaced by trucks travelling by road, especially for the movement of freight traffic. People too are travelling more by road than railways though train journeys are relatively safer than buses and cars. There has been a slow growth in freight traffic, of around 6 per cent, and of passenger traffic, of less than 3 per cent. Railways also have the added advantage of not contributing to pollution. Out of the 63,122 km route of railways, about 26 per cent is electrified. Rationalisation of fares and freight structures has been undertaken to increase the freight and passenger traffic. The number of classes for freight tariff have been reduced from 59 to 24, reducing the ratio between the highest and the lowest freight rates from 8 to 2.8 only. Also, certain reduced rates have been introduced for high rated commodities like petroleum, iron, steel and cement. Internet ticketing has also been introduced.

Railways are also in need of drastic repair, replacement and modernisation as indicated by the frequency of accidents that have caused thousands of deaths. In the recent past, train accidents per million passengers has dropped slightly through steps taken to prevent human error.

Efficient railways could have saved industry transportation costs. Unfortunately, Indian Railways has been burdened by huge deficits in its budget year after year and is never able to undertake the required modernisation.

Ports

Lothal was India's first port; access to the sea through the inland port led to a flourishing maritime trade. Throughout history, trade has been very important to India and various ports developed along the coastline. But today, the ports are not sufficiently equipped to carry out international trade and commerce efficiently. There is a perpetual congestion problem in Indian ports. There is not enough capacity to handle all the cargo in the docks. Ports have to be modernised to make exports reach their destination on time. India has 6,000 km of coastline and 153 ports of which 11 have a special status as major ports under the authority of the central government. The rest are under state governments and the majority are operated as port trusts.

The current capacity of major ports is overstretched and is substantially below the 'throughput' levels which basically means that the number of ships entering the ports are far too many as compared to their capacity to provide them with berths. The average 'turnaround' time of ships has to be decreased. The average speed of cargo handling operations around the world is much higher than in India because development of ports received top priority in most industrialising countries. Besides, the total costs of moving the container through a terminal are on average 70 to 80 per cent higher in India than in Japan and the US where, ironically, the labour costs, of dock workers is much higher.

India has a low handling productivity rate which mean that ships spend a long time at berth. According to the Shipping Corporation of India, ships spend 52 per cent of their time in ports. Consequently, ship turnaround time in Indian ports is between 5 or 6 days compared to 1 day or less in other ports of the region. Waiting time for a ship to get alongside its berth is also considerably longer than in other countries. Waiting time for a berth in Chennai in 1998 was 5 days. Containers spend much longer, 10 to 25 days, in ports where as the acceptable standard is 2 to 4 days. Customs clearance can take around 5 days when the world average is 3 to 4 days.

In any case, the increase in demand for port services would require more than 70 per cent increase in the capacity of ports. Minor ports have to play an important role.

Some states like Andhra Pradesh have privatised ports. In any case, greater commercial autonomy has to be given to ports to encourage competition amongst them. Tariff Authority for Major Ports (TAMP) was established in 1997 and it determines tariffs on goods independent of the Port Authority. There is a big question of dock workers and their employment that surrounds the development of ports because there are 35,000 dock workers in Mumbai, 13,000 in Kolkata and 11,000 in Chennai.

Airports

The first impression one gets of India is through its main airports. India's airports cannot compare with the modern airports that have come up in the region recently—in Bangkok, Dubai, Singapore and many others. There is no doubt that all Indian airports, which are under the Airport Authority of India (AAI), need refurbishment. The AAI was established in April 1995, by merging International Airport

Authority of India and National Airport Authority, in order to bring about an integrated development, modernisation and expansion of operational, terminal and cargo facilities at airports conforming to international standards. It manages the entire Indian air space.

Almost all the eastern neighbours have ultra modern airports and facilities. Indian airports have to be upgraded and it would requ.re a huge amount of money. Whether to let the AAI handle the upgradation and modernisation or let foreign investors bring in their money and expertise in transforming airports into modern ones is the question. There has been much debate about privatisation of airports and whether foreign companies should handle everything except the security aspects.

A partial open sky policy was adopted in the 1990s because of the declining performance and profitability of Indian Airlines and Air India. There was also a big increase in passenger demand for additional services and Indian Airlines alone could not manage. Thus, private firms were allowed to operate scheduled and non-scheduled services. The aircraft size and type were left to the discretion of the private operator. Foreign equity was allowed up to 40 per cent and for NRIs it was increased to 100 per cent—but only in the domestic air transport service. Subsequently, an open sky policy was also adopted for cargo operators on a permanent basis. Fares were deregulated and left to the market. No private operator was, however, allowed on international routes.

Competition from the private sector has led to an improvement in the services of Indian Airlines and Air India. With a number of domestic private operators in the field, (7 scheduled airlines operating on routes according to a published timetable and 27 non-scheduled operators) air fares have become cheaper and competition has proved to be healthy. But many who started out with great fanfare had to withdraw because of many reasons, among which route guidelines by the government, especially insisting on uneconomic routes, high cost of aviation turbine fuel, high taxes and high airport charges and uneconomic fares were prominent.

There are 449 airports/airfields but most are non-functional. The AAI manages 87 domestic airports and 28 international enclaves. But about 50 per cent of the total air traffic is routed through Mumbai and

Delhi. All airlines operate only through 61 airports and thus there is a problem of underutilisation. There is also a problem in handling cargo on the ground, and overcoming problems of congestion. Additional capacity is needed in many airports and there is a need for more international airports.

There is no doubt that Indian airports cannot compete with neighbouring Dubai or Bangkok or Singapore. If one wants to attract tourists as well as foreign investors to come in much bigger numbers, either the government has to undertake the necessary investment or give it to private hands for all the operations. The unions as usual are against such privatisation as they point out that the Airport Authority is doing well and profits are being made. Privatisation will bring about a change in management style and there is fear of mass scale retrenchment.

Recent initiatives in modernisation have been undertaken and joint ventures have been signed between foreign investors and AAI in order to modernise Mumbai and Delhi airports. Two new Greenfield airports with private sector participation have been proposed for Bangalore and Hyderabad in which 74 per cent of the equity would be in private hands. These would be in the form of joint ventures between state governments and foreign partners and AAI would hold 26 per cent of the equity. Technical consultants have also been appointed to make 10 more airports world class and 15 more airports are being studied for upgradation.

A limited open sky policy has been adopted to enable passenger traffic to come to India during the peak winter months. Some designated airlines have been allowed to operate additional services to and from India subject to the existing terms of agreement with Air India/Indian Airlines. In fact, around 2,400 additional flights have been arranged; Indian government is also allowing private airlines that have completed five years of domestic operations to operate to any destination in the world excluding the Gulf and West Asia. The main problem confronting the airports today is not just expansion and modernisation, but safety. How the AAI handles this would be critical for the growth of air traffic, both domestic and international. There has been a double digit growth in both domestic and international traffic in 2004 and private airlines account for 61 per cent of the domestic traffic.

In 2006, modernisation of Delhi and Mumbai airports were handed over to two joint venture companies—Delhi International Airport (P) Ltd. and Mumbai International Airport (P) Ltd. For Delhi, partners are GMR group and FraporT & Malaysian Airports and Indian Development Fund as other members. Joint Venture partners hold 26 per cent of the equity and AAI holds 26 per cent.

Telecommunications

India has been slow at developing a telecommunication network in the recent past; getting a phone was an arduous task often involving bribes and a long waiting period. Today, India has had a telecommunication revolution, especially in the area of mobile phones. But China is ahead of India because it has six times as many mobile line phones and fixed line telephones per 100 people.

The telecommunications sector has grown rapidly. Though fixed line connectivity is still small, mobile connectivity is rising fast. There is a big private sector participation in telecom, allowed since 1991, even though the public sector still dominates. Until 1994, telecommunications was a government monopoly. The National Telecom Policy of 1994 introduced private sector's participation in the provision of basic fixed telecom services and allowed cellular services in non-metro areas.

The new Department of Telecommunications is the policy maker and licensor. The Department of Telecommunications provide fixed services throughout India. MTNL provides basic services in Delhi and Mumbai VSNL had a monopoly on international services. The Telecom Regulatory Authority of India (TRAI) was established in March 1997 to act as a regulator.The government announced the New Telecom Policy in 1999 to regulate the sector with respect to services like basic, international, national long distance and Wireless in Local Loop (WLL).

The liberalisation of the sector was aimed at ensuring that telephones would be available on demand, universal access would be granted to basic telecom services at affordable rates, and India could emerge as a major manufacturing base and exporter of telecom equipment. It also intended to introduce all value added services that are available internationally and, in general, to increase the penetration of telecom in the country.

India remains a country where teledensity in the population (100 persons) though rising rapidly, remains quite low as compared to China. It was only in 2004 that fixed lines touched 44 million and the cellular user base reached 48 million mark. In 2004, teledensity reached 8.6 per cent as compared to 6.6 per cent a year before. The non-voice market comprising of message and data service for mobile operators also registered a huge growth recently.

India is among the top 10 countries in the world in terms of telecom network and has a huge foreign investment potential. The foreign investment allowed by the government has been raised to 74 per cent but FDI beyond 49 per cent requires government approval. No equity cap is applicable to manufacturing activities and FDI upto 100 per cent is allowed. Competition has been introduced in all service segments and national long distance services have been opened to free competition. WLL has been introduced for providing telephone services in urban, semi urban and rural areas. Full repatriation of dividend income and capital invested has been allowed in the telecom sector.

Getting telephones to India's 6.07 million villages remains a big challenge. The National Long Distance Service was opened to competition in August 2000. Convergence of services and a single license regime was introduced in 2002. A revenue sharing regime has replaced the fixed license fee regime for both basic and cellular operators. In 2002, the disinvestment of VSNL was completed and the government's equity was reduced to 26 per cent. The management of the company has been transferred to the Tata Group, a strategic partner. Internet services have been opened for free competition and permitted to establish own international gateways (through satellite or submarine cable) for carrying internet traffic. National Internet Backbone has also been commissioned. Corporatisation of the Department of Telecom Services and Department of Telecom Operations has taken place by creating Bharat Sanchar Nigam Limited with effect from October 2000.

In fact, India has made rapid strides in the area of telecommunications and Indian companies have gone abroad to provide telecom services.

10

Labour and Unemployment

In a country of over one billion people, the main strength is its labour power. There are around 400 million people who can be included in the work force in India. There are various degrees of skill and education that the Indian labour force possesses. The quality of labour force, whether it is skilled, disciplined and healthy, is very important for foreign investors who prefer to locate their factories in countries with cheap and abundant manpower. China has great advantage over India in possessing a skilled, educated and disciplined labour force. The productivity of labour is of great importance both in terms of quality and quantity of output.

In all developed countries, labour is more productive than in India; their production of output per hour is higher. As a result of higher productivity, the workers are able to enjoy more leisure and also command higher wages. In India, the productivity of untrained labour, working in small and medium sized units, is low. They work long hours but continue to earn low wages. In fact, when labour is cheap but unskilled, there is a tendency for industrialists to employ more capital than labour. It affects the growth of employment and unemployment can become an important issue for the stability of the government. In India, in recent years, job opportunities have been growing at a slower pace than the growth in the labour force, specially in urban areas. This slowdown in the creation of jobs has to be corrected, otherwise, there will be a rise in unemployment which is always a grim warning that the country is not experiencing equitable and sustainable growth. The jobless also feel frustrated and low, especially when there are no unemployment benefits or dole. Undoubtedly, after a long spell of unemployment, people are too demoralised to actively seek work. It also means GDP lost as labour is wasted.

While India's GDP between 1992-93 to 2000-01 grew at 6.4 per cent, the rate of unemployment as measured by the National Sample

Surveys (NSS), kept on increasing. The unemployment rate increased from 6.03 per cent of the labour force in 1993-94 to 7.32 per cent in 1999-2000. According to the 55th Round of NSS, the growth of employment dropped from 2 per cent in the period between 1983 to 1993-94 to less than 1 per cent in the period between 1993-94 to 1999-2000.

The Task Force appointed by the Planning Commission to look into the problem of rising unemployment pointed out that there was a sharp deceleration in the growth of the labour force from 2.3 per cent in 1983 to 1993-94 period to little over 1 per cent in the 1993-1994 to 1999-2000 period. There thus seemed to be a direct link between the decline in the growth of the labour force and the decline in the rate of growth of employment because of the lower labour participation rate. What could have elicited such a decline in the labour force? Could it be due to the withdrawal of women because they preferred more leisure as they felt better off or was it due to the decline of children joining the labour force as they were now in school due to a general increase in household incomes? It could only be rise in the real income that could have led to this phenomenon.

In future, however, the growth in labour force participation may not be so low which means that there is an urgent need to create more jobs in order to absorb the normal growth in labour force accompanying population growth.

There has been a decline in employment elasticity also. (Employment elasticity is the ratio of employment growth to the growth of value addition in production). This ratio has been declining slowly through the 1960s and 1970s and the trend has continued in the 1980s and 1990s. The decline is both due to the use of technology and the changing composition of production. Perhaps when more capital is used in production, as has been the case in recent years in Indian industry, the result is that less labour gets hired and there is a slow growth in employment. This trend is, however, in keeping with recent advances made in the field of technology and the availability of such technology for enhancing competitiveness.

Many studies have been undertaken and many policy measures have been adopted but complexities remain regarding the phenomenon of jobless growth in India which indicates that the underprivileged groups, especially, have been severely affected.

The decline in employment has been more in the rural areas and mainly in agriculture. Total employment in agriculture dropped from 60 per cent of the population in 1993-94 to 57 per cent in 1999-2000. Low productivity in agriculture combined with frequent crop failures due to drought and lack of adequate and alternate irrigation facilities, have made agriculture less profitable in some states. As a result, the number of workers employed in farming, has been declining. On the other hand, in some areas, higher agricultural growth due to increased use of mechanisation has led to a fall in demand for full-time agricultural labour. Low productivity and falling incomes in agriculture in some states has led to an increase in the use of casual farm labour. Many small farmers were forced to sell their land and become casual labourers; hence, the supply, has not been a problem.

Over the years, the government's response to the problem of stagnant agriculture has been to focus on poverty alleviation programmes for income generation and self-employment so that incomes of rural households increase. Self-employment has been promoted by various poverty alleviation schemes for both men and women in rural areas but the delivery of these programmes has not been very satisfactory due to numerous leakages. At best, these programmes have played an important role in providing supplementary employment, especially to vulnerable groups in areas under stress—often in times of natural calamities.

Many believe that crop diversification and setting up of more agro-processing businesses in the villages would lead to higher employment growth and income generation. Accordingly, the annual central budgets have been giving incentives to agro-processing industries.

It is also important to raise public investment in agriculture, especially in irrigation works as well as remove the controls on agriculture marketing that are constraining the free movement of agricultural commodities. Due to the declining investment in agriculture from mid-1990s onwards, a growth of 1 per cent in agricultural output has resulted in 0.13 per cent growth in employment as against 0.4 per cent growth experienced during the late 1980s and early 1990s.

The other avenues for employment generation in the economy are the industrial and services sectors. If we look at the organised manufacturing sector, growth has been lacklustre in the 1980s and 1990s and there is hardly any scope for increasing employment in this sector. Industrial growth has not been high enough, especially in the older industries that traditionally absorbed the maximum number of workers. The stagnation and decline of textile and food industries, especially in the 1980s, led to a period of low employment growth in the organised sector. A number of reasons like inadequate infrastructure, falling investment and lack of modernisation have been responsible for the low level of industrial growth in general.

The organised sector, which includes all public sector establishments and all private, non-agricultural establishments employing ten or more workers, has faced declining growth also because of the downsizing and closure of many of the public enterprises engaged in manufacturing. But only 7 to 8 per cent of the total workforce is employed in it. The public sector accounts for more than two-thirds of the total organised sector employment and its slowdown has had a severe impact on job expansion in that sector.

Many such enterprises have faced rising wages and declining profitability and reacted by shedding labour. They have increasingly resorted to restructuring in order to gear up to global competition. The consequence of reorganisation of production, which has taken place both in the public and private sectors, has been an increase in joblessness.

Since the possibility of increasing jobs in the public sector is rather limited because of restructuring, cost cutting and downsizing, the private sector, especially the private manufacturing sector, can offer more jobs in the future. Though it constitutes more than 75 per cent of total organised manufacturing output, in 2003, only 47.44 lakhs out of a total of 60 lakh were employed in the manufacturing sector. Most manufacturing units are trying to stay trim and slim in order to remain flexible. They are not tending towards greater labour intensity in their processes and like the foreign investors, are using more IT and other advanced technology. In fact, they are keen on giving voluntary retirement scheme (VRS) packages to employees who want to opt out.

Though retrenchment of labour has taken place in most countries on account of restructuring and reorganisation of industry, sometimes with increased frequency, as in the US in the 1990s, in India getting the 'pink slip' or being offered VRS, is something new. People are not used to voluntary or premature retirement and making people accept the VRS has not been very smooth. Many of the unlucky ones (working in loss making enterprises) were simply laid off without any severance pay. Job insecurity has increased human trauma which could be reduced only by setting up facilities for retraining and skill development centres. Such restructuring would assure the workers new jobs and proper rehabilitation.

The restructuring exercise has been aimed at increasing productivity through a trimmer labour force. In many cases, retrenchment has thrown families off balance. Not only did the employees lose their jobs but they also lost their housing, schooling for their children, healthcare and an 'address', that is so important in India.

In the last few years, persons receiving VRS witnessed a new phenomenon—their children were also not able to find jobs. Most of the younger generation who voted in the last election (2004) have remained jobless. Rise in unemployment among the youth calls for immediate measures like implementing some form of unemployment insurance. Increasing job opportunities for young jobseekers is thus the main challenge before the government today. They are not able to find jobs in the manufacturing sector because the demand for unskilled labour has been declining.

New industries in the manufacturing sector have also tended to absorb only technical and educated personnel. One of the main reason is that they want to be trim and flexible. Since under the old labour laws, hiring and firing became difficult, they prefer to have only contractual labour. The labour laws in the country, according to many, are responsible for the rise in the capital intensity of production. Though the labour laws have been blamed for keeping millions of workers out of jobs and protecting the jobs of those already employed, most employers today try to bypass the labour laws in many ingenious ways.

The same labour laws have not prevented skilled, labour intensive manufacturing units such as automobiles, auto parts and pharmaceuticals from entering global markets successfully. Large scale units have also increased the employment of casual and contract workers in non-core areas.

The decline in productivity in the small-scale sector has also been blamed for a rise in unemployment. If the small-scale sector grew rapidly, more jobs would have been created. The reservation of the small-scale sector has been carried forward; this was meant to increase FDI flows to the sector and enable it to reap the economies of scale that would lower production costs. But this has not happened in a significant way and the employment potential of the sector has not risen much.

Lack of infrastructure, marketing channels, proper quality control and lack of innovative designs have bogged down the productivity of the sector. Since the small-scale sector uses labour intensive processes, its expansion could have led to more jobs and more low technology products.

India's exports of low technology products has also not grown rapidly over the years—they rose from $ 2.5 billion in 1985 to $ 13 billion in 1995, while Chinese low technology exports grew from $ 3 billion to $ 72 billion in 1995. The same relative position of the two countries has been maintained till today.

Perhaps the reason is that small and medium enterprises (SMEs) are not growing in the right direction and are becoming inefficient. These enterprises were promoted for their employment potential since Independence but instead of availing of all the special incentives to become more cost effective, they have been faced with rising costs as a result of which they have lost out to more competitive neighbours. The quality of workers they get is also not as good as in China or Korea. Besides, many SMEs have also indulged in rent-seeking instead of trying to raise productivity. They have been inclined to move horizontally and build a number of small units instead of reorganising production in higher productivity units. If large-scale units could grow faster (greater flexibility of labour laws could be one of the reasons) through easier capital availability and improved infrastructure, they could also get more involved in supplying to large volume markets. Such large-scale orders cannot be supplied by small-scale units with or without cluster support. Labour intensive large-scale manufacturing would also increase the demand for educated and literate labour.

Education and Skill Training

It is also the lack of skills and training among workers that encourages industrialists to opt for more technology rather than labour. The Indian labour force is amongst the least skilled and literate as compared to the skill level of workers in countries like China and South Korea, especially in the manufacturing industries. Only 5 per cent of the labour force in the age group of 20 to 24 have vocational skills compared with 28 per cent in Mexico and as high as 96 per cent in South Korea. Almost 44 per cent of the labour force in India in 1999-2000 was illiterate and only 33 per cent had schooling up to secondary level and above. Only 19.6 per cent of males and 11.2 percent of female workers in urban areas have work-related skills. The importance of vocational training and universal compulsory primary education for a better quality labour force is obvious.

Educated Unemployed

Even with a rise in the number of educated persons in the labour force, such persons may find it tough to get appropriate jobs. The sectoral shift in occupations—from agriculture to industry or non-agricultural sectors, which is supposedly driven by the labour force getting more education and skills, has not been happening at a rapid pace in India.

Studies have shown that there is stagnation in the employment structure with increase in education. While the educational qualifications of persons joining the labour force has risen significantly, there has not been a commensurate increase in jobs that require higher education. The likelihood of being in a white collar job for college educated individuals is declining. In general, the rate at which white collar jobs have been expanding is lower than the turn-out of college educated persons. They usually keep searching for such jobs and do not take up second tier jobs like owning shops, petty businesses or small-scale production units. They thus become the educated unemployed. They would rather remain unemployed than work as farmers. In recent years, however, they have been accepting manual jobs, but still about 60 per cent of the educated are unemployed. Without significant expansion of opportunities in the formal or organised sector in the foreseeable future, agriculture and petty commodity production would thus continue to be major sectors of employment.

Absorption in the Informal Sector

Workers released from agriculture and the organised sector, as well as from the small-scale and medium-scale sector, are entering the informal or unorganised sector every day. The informal sector is absorbing around 92 per cent of the workforce and is characterised by unprotected jobs without regular salaries, job insecurity and no benefits. Even the minimum wages are not enforced and migrant workers, entering the service sector in big cities in a big way, are forced to live in slums. In a big cyber city like Bangalore, 20 per cent of the population lives in slums. Growth in high wage jobs in big cities has been accompanied by a deepening of urban poverty because low paid service workers are living in shanty towns and slums to cater to the needs of the affluent. There is an urgent need to improve the infrastructure of the informal sector in order to create more jobs and better work conditions.

Services Sector

The services sector is poised for creating about 70 per cent of the new job opportunities in the economy. It has been growing at a fast pace and job growth has been at 5 per cent (community, social and personal services, however, have had a negative growth). There has been a big increase in jobs in BPO (business process outsourcing) centres and in IT enabled services and exports. But the IT sector can absorb only around 2 to 3 million persons at most. According to a McKinsey study, direct employment in India's software industry is expected to rise from 180,000 in 1998 to 2.2 million by 2008. Besides, the requirements of IT training and knowledge of English would automatically exclude millions of rural and urban poor who do not have access to computers or English medium schools. More technical education in schools is thus very important because IT also indirectly contributes to job creation which leads to higher growth. But the catch is that it would depend on global trends and demand for IT and IT enabled services. A concerted revolt against outsourcing or finding alternative sources of IT expertise by the developed countries could trim down the demand for such services drastically and reduce the number of jobs.

Other expanding sectors, if they grow fast enough, like tourism too can give jobs to up to 66 million people per year. Similarly, construction, road transport, distributive trade, education and health services can also create many jobs.

Investment and Empowerment

A significant rise in investment in agriculture, industry and services would lead to a faster rate of job creation. And labour intensive techniques in all activities, especially in agriculture and allied activities, would be helpful in job creation. Since there are large interstate differences in the unemployment figures, more investment in laggard states is probably needed more urgently. In states with disproportionately high unemployment rates, there has been increasing migration of labour. Reducing the disparities through prompt action, especially through creation of jobs, would stabilise the migratory flows. An employment strategy that aims at reducing these disparities would involve faster growth of state domestic product. A faster GDP growth would also create more jobs; universal primary education and healthcare would enhance the basic skills and quality of the labour force.

Empowerment of women through development of skills and education could arrest the recent decline in the female workforce participation rate in rural areas. Equality of wages is also something to be looked into. Though participation has increased in urban areas, the average female wage in urban areas is only 80 per cent of the male average wage. In rural areas it is less than 60 per cent. This differential has to be reduced in the future. Clearly, there is a link between female literacy and their employability in the organised sector. More women are getting better jobs in states with a high level of female literacy.

Rural unemployment, often stretching for months, is an endemic problem in the poorer states. If the rural population has to live a life of dignity there should be guaranteed jobs for at least 100 days in a year. The UPA government, which came into power in May 2004, has been concerned with rural unemployment. It has passed the Rural Employment Guarantee Act.

The Employment Guarantee Scheme

The Bill involving the Employment Guarantee Scheme (EGS) was one of the key electoral promises of the UPA government under the Common Minimum Programme. It has combined the dual goal of providing unskilled work in rural areas for the unemployed and generating productive assets. It is based on the Maharashtra Employment Guarantee Act (MEGA) which came into force in 1977.

MEGA guarantees unlimited employment to rural adults provided there is a recognised need in the locality concerned and the people are willing to appear for work regularly. By contrast, the EGS limits employment to one member of a family which is below the poverty line (BPL) and has been identified by the *gram panchayat*. The employment is for a maximum period of 100 days in a year. While MEGA applies to all rural areas in the state, the EGS is proposed, at least initially, only in the poorest 200 districts in the country. Critics point out that EGS may not have an impact on poverty through such public works that the scheme may help to generate. But most research on Maharashtra's scheme indicates that it has helped to provide income to the poorest during lean periods and reduced seasonal migration. The landed classes have also benefited from the infrastructure created by the public works in the scheme. Since the late 1980s, demand for the employment guarantee scheme from Maharashtra's rural poor appears to have diminished. Some observers feel that it is because MEGA has been successful in creating infrastructure that has increased agricultural productivity and incomes. Whatever it is, it seems indisputable that MEGA has benefited the poorest by boosting their incomes and has somewhat increased their bargaining power *vis-à-vis* agricultural employers.

Some have argued that the infrastructure created through the workers under the scheme will not be productive. But the planning of the projects will be in the hands of the local *panchayats* and one might expect them to have an interest in constructing and maintaining projects that are genuinely useful.

Another criticism is that there would be corruption in the execution of the schemes. A certain amount of corruption is present in all anti-poverty programmes, in most public programmes and in the public distribution system. The EGS may not be more corrupt because the beneficiaries will be self-targeted and everyone who is willing to carry out hard labour will be entitled to gain employment under the scheme. Undoubtedly, there will be many non-poor who might be included. But the deserving poor cannot be entirely excluded either as often happens in administratively targeted schemes. It is unlikely that the non-poor will volunteer for low wages for hard labour required in the public works.

Simultaneous enactment of the Right to Information has enabled civil society organisations to monitor implementation and expose corruption.

Better supervision and ownership can be effected by increasing the role of *panchayats* and, more importantly, the people through the *gram sabhas* in the planning, implementation, evaluation and even auditing of public works. In Kerala, 40 per cent of the state's plan expenditure is carried out through *panchayats*. Thus, having a greater devolution of power in the area of finances to the *panchayats* should take care of corruption. Simple measures such as provision of job cards to workers, and exhibiting muster rolls on the notice board of the *panchayats* can make a great difference and make people more vigilant.

It may be true that open unemployment in rural areas is concentrated among casual labourers because their share in the working population has increased from 27 per cent in 1977 to 36 per cent in 1999 for men. It has increased from 35 per cent to 40 per cent in the case of women. Casual workers will thus be the principal claimants and the potential beneficiaries of the EGS. Farmers and other self-employed persons, as well as those with regular employment, are unlikely to offer themselves for unskilled manual work at the wage rates offered.

For women, greater participation in the EGS will enhance their status within the family and within rural society in general. The productive rural assets created within the scheme can include minor irrigation works, works for conserving soil and soil moisture and watershed development. The employment and income can assure labourers two meals a day and this would induce them to send their children to schools.

Many also think EGS should be a standing offer open to all without any means test and without any restrictions on the number of members of a family taking part or the number of days of participation by one of the members. According to noted economist Jean Dreze, who drew the blueprint of the NAC draft of the EGS, the twin principles of universality and self-selection should be respected in the EGS.

He has also pointed out the BPL list is known to be highly unreliable and this restriction is bound to exclude many poor households from the scheme. The Bill passed in the Parliament has included non-BPL families as also being eligible for the scheme.

India has one of the lowest tax to GDP ratios in the world and the question of whether it can afford an EGS is almost farcical. The Maharashtra scheme has worked for almost 30 years with a cross-section of civil society, politicians, business people, academics and concerned citizens who expressed their social obligation to find resources through four new taxes dedicated to MEGA. It was a recognition of the fact that the poor wanted to contribute to the economy and that they must be given the opportunity to do so through resources that could use their labour.

The EGS will cost only 1.55 per cent of the GDP and in a democracy the poor majority of around 30 per cent can justifiably demand their share in a country which is experiencing 6 to 8 per cent GDP growth.

Even if such employment generation as envisaged in the scheme does not yield any other positive result, the fact that there will be an increase in wage incomes in rural areas could generate more demand for rural goods and services and generate a positive multiplier effect. It may be able to give the unemployed the dignity and confidence they badly need in finding jobs and sticking to them. It could even contribute to increased tax revenues because of a higher level of economic activity.

Activities could include maintenance and support of educational and health institutions, providing mid-day meals in schools, sanitation services, etc. This would improve the rural quality of life. According to the Employment Guarantee Bill, the "expenditure under the Scheme will depend on the number of persons reporting for work, wage rate and the composition of the wage and the material components of the works. Assuming the wage and material components would be in the ratio of sixty is to forty and the average wage rate would be Rs. 60 per day, the cost of generating employment is estimated to be Rs 100 per person per day. Hence the cost of providing 100 days of employment to the poor household in a financial year is estimated to be Rs. 10,000. If the whole country is covered under the legislation, the total requirement on material and wage components, including the state share of funds is estimated to be approximately Rs 38,600 crore of which the central share will be Rs. 34,740 crore (this does not include administrative expenses)."

But a new clause has been added that where the food for work programme is already there, a much smaller amount would be needed from the Centre. It says, "Although the total expenditure would depend on the extent of coverage of areas of the country under the proposed legislation, it has been estimated that if the legislation is extended to 150 districts where the National Food for Work Programmes is being implemented, the requirement of central funds will be approximately Rs. 8,984.70 crore. The state government will bear 25 per cent of the material component (including the wages of skilled and semi-skilled workers). Since the employment is to be provided every year, this expenditure would be recurring expenditure." Clubbing with any other anti-poverty programme would mean further dilution of the scheme.

The outlay for the EGS on its own, however, is well below the defence expenditure and even below the projected expenditure on subsidies. It is also below the proposed increase in expenditure on education. And even though employment guarantee is a legal guarantee provided to every rural household, every household would not take up the offer. It will not require targeting and anyone who can get an income above the minimum wage through any other activity, would not be interested. Therefore, only a proportion of rural households would choose to avail of the offer and even among such households, not all of them would choose to take up such employment for the full 100 days. Chances are that between one-third to around 40 per cent of all rural households would choose to exercise this right across the country, which means only 49-50 million households.

Rural employment can also be provided by starting light industries in a cluster based setup. For these clusters to flourish, a lot of initiative and ground action would be needed in providing credit, infrastructure (power, water) and marketing channels.

Rise in Unemployment

The latest 61st Round of National Sample Survey conducted during July 2004 to June 2005, has revealed that India's employment growth at 2.5 per cent is still lagging behind the growth of labour force which grew at an annual rate of 2.5 per cent. Thus, though employment growth has been faster than in the past, unemployment has risen to 3.06 per cent of the labour force in 2004-05 as compared to 2.7 per cent in 1999-2000. The rise in unemployment was mainly due to rise in female unemployment both in rural and urban areas. More employment opportunities for women are thus required.

11

Savings and Investment

Savings are important for a developing country because they become available for investment for the country's growth through the financial sector. Savings in a vast country like India also give the government access to the financial means and resources for carrying out various developmental programmes. And unlike in the developed countries where the government tax mechanism is more efficient, in India, access to savings of households, corporate houses and the government's own savings are important for the financial system. As most Indians are usually insecure about their futures, especially in the absence of any social safety nets, they do save quite a significant part of their incomes every year but not as high a proportion as the Chinese. They are not used to changing their gadgets, cars and other durable goods frequently, a factor which was not taken into account by many MNCs when they set up their businesses in India.

Household savings comprise the most important part of total savings of the nation and, fortunately, they have been growing at a healthy rate. The savings rate has been rising, falling or remaining stagnant over the years mainly because of the changes in the household sector's contribution to the domestic savings of the economy. Its contribution has been around 70 to 75 per cent of the total savings. It is due to the steady rise in household savings that the percentage of total savings to the GDP has gone up from around 8 per cent in 1950, to around 25 per cent of the GDP in recent times. It rose to 28 per cent in 2004 and 31 per cent in 2005 but that was mainly due to the fall in government's saving, mainly public sector's 'dissaving' (a cutting down of losses). Corporate savings and the public sector savings, however, have not been growing in a steady manner. The private corporate sector has been lagging behind the household sector in savings and in the last few years its contribution has been only 10 to 12 per cent of the GDP. Corporate savings declined further in the 1990s and even became negative. Today the private sector's savings are more important as compared to the public sector's savings, which have been going down and have even become negative.

The public sector has a problem with regard to its high level of current expenditure which is eroding its capacity to save. There has been a sharp rise in both non-Plan or non-productive expenditure and Plan expenditure and the consequent sharp decline in public savings has meant that the government has a lower proportion of the total savings at its disposal for the maintenance of existing capital assets and their replacement. This has resulted in a long-term neglect of assets and has led to a lower output. When there is a lack of maintenance, the capital employed per unit of output rises and results in an inefficient production method. The growing number of loss-making public enterprises has been the main cause of the decline in public savings. By siphoning off funds for their survival from the public exchequer, the government has been vigorously 'dissaving'.

How to increase the flow of savings is a question that is crucial for India because other countries in Southeast Asia, which have done well, have all got higher rates of savings. China, and members of the Association of Southeast Asian Nations (ASEAN) have high rates of savings at above 30 per cent of the GDP. High savings have helped China's rapid economic growth. India's current rate of savings, till recently, was not considered adequate for a faster GDP growth.

Most people save in the form of assets like gold, land, houses and financial instruments as well as other types of moveable and immoveable property. People will save more in financial assets if their propensity to save is higher and they are looking for good returns for their money. If attractive saving instruments are made available by the banking sector, then people would be tempted to save more—especially if the interest rate is high.

Inflation is a factor that people take into account while saving money and it has to be controlled because people are inclined to save less if they see prices rising because then their savings would be worth less in terms of goods and services which they can buy in the future.

Giving tax incentives to save also works in the case of individuals and households. Corporate savings depend on concessions that they get on saving more and investing more. Similarly, the public sector's savings would depend on the efficiency of the units and how much profits they can make. A high rate of saving is also sometimes associated with high degree of inequality in the distribution of incomes. If more rich people, with a high propensity to save, get a bigger proportion of the national income, savings would go up. But efforts have to be made by the government so that those with low incomes also can save more in due course. If they are given training in skills and are educated, they too can have better income prospects and save more. Better healthcare will also induce people to save more with a rise in incomes as their life expectancy would go up.

Savings are needed for investment or additions to the capital stock of the country. And investment promotes growth, both in agriculture and industry. The more the farmers spend on improving their irrigation systems, wells, and buying better seeds, the more secure they can be of their future incomes. Unfortunately, most farmers have low incomes from which they can hardly save and thus their investments on farm improvements are also low. Rich farmers, on the other hand, spend mostly on consumption.

In recent years, the interest rates were first hiked to attract funds from home and abroad as well as to control inflation, and then lowered in order to promote a higher rate of investment but such low interest rates have also led to a rise in consumerism. People have been buying more on hire-purchase and borrowing money from banks to buy houses, flats, cars and other consumer durables. Increase in consumerism would mean higher demand for domestic goods. But if the demand is mainly for imported manufactures, then the domestic industry will suffer.

Raising the rate of savings involves increasing public sector's savings which involves cutting down bureaucratic expenses and subsidies that do not reach the poor. Creation of financial institutions which have attractive savings schemes and mutual funds that are reliable would also make people save more. The private sector can also be given appropriate tax incentives to save.

There is another form which India's savings have taken—gold. India's appetite for gold is vast. It imports 70 per cent of its gold requirement at a huge cost. Gold is a form of saving favoured by the people since ages. Getting access to the 'gold horde' of the country has proved to be a difficult task for finance ministers in the past.

Savings that are put in banks become investible funds in the hands of business which borrows from them. Any increase in investment leads to increase in production; that increases the demand for goods and lead to higher output and incomes, and results in a higher rate of economic growth. Huge investments were made by China to achieve a high rate of growth over the last two decades. In 2003, to achieve a growth rate of 9.5 per cent, China's investment requirement was 42 per cent of its GDP. India has in the past invested 22 to 33 per cent of its GDP for a decade and achieved an average of 6 per cent GDP growth. Its 'efficiency of capital' is higher because China has invested twice as much annually and its rate of growth has only been 50 per cent higher.

When domestic savings are not adequate for financing the development needs of the country, then foreign savings in the form of FDI is critical because foreign savings can bridge the gap between domestic savings and the investment needs of the country. Foreign investment has been unshackled since 1991 and allowed to flow in more freely than before. Before 1991, foreign investment played a much smaller role in India's development because the main emphasis was on 'self-reliance' but heavy industry was built with foreign collaboration.

Foreign Direct Investment (FDI)

Since Independence, the government was aware of the advantages of foreign investment and its ability to bring in technology in addition to funds. Certain companies were therefore allowed to have majority control of an enterprise. A number of tax concessions were given and the government streamlined industrial licencing procedures to avoid delays in foreign collaboration approvals. Foreign investment partners could only have up to 41 per cent of equity.

Somehow foreign investment was not viewed as wholly good for the country and certain restrictions were imposed on its expansion and the repatriation of funds. Indianisation or change over to fully Indian ownership was also insisted upon over time. There was always a suspicion about the role of foreign capital and dependence on it; same was the case with foreign aid and the government was never happy with dependence on aid. Self-reliance was regarded as the major plank of the development strategy and though Indian industries needed foreign technology and foreign money, foreign investment inflow was always subject to control, regulation and screening.

Only since 1991, the automatic approval for foreign investment of up to 51 per cent equity was allowed in 34 industries. The Foreign Investment Promotion Board (FIPB) was concerned with industries not covered by automatic approval. The emphasis on foreign investment as a major vehicle of funds and technology began since 1991. Only around 30 per cent of the approved foreign investment ventures actually culminated in actual investment.

Foreign investors have been attracted to India, especially because of India's huge market of at least 190 to 200 million middle class consumers. The prospect of selling to a growing domestic market has been important to all producers of consumer goods and durables. The difference between foreign investment in China and India however is that most investors in China have been interested in export production but in India, it has been the huge market of middle class consumers that has remained the main attraction.

After China, India with its second biggest population in the world and with over 240 million people with rather attractive disposable incomes has been a favoured destination of several multinational companies' investment. One of the reasons why all types of MNCs want to sell their products in India is the size of the market and the high rate of economic growth in the new millennium.

From cosmetics, watches to hamburgers and pizzas, foreign brands have arrived in a big way. In India, foreign investment has gone mainly to the consumer goods and consumer durable goods sector. The average middle class Indian's mind however is not so easy to gauge. Many foreign multinational firms however were disappointed because certain indigenous brands were hard to replace (Nirma, Bajaj autos) and they wound up their businesses and left.

Foreign investors, according to the FICCI survey of 2004, seem to be satisfied with the telecom facilities in India though all have reservations regarding procedural delays and the general ground level hassles. They are not satisfied with the state of India's transportation network, power, water availability, ports and airports. They are keen to see political stability, a stable policy environment and the continuation of economic reforms. They also are apprehensive of the exchange rate instability because it would affect their take-home profits.

Foreign investors in India are banking on the rise of consumerism as affluence spreads amongst the middle class. There is no doubt a visible desire and ambition amongst the urban middle classes to move up the social ladder by copying the lifestyles of the rich and the famous that they see on the TV screens or in Bollywood films. Many are also working harder at making money and many more lucrative opportunities than before are available. People want to acquire consumer durables and emulate the lifestyle of the upper crust. All this has led to a visible change in the consumption pattern of the urban population.

Peer pressure and copying one's own generation in western countries has also led to a distinct urge for upward mobility. The youth of today, especially from the well-off families, have more opportunities of going abroad and seeing first hand the way people live. They want to have the same icons and ideals and the same lifestyle. They want to wear the same type of clothes and use the same brand names as their foreign counterparts. Their eating and drinking patterns are similar.

Unfortunately, the impact of an imported lifestyle is clashing with traditional values. Children are growing up on junk food and do not like wearing Indian style clothes. Due to an entirely different lifestyle which people are following today as a result of the new exposure to global culture, diabetes and high blood pressure are becoming common among children and adults. Obese children are a common sight in India today among the middle classes. As many of the middle class families are connected with the NRIs abroad through family or friends, emulating the NRI lifestyle in terms of clothes, attitudes and ambitions has become commonplace. Buying the foreign brands available in India has helped them to acquire a similar lifestyle.

But the average middle class person still remains very sensitive to prices. If Indian goods are cheaper they would prefer them to branded ones. Till now, they have not been so hooked on brand names alone (unlike Southeast Asia or China) and that is why some famous multinational brand names failed to take off in India when they opened up franchised shopping outlets.

At the beginning of India's development experience there were only two or three varieties of cars till Sanjay Gandhi introduced 'Maruti'. Today, the variety has increased to over 20, and there are many car manufacturers in India who have joint ventures with well-known foreign car companies. A number of consumer durables are also being manufactured under famous brand names from Korea, USA, UK, Japan, Germany and France. Many of the foreign investors have their own 100 per cent subsidiaries.

In the initial years, there was a huge rush for cars and consumer durables; foreign ventures in these two areas came in with great fanfare. But after the initial spurt in demand, there was a much slower pace of growth. Indians have still not followed the west in its 'throwaway culture'. Yet, a majority of foreign investors view Indian operations as profitable because they see a distinct 'demonstration effect' at work amongst the people in India in clothing, way of living and recreation.

As compared to China, India still has less disposable income per family. Due to the one child family formula the average family size in China is 3 per family as compared to 5 per family in India. In 2002, 70 per cent of urban Chinese earned between $2000 and $7500 a year. In India, there is a greater inequality than in China. Around 6.4 per cent of the population in India as compared to 1.2 per cent in China earned more than $7500 a year but a much higher proportion (73.5 per cent) of the population earned less than $2000. It shows that India has a much narrower affluence base.

The foreign investors also do not rank India high on the list of their chosen destinations. India is below the first 10 'favoured' countries. Within India, their chosen destinations are Maharashtra, Karnataka, Andhra Pradesh, Tamil Nadu and Gujarat (in that order).

With the expansion of the EU to 25 members, India is going to have to compete with the newly acceded members for FDI from the EU which was one of its main sources. Intra-EU investment is bound to rise in the future and India will have to take drastic promotional measures in order to attract more investment.

Unfortunately, the impact of foreign investment has not been too good on the job creation front. Foreign investment also seems to be concentrated in towns—perhaps due to easier access to skilled personnel. But in order to remain flexible and also in order to wind up their operations quickly, foreign investors have tended to use more technology than labour. They also use more skilled and educated labour.

Since the opening up of the economy in 1991, the government has been wooing foreign investors in a big way. All kinds of sops have been offered to them. An investment of around $13.3 billion came between 1996-2000. But China received $209.3 billion during the same period. Between 1979 and 2004, China absorbed $560 billion in FDI.

A hundred little irritants come in the way of setting up a business in India even though the licence-permit *raj* has been dismantled. The bureaucracy still has its network and retains its authority on the economic system through various ingenious means. The Kafkaesque ministries drive foreigners crazy at times.

Investors were invited to undertake green field projects and the equity share limit of foreign investors was raised. But in some areas a cap has been placed on the extent of foreign participation.

In many manufacturing activities (as pointed above), 100 per cent foreign owned subsidiaries have been allowed. In 2001, FDI was further liberalised and 100 per cent equity was allowed in certain areas like integrated townships, including housing, commercial premises, hotels resorts and urban infrastructure. Yet the mandatory environmental clearances from the state governments, have created problems and delays.

The government has allowed 100 per cent FDI through the automatic route for mass rapid transport systems in all metros and also commercial development of real estate. Further, 100 per cent FDI has been allowed in drugs and pharmaceuticals. The government also has opened the defence industry for up to 100 per cent for Indian private sector participation and the FDI limit has been set at 26 per cent. NRI investors, who were major direct contributors to the inflow of foreign investment during the first half of the 1990s, have been less conspicuous in the latter half of the 1990s.

The FDI flow could have been higher if the infrastructure projects it went to, had fructified. The experience of Enron's Dabhol project in India left much to be desired.

There have been other problems also in attracting FDI. These range from corruption in India (as also in China) and problems in the continuation of the same framework in economic policies (not so in China). Perhaps the biggest irritant is the uncertainty of policies and the continued stranglehold of the bureaucracy.

Foreign expatriate personnel also face many problems—from paying half the rent in 'black' to encountering various difficulties in setting up office, including getting basic amenities like gas, telephone, menial and administrative staff, etc. Not used to the round about ways of getting things done in India, some of the foreign investors left after sometime. There could be a problem of security that many have faced, especially in big towns. India may seem to be moving slowly and gently but underneath, among the youth, there is a distinct discontent and envy for people who are better off than themselves and are enjoying a higher standard of life. In the big cities, no foreigner feels safe without a heavily guarded home.

Some foreign investors would also like to see a faster pace of economic reforms and amendment of the labour laws that they see as 'inflexible'. For higher foreign investment flows, 'mergers' and 'acquisitions' should also become easier. Some provision for an easy exit by foreign investors should also be there. If they want to exit and wind up, there are a hundred procedures to be followed. They are put off by the lack of a proper 'exit policy'.

Foreign investors are also afraid of political unrest. Recent attempts to increase the foreign investment equity participation in certain select sectors like insurance, telecom and airports have been met with political resistance from the trade unions and political parties backing them. India would certainly be able to attract more foreign investment if the labour force was more skilled, disciplined and educated and there was a general atmosphere of continuity of economic policy and commitment to reforms.

China has been the big success story of high growth with the help of foreign investment. Most foreign investors feel comfortable with the continuation of policies in China, the availability of skilled, disciplined labour force and the clockwork routine of the special economic zones. Rules, regulations, concessions and general policies are not changed with every change in the government as is the case in India, that is why they have been able to get so much more FDI than others.

India also does not have a great track record of enforcement of rights and contracts. There is a judicial backlog of 26 million cases. Foreign investment in insurance and the media is limited to a minority stake and the retail trade has not been opened to FDI. But in general, a much more lax, open and transparent policy has been followed in recent years. FDI cap or limit has been increased from 49 per cent to 74 per cent in basic and cellular telecom services and FDI in domestic airlines has been enhanced from 40 per cent to 49 per cent. Special concessions have been given to NRIs and they can invest up to 100 per cent.

As a result of focused efforts, FDI inflows have been increasing and increased by 33.8 per cent in 2005. India's share in the global FDI has also increased from 0.5 per cent in 2002 to 0.8 per cent in 2004. In 2005-06, FDI was $4.7 billion and shared a growth of 27.4 per cent.

Mauritius tops the list of the countries from which FDI originates. Some of it is 'circular flow' of capital from India which is opting for the Mauritius route in order to take advantage of the concessions allowed in investment. Same circular flow takes place in China through Hong Kong. Mauritius accounts for 37.2 per cent of the total inflows. USA is the second most important country of origin and its share is 15.9 per cent of the total FDI coming to India. Among the sectors receiving FDI, electrical equipment is the largest; over 70 per cent of the FDI is accessed by only 10 sectors.

12

Foreign Trade

Exports and Imports

Indians have always been engaged in trading with far off countries and people from the coastal areas especially have been active traders. Indian made handicrafts and cotton cloth have been found in the ancient ruins of Egypt, Greece and Rome. Indian made metal mirrors with handles of carved *yakshis* have been found in Pompei. Indian merchants traded from Lothal (Gujarat) a marvellous inland port in prehistoric times. Indian textiles were very famous in Southeast Asia from the 17th till the 19th centuries. Strangely, the goods that were most traded thousands of years ago, are still some of the most important traded items in the present century. Indian textiles and jewellery have been famed across the globe and they continue to be the most popular items. India's share in world exports is still low at 0.8 per cent though it was 2 per cent in 1950. Obviously, there is a lot of scope for export expansion and increasing India's presence in the international market. The government of India currently wants to raise India's share in world exports to 1 per cent.

A high rate of export growth has helped many countries in ASEAN to achieve rapid progress through enhanced incomes and job creation, especially for women. All countries in the world are today promoting exports in order to earn foreign exchange for essential items like oil, food and technology. There is not a single country which believes in autarky.

Many experts feel that soon after Independence, Indian policy makers did not encourage exports which could have taken India on a different and perhaps higher growth path. In fact, as pointed above, they believe that there was an 'export pessimism' which meant that only whatever was leftover from domestic consumption was exported. The policy makers perhaps did not see much future gain in promoting exports as the level of industrialisation was quite low, instead, they wanted to establish economic independence through rapid industrial growth. By contrast, exports were vigorously encouraged in the neighbouring Southeast Asian countries, especially when they entered the first stages of industrialisation—in the 1960s and 1970s. Being much smaller and more homogenous, they were able to take advantage of the big expansion in world trade that occurred in the 1960s and 1970s. They oriented their development policies around export growth in an aggressive manner. It later became the prime mover of such economies towards a higher GDP growth.

In India, the import of heavy machinery, capital goods, oil, defence equipment and food remained essential during the first two decades after Independence and required massive doses of foreign exchange. Foreign aid came to our rescue but self-reliance was the aim of planners and policy makers soon after Independence, by controlling imports of consumer goods and conserving precious foreign exchange. Promoting exports through vigorous export promotion measures did not seem the right alternative, given the fact that India's industrial capability at that time was rather low.

Exports of essential raw materials and food items were discouraged and reserved for domestic consumption and various bureaucratic procedures were imposed on any one wanting to export anything out of India. Taxes were imposed on raw material exports like raw cotton in order to restrict the exporters from sending out what could be consumed by the domestic handloom and textile industry.

The amount of paper work required to export a simple item was mind boggling. Even now with easing of many restrictions, various rules still apply while exporting goods and much time and effort is lost in the process. There seemed to be a lot of suspicion surrounding the business of exports at that time and harassment through paper work and controls was common.

Regarding imports, even more strict norms were applied. After India undertook planned industrialisation in the 1950s, conserving foreign exchange for essential items became not only an important policy objective but an obsession and restrictions were imposed on most imports, especially of consumer goods of any kind. Domestically produced shoddy consumer goods ruled the market. But due to the droughts in the mid-1960s, food had to be imported to feed the people. The first 20 years thus showed a lot of import compression.

Due to reasons mentioned above, in the first thirty years, exports and imports grew slowly and because of the three wars India had to fight—one with China in 1962 and two with Pakistan in 1965 and 1971—there was a heavy foreign exchange outgo on defence equipment. Import of defence equipment took precedence during those years and import of crude oil continued to be a major item. Imports exceeded exports in the earlier decades even though the import of non-essential items was heavily restricted. Exports minus imports, i.e. the trade balance, was mostly negative, showed a deficit.

Further, the first oil shock in 1971 led to a big rise in the trade deficit because of a huge and sudden jump in the price of oil. But since Indians started going out to the Gulf countries and their remittances started flowing in, the current account of the balance of payments began to improve. (The balance of payments is a statement of the money value of all transactions that India has with foreign countries and international institutions. The current account is made up of visible and invisible trade. The visible trade includes the export and import of goods and invisible trade includes income and expenditure from services like banking, insurance, tourism, shipping, profits, remittances, and interest payments on investment. The capital account includes all payments arising from the transfer of capital or assets from official or private sources. The current account and capital account together reveal the 'balance' which is either in surplus or deficit. The capital account shows the implication of current transactions for the country's international financial position. A surplus or a deficit on the current account gets reflected in the capital account through changes in the foreign exchange reserves of the country).

In 1977-78, there was a balance of payments deficit of $1.5 billion and in 1980-81, it was $2.9 billion (1.7 per cent of the GDP). It rose to $3.5 billion in 1984-85 and to $9.9 billion in 1990-91. In the 1980s, though exports grew quite rapidly at 14 per cent in dollar terms per year, there was a rise in the current account deficit due to heavy borrowing by the government and the private sector firms from abroad in the form of short-term loans. India's foreign exchange reserves fell from $5.85 billion in 1980-81 to $4.1 billion in 1989-90 and to $1.6 billion in 1990-91.

During Rajiv Gandhi's time, some amount of introspection about the controlled trade regime took place and there was gradual liberalisation in the import of raw materials and embellishments, components and spare parts. An Open General License Category (OGL) was started in the 1980s. The strict import regime was thus gradually relaxed. In general, India's foreign trade remained controlled as compared to the ASEAN countries.

On the export side, there were both export controls and export incentive schemes. About 190 items were subject to some kind of control, and some were canalised, that is exported only through the state trading agencies.

Several export incentive schemes were also in place to offset the impact of so much control. Most important was the duty drawback scheme that reimbursed exporters for either tariff or excise taxes and cash compensatory support that compensated exporters for indirect taxes not offset by duty drawbacks. There was also a replenishment license scheme (REP) that enabled exporters to import free of quantitative restrictions (QRs) items for their own use or resale of up to 5 to 20 per cent of their export. There was the advance import licenses that allowed duty free imports of inputs.

On the import side, there were QRs that were based on a complex licensing scheme for exporters. The Actual User Policy, Phased Manufacturing Programme (PMP), Government Purchase Preferences and canalised import scheme, were all being used for controlling imports. The Actual User policy banned imports for resale. PMP allowed imports by firms committed to increasing the local content of their production. They were asked to follow a predetermined schedule. Government Purchase Preference consisted of procurement rules for the Central government and gave preference to domestic suppliers. Canalisation of imports was for specified items and could be procured by designated state trading agencies.

The tariffs were set high and basic duties ranged from zero to 355 per cent, auxillary duties were from 0 to 45 per cent and countervailing duties were from 0 to 50 per cent. High customs duties helped the government to earn more money for financing the fiscal deficit. The government could afford to splurge on its current expenditure (that includes subsidies, salaries, benefits) because customs duties raked in substantial amounts of money.

The export-import regime underwent a big change after India went to the IMF for help and secured a substantial loan in 1991. The export growth improved for sometime following liberalisation but again started to deteriorate at the end of the decade. In the new Millennium, export growth has again become robust and in double digits. The sustainability of high export growth, however, is not completely assured because it depends on the world demand.

A number of factors led to the crisis of 1991 among which was the third oil shock of 1990 which raised the oil import bill hugely. The Gulf War and its negative impact on remittances from West Asia also was responsible for exacerbating the crisis. Foreign exchange reserves dwindled to an alarming extent and the withdrawal of money by NRIs from their special foreign exchange accounts did not help the situation. India's trade with the Eastern bloc countries dwindled with the collapse of the Soviet Union—it had a disastrous impact on India's tea trade. India's international credit rating by Standard and Poor went down and the Indian government was forced to sell 20 tonnes of gold to the Union Bank of Switzerland. There was a fear of default on the external debt front. India was forced to revise its trade and industrial licensing policies after the IMF package and an era of economic reforms was ushered in.

Since trade liberalisation gathered momentum in the 1990s exports have been encouraged mainly through liberalisation of imports. A fast rate of export growth was made an important goal for the economy because it would provide employment and earn foreign exchange for importing essential inputs. The employment creation ability of exports, however, depends on the labour intensity of exports. Between 1995-96 and 2003-04, there has been a decline in the labour intensity of exports and the share of medium technology intensive and knowledge intensive products in the total exports has risen.

Freer imports would make India's exports more competitive internationally as all the best internationally priced inputs could be used. The liberalisation of import regime has vastly increased competition from imports. India's exports could use appropriate imported components, embellishments and designs which would improve the quality of Indian products. But in quite a few cases, the opening up of imports has threatened the existence of many industries, for example the toy industry, and other small goods industries.

In general, import liberalisation has made a big difference to the quality of Indian products because of the competition offered by foreign goods in the domestic market. It has also led to better quality of exported goods and more sophisticated manufactured products. There has been a change in the export composition as mentioned above and a decline in the share of exports like tea, spices, textiles, marine products, and leather manufactures. Despite high growth in the gems and jewellery exports, its share has not risen. Exports like metal manufactures, including iron and steel products, manmade yarn, fabrics, petroleum and crude products have become important. Most important are knowledge based products like drugs, pharmaceuticals, plastics and linoleum, machinery, transport equipment including auto parts, ancillaries and, more importantly, electronic items.

Cheap imports of all items including processed food have been flooding the market after the quantitative restrictions were lifted in April 2000. As a member of the WTO, India can no longer stop imports in a big way by applying quantitative restrictions and all import control is only through tariffs or customs duties that have been reduced across the board. It has been a loss to the government's coffers, especially when custom duties were high and a big amount was collected.

Customs duties have been high in India as compared to the duties in neighbouring countries. The peak rate was almost 400 per cent in 1990 but it has been reduced to 50 per cent and more recently (2007) to 10 per cent. These were imposed in order to discourage imports that competed directly with domestic goods and also to protect the industries concerned. The Indian industrialists had for years welcomed the high tariff wall as their inefficiencies and high cost of production could be hidden and consumers, who had no other choice, were forced to buy their goods. Today, with most duties brought down to the levels prevalent in other Asian countries, industrialists have had to become more competitive through cost cutting innovations and improved technology.

There are many reasons why India could never become like one of the ASEAN countries in achieving a fierce rate of export growth. Perhaps one of the main reasons was the attraction of the domestic market. Because the domestic market is so big there has not been a strong export culture. Striving to compete with foreign products in the international market has not been the focal point of manufacturers. They could always sell at home and make a comfortable living. Export rejects became a common feature in the 1970s and 1980s when exporters could not maintain quality. Perhaps the high duty structure made imported inputs too expensive and often details like a zip or a clasp led to their shoddy look and to their rejection by buyers. Getting the 'finish' right seemed to be the main problem of many Indian exports. Proper quality control and pre-shipment checks would have minimised such defects.

In recent years, under the rules of the WTO, even export incentives have been modified so that Indian exporters get incentives that are on par with those given in other competing countries. Monetary incentives like cash compensatory support and subsidies have been withdrawn.

High Transaction Costs

Exporters have been complaining for ages about the problems they have had with the bureaucracy and the lack of proper infrastructure. It all led to higher transaction costs. Such costs are related to the logistics of moving goods through ports and are incurred when there is a lack of efficiency in such movement mainly due to cumbersome documentation during cross-border trade. Customs clearance, when goods for export and import are brought to the customs stations and kept at customs areas for clearance by customs authorities, is a big hassle for the exporter or importer. The documentation required for exporting and importing consignments in and out of India is cumbersome and costly. There are 29 types of documents required and there have to be 118 copies made, with 256 signatures. The total manpower required is seven persons. The cost of such procedures is around 10 per cent of the consignment value.

There are direct and indirect transaction costs also. Indirect ones are delays, lost business opportunities, lack of predictability and stress. An Exim Bank study estimated that around 10.7 per cent of the export revenue was lost through transaction costs. On the import side, trade facilitation would make imported items cheaper. This would specially benefit the SMEs.

Exporters have also been cribbing about lack of adequate financing available and aggressive export support by the government. In some countries like South Korea the President has been directly involved in solving problems for exporters. It is to the exporters' credit that despite these problems, India's exports rose moderately in the 1990s and in the new Millennium, India has managed to capture a niche in a few items, some are traditional items and the others are new.

In recent years, gems and jewellery, textiles and garments have remained important export earners. Efforts at diversification of exports into newer areas have also borne fruits and many new items like pharmaceuticals, minerals and electronic products are now being exported very successfully. Software exports, (non merchandise export) rather surprisingly have become most important in terms of earnings. Many think that the success of software exports is due to the fact that these do not involve either bureaucracy or the inadequate physical infrastructure like roads, ports, airports and thus can avoid all physical infrastructural problems. But the fact remains that the government has played a part in encouraging higher education in electronics and engineering in the last five decades. It has helped to establish various institutions of higher learning in engineering and science and has laid out software parks.

In the last decade imports also have been growing equally fast. The main items of import are crude petroleum, fertilisers, edible oils, semi precious and precious stones for processing. Semi precious stones and uncut diamonds are imported and cut and polished in the small villages of Gujarat and Rajasthan. It is an age-old craft in which entire families are involved. India has become an exporter of polished diamonds and now increasingly, of studded jewellery. The cost of cutting and polishing of small diamonds remains lower than in any other country in the world. Except for very contemporary designs and machine finish, Indian jewellery is most competitive in terms of price and craftsmanship. But because of latest designs catering to western tastes, Thailand remains at the top. Branded jewellery is also an unexplored area though hallmarking of gold and diamonds is becoming very popular in India.

As there are no physical, quantitative barriers to imports any more, higher tariffs would be the only way to stop certain types of imports from flooding the markets. In certain products in which there has been a threat from foreign competition, industrialists have been pressing for higher tariff walls because they have pointed out that they are at a disadvantage *vis-à-vis* India's competitors who have a better infrastructure, cheaper finance, and more flexible labour laws. Being able to hire and fire labour and vary the numbers according to the health and state of the industry leads to flexibility in production as it keeps the size of the enterprise under control. All these factors help competitors abroad to keep their costs down. Some competitors also have a more efficient banking system in their countries.

Though everyone was initially very worried about the onslaught of imports, only a few industries have been affected adversely. Most domestic industries have restructured themselves in order to remain afloat.

Naturally, there will be less of an assured market at home when there are many imports. This means 'wait and watch' for a few years before they decide to invest heavily or simply wind up. That is why domestic producers have been cutting back on fresh investment and innovations at certain times in the past few years.

Between 2001-2003, this attitude of industrialists led to recessionary conditions that affected India's capital goods production. Its growth rate remained negative for some years. Other core sector production like power generation also received a setback and this inadequacy in turn affected export production. Exports picked up again in 2005 and 2006, growing at nearly 20 per cent. From 5.8 per cent of the GDP in 1991, exports rose to 9.4 per cent in 2001-02, and to 11.7 in 2004-05.

But for most exporters, the main concern is quick and effective means of transportation to foreign destinations that include efficient services at ports and airports. A serious bottleneck can lead to huge losses if exports arrive late, especially in the fashion and food industries.

One of the problems with India's exports is the narrowness of its export markets—other than US and Europe, there are few other lucrative and dependable export markets. There is also a lack of variety in India's export items. In most of the traditional products, there seems to be a saturation problem as competitors (specially from South Asia) try to flood the markets with similar products. Apart from the biggest trading partners (US and EU), new markets have to be found since the loss of the market in the Soviet bloc countries. The competition in manufactured goods is very tough, especially with China becoming the dominant player. In agriculture there has been a decline in export growth mainly because of the limited access to markets in Europe. Hopefully, the agricultural market in Europe would open up further in the future.

It seems from their recent moves that EU and US are devising new ways to keep third world exports out by imposing a variety of non-tariff barriers that are hard to overcome. These include strict sanitary and phyto-sanitary measures, hard for poor countries to measure up to. This is especially true of agricultural goods and marine products. India started off well in the area of marine exports but huge consignments were refused on grounds of lack of proper hygienic standards.

Anti-dumping action is another device used by industrialised countries to ward off third world exports. India has faced anti-dumping measures in US and EU since 1995. It has had 98 anti-dumping cases and 39 subsidy cases brought against its exports, mainly of chemicals, pharmaceuticals, fibres/yarn, and steel. Often India has won against such action at the WTO's dispute settlement bodies.

Diversification into other areas of exports would help in boosting export growth but it would depend on a large number of favourable factors. Recession in any of the major industrial countries will also affect export growth adversely. For export growth, the world demand situation is of utmost importance.

Imports and exports in 2005 accounted for 23 per cent of the GDP as compared to 15 per cent in 1990-91. The current account balance has been in surplus in the first few years of the new millennium which means that the current external receipts have been good enough for the current external liabilities. It indicates that there has been a rise in the invisible trade inflows and foreign exchange has been coming in through remittances, software exports and services.

From 2004-05, once again due to the rise in petrol prices, the current account has been in deficit.

Many fiscal incentives have been offered by the government to textiles, pharmaceuticals, telecom, biotech, gems and jewellery and IT exports. In recent years exports to China have been rising fast. China is buying steel, iron ore, plastic and linoleum products, machinery and instruments. India is importing electronic goods, chemicals, medicinal and pharmaceutical products, coal and coke, silk yarn and fabrics. China is becoming India's third most important trading partner after US and UAE.

Special Economic Zones (SEZs)

In 2005, the Bill on Special Economic Zones was passed by both houses of Parliament; the details and guidelines are awaited. The purpose of having a separate Bill on SEZs is to clarify all policy initiatives relating to such special zones so that many more foreign and domestic investors can establish their manufacturing units in these areas. There are 11 functioning SEZs in the country already and they are producing 5 per cent of India's total exports. Yet it has been felt (by exporting firms mostly) that there are certain areas that need attention in order to make India's SEZs as attractive as those located in China. With better and clear cut incentives the government hopes to attract $2 billion more in FDI.

Most countries in South Asia—Nepal, Bangladesh, Sri Lanka and Pakistan—have all tried to promote their exports and create jobs by establishing these SEZs. Since all are highly populous countries, they are heavily into exports of goods requiring cheap labour. In fact, they are all competing with each other in almost the same products— ordinary garments, sports goods, knitted garments, textiles, gems and jewellery. Bangladesh and Sri Lanka have really done well in garment exports and 90 per cent of the workers in Bangladesh's garment sector are women.

Basically, all the countries in South Asia have been able to cut costs by locating their industries in these special zones where many tax concessions and tax holidays are available. In these SEZs, a different set of laws is applicable and a smooth and well functioning infrastructure is specially created to meet the needs of different exporting units. Other attractive incentives relate to repatriation of profits and these have also been given to invite foreign investment. A regular supply of power and water as well as regular supply of labour through an efficient transportation system to the factories has been ensured to all the units in these special zones.

India's SEZs are scattered around the country, from Surat to Kochi, to Noida near Delhi. But they have not been as successful as those in some of the neighbouring countries and specially those in China. The SEZ Bill will clarify various policies relating to income tax concessions and there would be a single window clearance and fast track approval for all future project proposals. These special zones will be treated as though they are foreign territories within India. The SEZ units and developers will get 100 per cent exemption from income tax for 5 years and 50 per cent of their ploughed back profits will also be exempted from tax for five years. They will also be exempt from customs and central excise duties for five years

There will be quick disposal of trials and disputes which will make foreign firms happy because they can 'exit' quickly if they wish. Hopefully, foreign investors will set up manufacturing plants in these special zones and take advantage of the facilities that are equivalent to those prevalent in the export zones in neighbouring countries.

India's export growth, which is already on an upswing, can get a further boost if the main problems of infrastructure and supply of labour are solved in these zones. However, the labour laws of the country will prevail in these zones. But since most employment will be on contract basis, the labour laws could be circumvented.

As in other countries where such zones attract a lot of women workers, India too has many women workers in the SEZs and in future too, more women are likely to be employed in them. Women workers usually earn salaries that they would not be able to earn outside the zone and, also, the difference between men and women workers' wage is not too sharp.

MNCs have typically set up their factories in these special zones in most South Asian countries and they employ thousands of women but their work is mostly repetitive in nature like knitting, sewing or fixing small parts of machinery. As a result, women often suffer from chronic illnesses because of the monotony and repetitive nature of their jobs and the highly restricted spaces in which they are confined during work hours. They suffer from various problems related to night shifts and close monitoring by tyrannical supervisors. They are also not given proper contracts and are hired and fired easily. No health benefits are usually given to women workers and with marriage or pregnancy their contracts are often terminated. But some argue that if the women did not work in these factories, they would have no income at all which would push them back into poverty, trafficking and an oppressive home situation.

The special zones indeed do provide jobs to women from the neighbouring towns but they have to be given more job security and health insurance to maintain the quality of the labour force. What is also required is proper training and skill upgradation so that there is scope for promotion and improvement in job profiles for women over time. Otherwise, women of a certain age will keep getting hired and fired, remain on the fringe of all industrial activity, and keep on getting only short-term employment.

There is another danger in having too many of these economic zones on terms that are on par with those existing in all our neighbouring countries. China has by far the most attractive terms and conditions. In this intense competition, there has been a tendency on the part of MNCs to keep changing their locations whenever they see a slight cost advantage. This can result in sudden closure of factories and resulting unemployment. Some workers often go back to their homes and supply goods to agents who are working on behalf of multinationals. Such outsourcing from very poorly paid workers by big firms located outside the SEZs is not uncommon in India and in many of the other South Asian countries. Since only 50,000 additional jobs can be created in these special zones as compared to the big monetary and fiscal concessions given to them, the best course would be to have a few really well functioning special economic zones that are properly and efficiently run without undue exploitation of women workers.

Foreign Exchange Regime and Exports

Export growth depends on export prices and these depend on the exchange rate between the rupee and dollar and other foreign currencies. If the value of the rupee in terms of the dollar is high, then the export price is high and importers would choose to buy from other competing countries. Naturally, the exchange rate becomes very important. As mentioned above, the government, in the initial years was very concerned with conserving foreign exchange but when the country had started borrowing from abroad heavily, the rupee's value in terms of the dollar, started to fall. India was forced to devalue in 1966 after it faced a balance of payments crisis. Similarly, in 1991, facing another major crisis in the balance of payments when India owed huge foreign debt, its exports were low and the remittances and foreign exchange reserves declined disastrously, India had to devalue the rupee by 22 per cent. The devaluation made India's exports cheaper *vis-à-vis* its competitors and gave them a boost.

When ever the dollar's value goes up due to the demand for dollars in the foreign exchange markets India's rupee experiences a depreciation which is different from devaluation which amounts to a forced reduction in the rupee's value in terms of the dollar.

The Indian rupee's value is determined by the demand and supply of the rupee *vis-à-vis* the dollar. When the demand for the rupee is higher, the rupee becomes strong in terms of the dollar. This is the floating or flexible exchange rate system that India has adopted since 1991. Previously, in the 1950s and 1960s, the rupee was pegged to the dollar and the pound sterling. And to keep the rate stable and to prevent excessive volatility, the RBI regularly monitored and still monitors the forex markets. It intervenes whenever abnormal swings in the demand and supply of dollars appear.

India has also adopted complete current account convertibility for exporters and importers since 1993. The rupee is convertible into dollars for receipts and payments of goods and services in dollars. People earning in dollars can convert them into rupees at the market rate anytime. When they want to import anything, they can do so by converting their earnings back to dollars.

India has still not adopted capital account convertibility which means that not everyone can go to the bank and convert their rupee savings into dollars. There is regulation of outflows of money from India and only certain types of outflow in dollars are allowed. There are many who have argued that capital account convertibility is important for foreign investment. China has it and many of India's competitors including Pakistan have it. But India is still going the cautious way and perhaps with good reason. It was capital account convertibility that exacerbated the Southeast Asian crisis in 1997 when there was massive capital flight out of those countries almost over night. Similarly, in the case of Mexican crisis, there was a similar flight of capital.

From the 1960s onwards, there were two rates for foreign exchange conversion, one was the official rate and the other was the market rate. The official rate was always lower than the market rate. Today, there is a unified rate of foreign exchange. It means less hassles for exporters, importers and common tourists.

India and the World Trade Organization (WTO)

Following World War-II, India was a signatory to GATT or General Agreement on Trade and Tariffs 1947 which came into effect in 1948. All countries or contracting parties were bound by the agreement of MFN or Most Favoured Nation clause which basically meant that members would give the same tariff treatment to each other. All this was undertaken in order to facilitate the multilateral trading system that would help all developing countries in their export growth. It was an agreement signed by 100 countries to reduce tariffs for developing countries. The Generalised System of Preferences or GSP proposed in the United Nations Conference on Trade and Development (UNCTAD) 1964, and accepted in 1969, proposed that industrial countries would charge no duty on imports from developing countries. But it was watered down and only 11 schemes were laid in which such a duty free access would be acceptable to the industrialised countries.

There were seven major trade negotiations under various rounds of tariff cuts. The Kennedy or Sixth Round was between 1964-1967. It entailed tariff reduction for a whole group of goods instead of commodity by commodity basis. The Tokyo Round was held between 1973-1979 and addressed the problem of access to industrial countries' markets due to tariff and non-tariff barriers for developing countries.

At the end of 1983, Japan and the US made a joint declaration in Tokyo that serious thought should be given to the preparation of a new round of multilateral trade negotiations. The focus would be on the liberalisation of agriculture. India was not very enthusiastic about the new round like many other developing countries as it feared that more concessions would be extracted and new subjects that were of little interest to the developing countries would be taken up for negotiations.

A new round of multilateral trade negotiations (MTN) called the Uruguay Round was launched in Punta del Este in Uruguay towards the end of 1986.

Many other issues related to trade cropped up and extended beyond the mere trade in goods to services, protection of trade related intellectual property rights (TRIPS), particularly the protection of patents, opportunities for investors and problems in the agriculture sector. Trade related investment measures (TRIMS) were also introduced. All these were to be brought under a new discipline which would guide trading between nations.

After much negotiation, a draft was presented that would form the rules and conditions for world trade. This was the famous Dunkel Draft. The developing countries were to aid and facilitate trade by systematic tariff reduction and opening up. India signed the Dunkel Draft on April 15, 1994, and like the 130 members of the WTO at that time, has been under obligation to abide by its agreements. China joined the WTO in 2005; it has 146 members today.

The Uruguay Round was finally concluded in the middle of 1994 in Marrakesh and the WTO was established in 1995 in Geneva on the basis of a mandate laid out by the Dunkel document. It established an elaborate set of rules and regulations regarding trade in agriculture, industry, services, trade related intellectual property rights (TRIPS), dispute settlement and investment measures. In all, 28 areas were covered.

It included agreements on 12 subjects in the area of goods, agriculture, sanitary and phytosanitary measures, textiles and clothing, technical barriers to trade, trade related investment measures, anti-dumping, customs valuation, pre-shipment inspection, rules of origin, import licensing, subsidies and countervailing measures and safe-guards.

WTO also had agreements on intellectual property rights, trade policy review mechanisms and dispute settlement processes. It also contained agreements, one each in the areas of government procurement, civil aircraft, dairy and bovine meat. These four agreements were applicable to only to those countries that had especially accepted them. All other agreements applied to all members of WTO.

India has availed of MFN or Most Favoured Nation treatment since the GATT days. It has given MFN status to all its neighbouring countries including Pakistan—whereas Pakistan is still dithering about reciprocating.

The WTO agreement has many clauses that affect the economic policies of the member countries in agriculture that include patenting of seeds and microorganisms, export subsidies, fixing of tariff rates and provisions for food security to people in developing countries through the PDS.

India has brought down tariff levels in agriculture. Whereas the bound rates (which are the maximum rates) for tariffs in WTO are 94 per cent, India's average applied tariffs in agriculture are 33 per cent. Tariffs on processed foods have been further reduced in the Budget of 2007 (World Bank: *India and the WTO 2003*). But there has been controversy within the country regarding patenting of seeds and microorganisms. The patenting of seeds has a component of plant breeders' rights and farmers' right to keep seeds for the next farming season. India has faced protests from farmers' groups wanting protection for India's biodiversity and huge indigenous knowledge.

Regarding agricultural subsidies, developed countries have been asked to reduce their subsidies by 20 per cent over 6 years and developing countries have been asked to reduce them by 13 per cent over ten years. In certain exceptional cases, subsidy could be granted and these came under Blue, Amber and Green box clauses. Under the Green box clause, the country could continue with subsidies if it went for agricultural research and under Blue box direct subsidies to farmers could be given for rural development.

The rich countries have tried to protect their agriculture because of the political clout of the farmers' lobby. They subsidise their farmers heavily ($1 billion a day) in order to produce their farm output cheaply but insist that developing countries should open up their markets to their farm exports and reduce their subsidies. Thus the rich countries pamper their rich farmers who, but for the heavy subsidies, would not have been able to compete in the international market. To fob off developing countries' exports they insist on various standards—and resort to various non-tariff barriers like standards for hygiene and presence of organisms in agricultural and marine products.

Patents and the Intellectual Property Rights

India enacted a Patents Law after Independence to protect people's scientific discoveries. It became necessary to change the law (Indian Patents Act 1970) in 1999 and 2002 in order to comply with the WTO norms. The TRIPS agreement had stipulated that India must revise its patent laws. It is widely believed that with greater patent protection more foreign investment would be attracted to India. There would also be greater technology transfer and Research and Development by foreign companies. It would also help innovations by domestic companies and they would be inclined to undertake bigger investments under new patent laws.

India always had process but not product patents in pharmaceuticals and agrochemicals. Process patents helped in keeping medicine prices low because famed generic drugs could be made indigenously through different processes.

With the WTO agreement, India agreed to change the Patent laws by 2005 and introduce product patents. It did so through an amendment. Naturally the prices of important drugs had to be increased and this created a controversy. Many have argued that only the old types of product prices would be affected and not new ones. Besides, India could join the league in pharmaceutical R&D and inventions that could be patented.

For important drugs there would be compulsory licensing arrangement and the price of drugs could also be controlled. This is true of lifesaving drugs and other popular drugs for diseases like AIDs, Cancer and TB.

Another big objection regarding the TRIPS agreement is from Indian environmentalists who feel that India's indigenous products, traditionally used in various ways, have been patented by the US in recent years. *Neem, jamun, basmati* rice are examples. The other objection is about patenting of seeds and whether the farmer has the right to use the seeds as he wants or is it the right of the seed producing company to dictate everything? In services, the General Agreement on Services (GATS) calls for the further opening up of telecom sector.

Soon after the establishment of the WTO, the first Ministerial conference took place in Singapore in 1996 and as feared by the developing countries, the agenda for WTO rules was enlarged. New issues were introduced (the Singapore Issues) and new agreements were generated in the area of investment, competition policy, transparency in government procurement and trade facilitation.

At Seattle, more new issues were introduced: industrial tariffs, global electronic commerce, trade and labour standards, trade and environment. India has objected to the introduction of labour standards and its link up with trade. It was perceived that application of strict labour standards would impact India's trade. Basically, there was an attempt to enlarge the agenda of the WTO by the industrialised countries in Seattle.

In the next Ministerial meetings also, new agreements were generated in the area of investment, competition policy, transparency in government procurement and trade facilitation. India has resisted these new subjects in the WTO except the one on trade facilitation.

The Doha meeting took place in 2001 and was followed by the Cancun meeting in September 2003. There was a lack of consensus on agriculture especially when the rich countries continued their trade—distorting domestic agricultural support policies. India and other developing countries demanded greater market access. EU and US agreed to reduce domestic support and increase market access. Members of the WTO adopted a Framework Agreement on Doha Work Programme after the Cancun meeting on August 1, 2004 because no agreement could be reached in Cancun. The most recent (sixth) Ministerial conference took place in Hong Kong in December 2005 and there was consensus regarding completing the Doha Work programme by 2006.

India as a member of G-20 has continued to negotiate on agriculture. It has argued that developing countries have commitments for the provision of livelihood and food security to their citizens and have to have flexible domestic policies towards agriculture. The G-20 asked for special and differential treatment for developing countries.

Market access for non-agricultural products was also brought up and India suggested a cut in bound tariff rates with greater cuts in tariffs for developed countries than in developing countries. The proposal of zero duty commitment for seven major sectors (including textiles, electronics, gems and leather) was not acceptable to India. India has bound tariff rates at 30 per cent in industry.

The developing countries pointed out that the advanced industrialised countries were demanding substantial market access in developing countries without regard to their legitimate food and livelihood security and rural development concerns. India has also submitted a list of non-tariff barriers it is faced with industrial goods exports.

The G-20 has also called forth the elimination of all forms of export subsidies given by rich agricultural countries within a specified timeline, especially on certain commodities like cotton that have adversely affected African countries.

In the service component of the Framework Agreement, India wants more liberal commitments from industrial countries in cross border supply of services specially the electronic mode of delivery (outsourcing). It has expressed the desire to ease the movement of natural persons and it has questioned the various barriers to free movement like the economic needs test, recognition of educational qualifications, administrative procedures relating to visas and social security contributions. It has offered various services such as engineering, health, financial, tourism, bookkeeping, medical, dental, midwives, nurses, paramedical and physiotherapists. It has welcomed the move to ease FDI inflows.

India has also called for patent rights under geographical indication to include products other than wines and has asked for inclusion of items that include traditional and folk knowledge under such patents.

On the whole, India's as well as other developing countries' motive in joining the WTO has mainly been gaining greater access to industrial countries' markets so that trade can become an instrument of growth. Many countries have gained enormous prosperity through trade in the past few decades and, naturally, our interest lies in exporting more to the industrial countries. But unfortunately, there has been a mismatch of interests between the rich countries and India and other developing countries.

Industrial countries are interested in selling more to highly populated, fast-growing countries like India which are not fully developed; they have problems in opening up their own markets easily. This is visible in all their proposals in which unequal treatment is meted out to developing countries. By not treating them as 'equals' in the liberalisation process, they are ignoring the head start they themselves had in becoming industrialised a hundred years ago.

They are also not giving freer access to industrial goods though they agreed to do so, earlier. As soon as some export from India makes a small mark in their markets, they come up with 'anti-dumping action' through the WTO. They define dumping by comparing the domestic price of a product with its export price. Whenever there is slight discrepancy, they bring a dumping suit and impose high duties. They insist that imports of woolen clothing or bed linen from India are causing damage to their own domestic producers. India, however, won the anti-dumping suit brought against its export of bed linen to the EU.

All disputes have been dragged to WTO for settlement. Instead of more multilateral trade, because of the problems involved, there is a growth in bilateral trade. Trade blocs have been flourishing in all parts of the world against the spirit of multilateral trade. Free trade agreements (FTAs) have become more widespread and free trade within such blocs and between two or three trade blocs is flourishing.

China's joining the WTO has had an impact on all developing countries because of its becoming the manufacturing hub of the world. Its share in the world textile trade has increased substantially. EU members are also outsourcing parts and components of various engineering products as well as office equipment to China, giving a big boost to EU-China trade.

13

The Financial System

The financial system is the backbone of the country's business—big and small. It comprises the banking system, the financial or capital markets which are made up of the equity market, bond market and the fund management sectors of insurance, mutual funds and pensions. While the commercial banks provide mainly short-term capital finances to industry, the capital market provides long-term capital to the government, business as well as individuals. The capital market is made up of a large number of institutions, both organised and unorganised. Many people wanting to raise loans may also have to resort to moneylenders and other indigenous non-banking financial institutions that comprise the unorganised sector.

Commercial Banks and the Central Bank

The mainstay of an economy is its banking system. An efficient and reliable banking system helps to achieve even paced, sustained development. Commercial banks finance industrial projects through loans, underwriting and direct subscription of shares and bonds, leasing and venture capital. The Development Financial Institutions (DFIs) provide long-term loans for industry and hold a high percentage of equity in many major Indian private sector companies.

Fortunately, the framework for a banking system was laid out by the British. But there were many problems after Independence with the banking system. Many banks were established and owned by business houses and they multiplied randomly to facilitate their own businesses.

After a few years, the government realised that banks could help development in a big way. If people had access to easy loans they would be able to set up their own businesses and earn incomes and employment would rise. Financial policy became important for business expansion and for increasing employment. Banking became an important instrument of development policy.

The banking industry was gradually nationalised from 1955 in order to make loans more accessible to the poor and the needy. Priority sector lending or lending to certain sectors selected on a priority basis like small borrowers, the rural and agricultural sector, was made an important segment of banking. All banks were made to charge lower interest rates for loans to the agricultural sector and the small-scale sector.

There were other reasons for bank nationalisation like the closure of 477 banks in the pre-1969 period due to bad management which had led to the pauperisation of many individuals between 1951-1969. In 1969, 14 commercial banks were nationalised. It started with the Imperial Bank of India which was nationalised along with 7 other subsidiary banks (belonging to princely states) in 1955. Between 1980-1986, more banks were nationalised and the number rose to 27.

Giving loans on easier terms to the industrial sector after nationalisation, led to certain distortions like industries choosing capital intensive techniques instead of labour intensive ones. But rural credit offered by nationalised banks played a major role in the Green Revolution which enhanced the nation's food security situation. There was, however, much political interference, nepotism and inadequate management and writing off of agricultural loans in the banking system. In loan *melas*, the benefits went to the rich farmers and landlords. A huge amount of unreturned loans also piled up. Vested interests also prevented banks from playing the role of removing regional disparities and encouraging investment in backward areas.

The Banking Commission appointed by the Central government in 1972 found that the ratio of equity and reserves to deposits in private banks fell from 9.7 per cent in 1951 to 2.2 per cent in 1969. This was a dangerous trend because it meant that the banks did not follow 'prudential norms'. Only 8 per cent of the total loans were given to the small-scale industrial sector and to small-scale agriculturists.

Various types of Grameen banks were set up and one-third of loans were given to priority areas, agriculture and the small-scale sector. Loans were also given for self-employment schemes. Interest rates were controlled on both loans and deposits. It made the government's interest payments on loans easier. Many abuses of the nationalised system of banking surfaced and it was felt that to have a faster rate of growth, the banking system had to be modernised and reformed.

The Narasimham Committee, which was appointed in 1991 recommended that the banking system should focus on maximising profits and diluting social objectives. Government's share in the nationalised banks was brought down to 51 per cent. In 2005, there were 70,324 offices of commercial banks in India and foreign banks had 245 offices. Regional Rural Banks (RRBs) had 14,762 branches and other scheduled commercial banks had 6,321 offices. Non-scheduled banks were only 25 in number and the nationalised banks had 35,075 offices. The State Bank and its associates had 13,896 offices.

Since the reforms, interest rates have also been freed or deregulated. The government intervenes through the monetary policy giving guidelines to banks in their decision to fix their prime lending rates. Private foreign banks have been allowed to operate and there is a bigger choice available to the public in banking services.

There are nearly 300 banks including public sector banks, Indian private banks and foreign banks as well as 200 RRBs. There was a big increase in the number of rural banks from 1969 to 1991. From 23 per cent of the total number of banks in the country, rural banks rose to 40 per cent of the total number of banks. Priority sector lending had also risen and comprised 40 per cent of the loans between 1969 and 1991.

But something was not going right with the banking system and by 1991, the nationalised banks had gathered a huge amount of non performing assets (NPAs) which accumulated due to non-payment of loans. Because of these NPAs, the banks were not able to perform efficiently and effectively in dispensing credit and in promoting growth.

Since the reforms, though the number of private banks and foreign banks has grown, the dominant position is still held by the public sector banks that control 82 per cent of the business. There are also 350 co-operative banks and 20 land development banks and a large number of primary agricultural societies and co-operative banks. The State Bank of India is the biggest of them.

With the reforms, the hold on banks by the government has been much loosened, especially since the flexibility in interest rates was introduced. Yet the reforms have not led to a more efficient banking system in terms of better services to the public. Even the Co-operative banks, which were meant to bring about easy banking to the people, have been involved in scams.

Access to microcredit is still not highly developed and lacks the leadership of Dr. Mohammad Yunus who started the Grameen Bank of Bangladesh. If more Self-help groups (SHGs) could be formed the poor could be made more credit-worthy, and they could have their own enterprises.

The importance of banking in the country emerges from the fact that if there are more banks in the rural areas the saving habit would be encouraged. Small savers are important for the collective savings of the country. In fact, the phenomenal expansion of public sector banks' branches between 1970-1985, especially in rural areas, encouraged the saving habit. But since there were few customers, the unit cost of administrating loans and deposits turned out to be high due to the small volumes. Thus, the geographical coverage increased but it led to low profitability and low efficiency of the banking system.

Indians are thrifty by nature. The saving rate which was around 24 to 26 per cent from mid 1990's has risen to 28 to 30 per cent during 2003-04 to 2005-06. However, public sector saving has been declining leading to decline in public investment. A redeeming feature of recent years is that the saving of public sector which had been negative until 2002-03, was positive for the third consecutive year in 2005-06. This has been due to higher saving of non-departmental as well as departmental enterprise.

Banks also provide loans crucial for industrial growth and 50 per cent of their business is with industry which borrows for innovations and industrial expansion. But if the interest rates remain high, there is excess liquidity and businesses fail to borrow much.

Since the reforms, interest rates have been deregulated and it has been left to the banks to decide lending rates. In recent years, the interest rates have been coming down but even so, they remain higher than in other industrialising countries. The real interest rate, defined as nominal interest rate minus the rate of change in the wholesale price index, or rate of inflation, still remains high. A high interest rate is very cumbersome for industrialists as it raises the financial costs of business and in the ultimate analysis leads to lower competitiveness. Actually one of the reasons for high interest rates, in the past few years, has been the proliferation of savings schemes in the market. The banks have been forced to remain competitive and maintain high deposit rates, which meant that their lending rates also remained high. But household savings held in banks did increase at the expense of the share of savings that were being held as shares and debentures.

The share of savings held in shares fell drastically from 10 per cent in 1992-93, following the stock market boom, to 2 per cent in 1998-1999. The high interest rate of banks could also be due to inefficiencies of the banking system. Efficient banking is defined as one in which banks earn a reasonable rate of return, have capital adequacy, and efficient customer service. Many public sector banks remain unprofitable because they are undercapitalised and rely on the government to take care of their bottom lines. One reason for the inefficiency is the huge amounts of non-performing assets (NPAs) or bad loans.

Why Such Huge Amounts of NPAs?

The strangest thing about the banking sector has been that while it scrutinises and examines small loans asked by farmers and small businesses, it is extravagant in its generosity towards big businesses. Any big businessman can ask for huge sums, spend it on whatever he likes and then declare that he cannot pay back the loans. There are various ways in which they dodge the recovery of loans and after a while the banks call these unpaid loans NPAs. India's banking system has a formidable amount of NPAs, which is blocking the path of reforms and efficient banking. One of the reasons why the banks are not able to modernise is also due to the burden of NPAs.

In recent years, due to help from the central government and due to their own efforts there has been a reduction in NPAs. (Net NPAs stood at Rs. 24,617 crore in 2003-04.) Even so, much more has to be done in order to bring the banking system on par with the banking practices of advanced countries.

In general, banks have been inefficient and non-profitable for other reasons also. Public sector banks incurred high administrative expenses due to overmanning. Another reason is the high reserve requirement that was required by the RBI from commercial banks in order to maintain a certain amount of liquidity. According to the Banking Regulation Act of 1949, banks had to maintain assets in the form of gold, cash, government securities and government guaranteed securities, equal to not less than 25 per cent of their total demand and time deposit liabilities. This is called Statutory Liquidity Ratio (SLR) and over the years, it kept on increasing. It led to inefficiencies and forced commercial banks to keep a high proportion of their funds in government securities and government guaranteed securities of public sector financial institutions. High SLR affected the financial institutions' capacity to grant loans and advances to business and industry. It also diverted bank funds away from loans to industry and trade to investment in government securities.

Another requirement from banks was the Cash Reserve Ratio (CRR) that was mandatory for all commercial banks under the RBI Act 1934. Every bank had to keep certain minimum cash reserves with the RBI. Initially it was 5 per cent against demand deposits and 2 per cent against time deposits. By the 1962 Amendment, RBI was empowered to vary the CRR between 3-15 per cent of total time and demand deposits. The RBI also paid much lower than market rate of interest on government securities. This affected banks' profitability and together, the SLR and CRR made banks keep as much as 53.5 per cent of their aggregate deposits in cash balances with RBI or in government securities. In recent years, following the Narasimha Committee report 1991, SLR was reduced from 38.5 per cent to 25 per cent. The Committee also recommended that the CRR should be reduced from 15 per cent to between 3 to 5 per cent. A reduction of SLR and CRR would leave more funds with the banks for allocation to agriculture, industry and trade. It also recommended that the government's borrowing rates should be market related.

The Prudential norms of banks have also been revised and they require that banks make 100 per cent provision for all NPAs. Banks would have to make at least 30 per cent provisions against doubtful and bad debts. Banks were also asked to follow the capital adequacy norm which requires them to maintain a capital to risky assets ratio of not less than 8 per cent. This was done to enable Indian commercial banks to be in line with norms set by the Bank of International Settlement in Basle, Switzerland. What is still bothering industry is the downward rigidity of lending rates even as/when deposit rates have been coming down.

Role of the Reserve Bank

To control the supply of money in the economy and to prevent the rapid escalation of inflation are the main aims of the RBI. It is the apex bank which gives guidance to all commercial banks and also acts as a lender of last resort. It also issues currency notes and coins. It has an important regulatory, monitoring and supervisory role.

It controls the money supply by giving instructions to the commercial banks regarding the CRR and the SLR. These are announced in the Reserve Bank's annual credit policy. By reducing both, the RBI can increase the amount of money circulating in the economy. By increasing the SLR and CRR, the RBI can reduce the money supply in the economy. It also announces the 'bank rate' in its annual credit policy which is the rate at which commercial banks can borrow money from the RBI against government securities; and in turn it gives them an idea of what their own interest rates (lending and deposit rates) should be. The bank rate as announced by the RBI influences the prime lending rate of banks.

It is also responsible for maintaining the official rate of exchange of the rupee *vis-à-vis* the dollar and intervenes in the foreign currency markets by either buying or selling dollars. When it feels the time is appropriate to prop up the rupee against the dollar, it sells dollars in the market. If it feels that the rupee's value is appreciating rapidly, it can sell dollars and thus increase the supply. Arresting the sharp rise in the rupee's value against the dollar is important because it can harm India's exports.

The RBI is supposed to supervise the monetary system mainly through a control of the money supply but it also gives guidance to banks for promoting development and fulfilling certain social objectives. In fact, many institutions have been set up by the RBI in order to promote the savings habit in the country and it also has set up institutions to mobilise savings for industrial and agricultural finance. It acts as the banker to the government and provides loans against government bonds as well. But there is a limit to such borrowing and the government borrows the rest of its requirements from the market.

Regarding fixing of interest rates, times have changed and RBI does not directly fix the interest rates as it used to in the past. In the first five years after Independence, cheap money policy was followed and the bank rate was fixed at 3 per cent. It rose to 3.5 percent in the 1960s and 1970s but between 1981-1991 it rose to 10 per cent. It was 11 per cent in 1991 and 12 per cent in 1992. The impact of high interest rates was felt by industry and the RBI has tried to bring about lower interest rates to encourage fresh investment. In 2005, interest rates were around 6 per cent. Lower interest rates since 2003 have encouraged housing construction and a boom in consumer expenditure which, along with more road building activity, stimulated industrial expansion.

The RBI also undertakes open market operations and deals in the transaction of securities to influence the volume of cash reserves with commercial banks. It thus influences the volume of loans and advances made by banks. When the RBI sells government securities in the market, it withdraws a part of the cash reserves with commercial banks and reduces their ability to expand credit. When it buys government securities from the market, it creates more credit and bank deposits and thus the supply of money expands.

Other Types of Financing in the Money Market

The call money market is a short-notice market in which money can be borrowed overnight and the lender has the right to retrieve money at a short-notice. It is in the form of cash. About 80 per cent of the call money funds are financed by non-banking financial institutions and only 20 per cent by the banking system. The call money rates are very volatile and vary according to season and demand.

There is also the Bill Market in which by selling and buying short-term bills, normally up to 90 days, money can be raised. A Bill of Exchange is basically an 'IOU' (I Owe You) where the drawer undertakes unconditionally to pay the drawee a specified sum at a specified date, usually after three months. It is in the form of paper money offered at a discount to face value. The discount annualised, is equivalent to an annual interest rate in synchronisation with the others in the market. The 'Bill' is endorsed by a public sector bank.

In India, the 91-day government treasury bills are most common bills and banks often raise money by selling them in the Bill market.

The commercial bill market is well developed in western countries but not in India.

There is also the 364-day Treasury Bill now in the market. The Treasury Bill is an instrument traded most in the money markets because it is a government backed short-term loan with a limited maturity period of one year. It is issued at a discount and its attractiveness depends on the discount rate and the yield. The yield curve shows the different interest rates on government bonds that mature at different times over the years. Normally greater compensation is required by bond investors for holding their asset over a longer period in which they are exposed to inflation and so the slope of the yield curve is upwards.

The repo market is also used for short-term borrowing by banks against government bonds and the repurchase agreement is one in which the issuer (the government) agrees to buy securities from a dealer for a stated period and to sell them back on a future date at a specified higher price. The difference between the buying and selling prices, expressed as a discount, is the interest payable over that period.

Repo auctions have been popular with the RBI for controlling the liquidity of banks. Such auctions are a regular feature of RBI's 'open market operations'. Government securities are repurchased from the market by the RBI, when an injection of liquidity in the financial system is required. In 1996, the reverse repo was introduced in which the banks could sell dated securities to the RBI through auction. It offered a good way to park surplus funds by banks. The RBI's 'Liquidity Adjustment Facility' was started in June 2000 to modulate and control short-term liquidity and give signals to short-term interest rates. By using repos and reverse repos as a policy instrument, it influences the volume of liquidity in the money market and through it stabilises the short-term interest rate or call rate. LAF has become an important tool for adjusting liquidity on a day-to-day basis over the last few years and is a major instrument of monetary policy.

CDs or certificate of deposits are also used by commercial banks to raise money in the market. They are freely transferable after 45 days from the date of issue. The maturity is between three months to a year; and the CDs are issued at a discount to the face value; and the discount rate is freely determined by the market conditions. Various development financial institutions like the IDBI, ICICI and IFCI have been allowed to issue CDs with a maturity period of one to three years. Such CDs allow financial institutions to raise resources from the market.

Inflation

One of the main roles of the Reserve Bank of India is to control inflation. When prices are rising rapidly, the poor, whose incomes are not indexed to prices, suffer. All persons with fixed incomes like pensioners and bond holders also suffer. It rewards only speculators and hoarders and thus hurts the vulnerable section of the population who have to cut corners in order to survive. A high rate of inflation puts pressure on interest rates leading to a rise in project costs and investment. It reduces the real interest rates (nominal interest rates minus the rate of inflation). This low real interest rate adversely affects the rate of saving in the economy.

Inflation is measured by two indices—the wholesale price index (WPI) and the consumer price index or CPI. The WPI includes prices of food items, fuel, manufactured products and essential commodities. The 'weights' attached to these constituents have been determined by the usual consumption pattern of common people. The highest 'weights' are attached to manufactured products (63.75 per cent), food items (22 per cent), fuels (14.2 per cent), and essential commodities (17.6 per cent). The CPI is based on actual retail prices and is used for calculating the dearness allowance of employees in the public and private sectors. It probably is more realistic because it includes services. Both WPI and CPI have been more or less stable and moderate during the 1990s, ever since the economic reforms were initiated as compared to the earlier decades after Independence. Food items in CPI have a higher 'weight' than in WPI. A moderate rate of inflation is good for business expectations because it induces manufacturers to undertake investment in the future. Falling prices, like in the case of Japan in the last decade, are bad for investment. They make businesses postpone investment as high returns are not guaranteed at all.

The base year for measuring the inflation index is changed ever so often in order to make comparisons with recent years easier.

The comparison between today's prices is made with a base year and in recent times it has been fixed at 1993-94. The rate of inflation is measured as a percentage change from one time period (point) in the past, to another time period (point) later. It is called a point-to-point measurement of inflation.

India witnessed a high rate of inflation in the 1960s, 1970s and some years of 1980s. Whenever inflation rose dramatically in the past there were reasons like drought, war, oil price hike or rise in government expenditure. Thus, either demand for goods and services rose due to scarcity of food items or the costs of goods and services rose due to price of fuel. Government spending also puts a large amount of money income in the hands of the people and they in turn increase their demand for goods and services which may not be matched by a rise in the supply of those goods. The result is inflation.

In recent years, the increase in government borrowing from the market in order to finance the fiscal deficit has led to an expansion in money supply in the economy which has pushed up effective demand for goods and services. Controlling government expenditure is thus very important for controlling inflation. The immense pressure of black money in the economy on certain prices should also be mentioned. Unaccounted money, due to non-payment of taxes and corruption, has resulted in the inflation of house prices and real estate. 'Slush' money with politicians and corrupt officials has also gone into black marketing and hoarding of commodities.

A high rate of inflation is politically destabilising and people have always agitated against rise in prices of essential commodities. That is why inflation control has been at the forefront of economic policies. A low rate of inflation is also good for export competitiveness and for attracting FDI.

When scarcity of goods temporarily hikes up prices, especially of agricultural goods, and speculation and hoarding are rampant (like in June 2006), timely imports of goods in short supply like onions, tomatoes or sugar can ease inflationary pressure. Distribution of food stocks through the PDS can also take care of inflation caused by failed monsoons. When inflation is due to general rise in costs due to an international oil price hike, the government can ease the pressure on the vulnerable sections by subsidising kerosene, LPG and diesel.

A prudent monetary policy is most important for controlling inflation, especially credit control and raising interest rates. People are attracted by higher interest rates and save more. But investment is adversely affected and can bring about a downswing.

14

The Capital Market

For raising long-term loans, companies and individuals as well as the government have to approach the capital market. The government can raise money through 'gilt edged' bonds and its borrowing is conducted through the sale of securities. The gilt-edged market is a relatively secure market and the RBI plays an important role in helping the government raise money through bonds which have fixed incomes. There is not much speculation in this market and it is patronised by institutions like commercial banks, Life Insurance Corporation of India, General Insurance Corporation, Public Provident Funds—all of whom have to buy these securities as part of their portfolio. It is not an auction market but an over-the-counter market and the average size of the transactions is huge.

Debentures and Shares

Industrialists may want to raise capital by issuing debt securities carrying a fixed rate of interest. These are debentures that are usually issued by a company and secured on its assets. The debenture holder is a creditor of the company and is entitled to be paid his interest regardless of whether or not the company is making profits and before any distribution of dividends. Debentures issued by a public company, provided they have a stock exchange listing, may be traded on the exchange.

Companies wishing to raise money through equity can go to the primary or 'New Issues' market and issue shares. These shares can be traded in the country's stock markets which is the secondary market. We have seen many people getting rich by playing the stock markets actively. But for most, the stock market remains quite complex and difficult to understand. India's stock markets are over a 100 years old and were started to trade in commodities like cotton and jute. The Bombay Stock Exchange (BSE) and the National Stock Exchange

(NSE) (also in Mumbai) are the two major stock exchanges of India. India's stock market is active and very big in terms of the number of transactions taking place. There are 23 stock exchanges in the country and millions of people are playing around with stocks and shares. Thousands of people derive their incomes from stock markets as brokers. In recent times, however, paperless trading and screen based trading has replaced the concept of floor trading in which thousands of brokers have participated in the past. 'Demat' or a share depository system has been introduced but most people in India still hold physical shares. The number of shareholders having a 'depository' account in July 2004 was just over 60 lakhs as compared to the total share-holding public of 2 crores.

The changeover to the electronic mode of exchanges is in keeping with the developments in stock exchanges around the world. The major stock exchanges are New York, London and Hong Kong. The Standard and Poor Stock Index (S&P 500 index) of the US is the most important market index in the world and is watched closely by all.

Though stock exchanges in India are well established, many Indians are still cautious and only 2 per cent of the population invests in shares. About 70 per cent of the amount that households save goes into fixed deposits and other debt instruments like bonds. Only 7 to 8 per cent goes into the capital market and the rest to postal savings, provident finds, and life insurance funds.

Until the 1980s, players in India's stock markets were the large financial institutions like the Unit Trust of India (UTI) and the Life Insurance Corporation (LIC), and these invested in corporate equity for reasonable returns in the form of dividends. They tended to make their investments in companies with sound fundamentals and kept their money for long periods of time in their purchased shares. The extent of actively traded shares was limited.

Indian stock markets were deregulated in 1991, the Capital Issues Control Act (1947) and the post of Controller of Capital Issue were abolished.

Today, Indian companies are free to access the market for their capital requirements and since 1991, they can freely price their shares. Thus, Indian companies' Initial Public Offers (IPO) have been made easier and companies can determine the value of the shares themselves. They can go for 'book building' also in which they reserve and allot shares to individual investors.

There are two types of shares, preferential and ordinary shares; these have to be issued subject to certain guidelines of the Securities Exchange Board of India (SEBI) which was established in 1992 to oversee and regulate the stock markets. Its job is to protect the interests of investors in securities and to promote transparent and efficient functioning of the capital market. SEBI regulates not only the stock markets but also non-banking financial intermediaries, brokers, bankers, portfolio managers and mutual funds. It prohibits insider trading and regulates any substantial acquisition of shares and take over of companies.

All shares that are not preferential shares amount to the equity capital of a company. Shares can be issued at a premium or a discount and the government has allowed companies to buy back shares subject to certain conditions laid out by SEBI. Buy back reduces the number of shares in issue and increases the earnings per share. The private placement market has become popular. Around 72.5 per cent of total resources were mobilised through private placement in 2006.

The guidelines from SEBI relate to the disclosure of various data about the companies issuing the shares like past track record. The promoting or share issuing company must have a minimum specified percentage of shares. There is a lock in period for such contributions and various disclosure norms justifying the price fixed, including past market prices that the company has to abide by. An assessment of risk in the project has to be undertaken.

The share accounts are maintained with a central depository. The Depository Bill was passed in July 1996 to provide a legal framework for the establishment of a depository to record all ownership deals in book entry form. The first depository commenced operations in October 1996. On the whole, the Indian public issues market has made important advances in terms of market design. It conducts purely computerised auctions in which price 'discovery' or the fair price of a set of securities that are up for sale occurs. By removing the human element, non transparency of transactions, has been removed. There has been an increase in resource flow in the primary market for equity as a result. The equity market is roughly the same size as the banking system in terms of financial intermediation.

The size of the various stock exchanges, as measured by the number of transactions taking place in India, is huge. While the average value of transactions is small by world standards, India has a very large number of transactions. Out of the two major stock exchanges—National Stock Exchange (NSE) and Bombay Stock Exchange (BSE), the former is bigger. In 2002, NSE displaced Shanghai in becoming the third biggest in the world, while BSE moved up to fifth rank in the world's stock exchanges.

The Sensex measures the BSE sensitive index based on 30 share prices (the weights are determined by the importance of the stock) and is watched by all interested as indicative of the health of the stock market. Nifty Index is composed of the average share price of 50 shares and is also important. There is a Nifty Junior index also. Every day millions of rupees worth of shares and debentures as well as government bonds and securities are traded in the stock market through thousands of brokers. At the end of the day, transactions are completed through 'settlement' between the buyers and sellers.

The characteristics of the stock market changed in the early 1990s which saw, due to the liberalisation measures, a wide range of shares, including new issues of relatively unknown companies. Many companies of dubious net worth also got themselves listed on the stock exchanges and sometimes even got oversubscribed. After giving good returns initially, suddenly some of these companies wound up.

Many companies that have listed shares in the stock exchanges however have negligible 'liquidity' which means they are not often traded. Some shares are actively traded and can be purchased in small lots and are attractive, not so much in terms of their offer of dividends but the promise of capital gains. Small investors have entered the market in large numbers in order to get higher returns from stock market investments but stockbrokers alone are entitled to transact business in a stock exchange.

The secondary market for equities now offers the capacity of seamless end to end electronic operation. The average size of a transaction in 2004 in BSE was Rs. 31,503. There are retail investors and institutional investors; there are two types of transactions—investment and speculative. An investment transaction normally involves the actual delivery of the security and payment of its full price. The spot market is a pure delivery market.

The speculative transaction, on the other hand, involves deferred settlement. The delivery of securities or payment of full price are rare and, instead, only the difference in prices is paid and recovered.

Speculative transactions are possible with smaller amounts of money. Forward transactions involve delivery and payment of securities within a fixed period—15 or 30 days. In forward delivery or system of carry forward, there is postponement of delivery by making a payment of a 'consideration' or premium, by one party to the other. For example, if buyers (bulls) want postponement of delivery—that is they have undertaken to buy but do not wish to buy, they pay an amount (*badla*) to the sellers (bears) who are pessimistic. Similarly, the bears can also pay a 'consideration' to the buyers for agreeing to accommodate them until the next settlement. This is known as 'backwardation'. Almost three-fourths of the outstanding position at the settlement period gets carried forward to the next settlement and involves a huge amount of money in which *badla* financing assumes importance. *Badla* has been banned in the market for some years as it was perceived to be causing much speculative activity.

Wide movements in share prices have become common in recent years and the Sensex has risen and fallen periodically. Sometimes it is due to market manipulation where some operator rigs up certain stock prices artificially. The stock market collapse after the scam of 1992 in which Harshad Mehta was involved and a number of small investors lost heavily, has not been repeated in recent times. The scam, that was mainly due to the unscrupulous operations of one broker, was the result of various loopholes in the functioning and surveillance of the stock market. Mehta siphoned off money borrowed from banks to rig the stock market and artificially hike up prices of some stocks like ACC cement. This was also a case of insider trading, which means an illegal dealing in shares by parties with knowledge of unpublished price sensitive data.

After the Central government's annual budget 1992-93, there was a huge manipulated stock market boom that crashed soon after, resulting in big losses for investors. The Janakiraman Committee also found that huge amounts of money was siphoned off from banks for speculation by Mehta. The banks involved did so because they faced low interest incomes since the economic reforms began, and were looking for opportunities for making quick profits. When they found that stock markets were booming and bulls (buyers) needed funds to finance their own bought positions, they saw an opportunity to make profits. Money received by banks from sale of PSU stocks was used to earn high returns and to finance stock brokers in a booming market. But the bubble burst soon enough as the boom was not a real one.

In 1993, the government decided to permit Foreign Institutional Investors (FIIs) to make portfolio investments in India's stock markets subject to certain conditions. They too concentrated on shares of leading companies. Given the huge funds at their disposal, even small investments by the FIIs meant big money for stock markets in countries like India.

Indian companies were allowed to access international capital markets through Euro equity shares. A range of non-bank financial companies including private mutual funds were also allowed to operate in the stock market. Investment norms for NRIs were liberalised also.

While the 1990s were marked by one major fraud by Harshad Mehta, in 2001 Ketan Parekh was accused of routing money held by Indians abroad back into the stock market through the overseas corporate bodies registered in Mauritius and a certain cooperative bank. This led to the collapse of the stock market soon after the Budget 2001. When Harshad Mehta's scam broke out on April 23, 1992, the BSE sensex crashed by 570 points. In Ketan Parikh's case, the market fell by 147 points and small savers of the cooperative banks lost heavily. Like Mehta, Parikh also tapped bank funds to play the stock markets and jack up stock prices in order to make big gains which were ultimately lost.

The problem has been that India's stock markets are shallow and they cannot bear the rise in speculative activity. Several 'bull' runs were followed by 'bear' collapses indicating that only a few operators who were also market 'insiders' could make or break the financial markets. The shallowness of markets means that only stocks of a few companies are actively traded—in India's case, only 5 or 6 stocks dominate the stock market and the top 25 companies account for 50 per cent of the total market capitalisation at the BSE. There are over 5,000 companies listed on the BSE and 1,500 companies have actively traded stocks.

Secondly, only a small proportion of these stocks are routinely available for trading, the rest of the stocks being held by promoters, financial institutions and others interested in corporate control or influence. Thirdly, the number of players trading in these stocks are also few. The net impact is that speculation and volatility are the essential features of such markets. The regulatory system has to be strong and effective to neutralise the influence of a small number of players.

Indian stock markets have been experiencing a higher and higher market capitalisation. It means that the total market value of the companies' traded shares, has been going up. In 1990, India's market cap was just about 1.26 per cent of the US and 4.5 per cent of the UK and 35 per cent of Korea. It has risen enormously in the last 15 years.

In 1991, India's 30 share Sensex was at 1,915 and the market capitalisation was at Rs. 35,778 crore. In 2005, the index and market cap changed significantly. While Sensex crossed 8,000, the market cap soared to over Rs. 700,000 crore. In January 2007, market capitalisation (NSE) was US $834 billion and was 91.5 per cent of the GDP. China's market cap is $1000 billion and is 33.3 per cent of its GDP. Market cap in terms GDP indicates the relative size of the capital market besides investment confidence and discounted future earnings of the corporate sector.

As the corporate fundamentals got better after 2000, and market related reforms such as online trading, paperless trading and banking reforms were introduced, stock markets have become very attractive for FIIs. There is a big increase in derivative trading which doubled between 2005 and 2006. Derivative trading relates to trading of a financial instrument derived from some other asset like a futures contract or option's trading.

In order to decide what stocks to buy, investors often study the P/E ratios of stocks. This is the market capitalisation of the company divided by the profit attributable to ordinary shareholders in its last financial statements: the share price divided by earnings per share. This ratio shows how many years it will take the company, at the rate of earnings used, to earn the equivalent to its full value. It also basically reflects investors' expectation of corporate income growth in future. It was 20 in December 2006 as compared to 17 to 18 a year earlier. India's PE ratios were higher than in most countries in emerging markets. EPS or earning per share is a measure of the company's performance. It equals the profit attributable to the ordinary shareholders (i.e., profits before ordinary dividends) divided by the number of ordinary shares in issue during the year.

Since the Ketan Parekh episode, SEBI has been empowered and made stronger to prevent excessive speculation and volatility. It has introduced rolling settlement in July 2001, under which settlement has to be made every day. In general, while SEBI is supposed to control excessive speculation in the market, it is essential that there is some amount of speculation otherwise it would be impossible to have a large volume of business necessary for mobility and liquidity. But reckless speculators should be controlled, especially since they risk little and operate largely on borrowed capital. Markets crash when there is a huge default. Such defaults have been prevented by the government's setting up National Securities Clearance Corporation (NSCC) which manages risks at the NSE. When a clearing member on the NSE defaults on payment obligation, the NSCC steps in to pay up. This prevents a contagion from taking place.

Foreign Financial Institutional Investors (FIIs)

India has been receiving a big amount of FII funds. These are private capital flows and they now dominate the total financial flows to developing countries. A big surge in portfolio investments is due to the low international interest rates. The low real rates of return in their own home markets has triggered the FIIs to seek the 'emerging' markets like India to park their funds. The number of registered FIIs in India in 2004 was 637. The net investment of FIIs in 2003-04 was $9,950 million and in 2004-05, it was $10,173 million. From 1992-93 till 2004-05, the total FII inflows have been $35.9 billion. The FII inflows have been aided by the deregulation of the financial markets, the growing competition among them to seek the most important emerging markets. Even though the number of FIIs has risen by 27 per cent in 2006, they accounted for only 10.4 per cent of the total gross turnover in the spot and derivative market.

Secondly, there has been institutionalisation of savings in developed countries that has made available large amounts of capital for investment. FIIs try to diversify their risks and seek higher returns through global markets. For example, pension funds alone constitute billions of dollars of investment. The increase in mutual funds has also aided international financial flows available for investment. Also, major advances in technology, especially in the field of communication and information, has played a role and helped in removing physical barriers of space and time. Twenty-four hour trading is now possible. Liberal tax concessions have also helped such inflows.

India has been deregulating its financial markets and further opening up is also in the horizon due to WTO stipulations. Institutional fund managers, as a result, are today managing trillions of dollars of assets.

To aid their decisions, there are rating agencies which try to give ratings to bonds and inform the investors whether their investment in a particular bond is risky or not at the global level. Standard and Poor and Moody's Investment Services also investigate the investment condition of the economy. Triple A rating means best quality with the smallest risks, and an exceptionally stable and dependable market. BBB and Baa are of medium quality.

In India, FIIs are important market players and when they enter, the stock market goes up and when they withdraw, it falls. In general, the FIIs are looking for high returns and stability.

Instruments of Investment

Life Insurance and Mutual Funds

Long-term capital can also be accessed from the insurance sector and mutual funds. Insurance is big business in a country like India and is worth more than Rs. 400 billion even though only 7 per cent of the population is covered by life insurance. In Japan, almost the entire population is covered by life insurance. Together with banking services, the insurance sector contributes 7 per cent to the GDP.

The first Indian life insurance company was the Bombay Mutual Life Assurance Society established in 1870. Before that, foreign insurance companies dominated insurance business and enjoyed a near monopoly. The rise of Indian insurance companies was connected with the national movement and gathered momentum in the 1920s and 1930s.

In 1974, the insurance business was nationalised and only LIC of India and the GIC were allowed to function.

General insurance deals with motor vehicles, marine, fire. In all, 140 different products. A well developed insurance sector can promote faster economic growth because by encouraging risk taking activity, it has the potential for mobilising long-term contractual savings. These can be used for infrastructure, where there is a big demand for such savings. Whereas banking institutions mobilise short and medium term savings, contractual saving institutions like insurance companies and pension and provident funds have long-term contractual liabilities and are naturally suitable investors in infrastructure projects.

The Indian insurance business has a huge potential because the market is large and mostly untapped. A government appointed committee's report on the Insurance sector in 1994 had advised the ending of state monopoly and setting up a strong insurance regulatory authority.

Basically, insurance business banks on people avoiding risks, illness, accidents, disability, damage to property. They are willing to pay a 'premium' in exchange for an insurance cover. Where there are many risk averse persons, an insurance firm, by pooling of risks, can assure an expected value of income to each person. The insurance business can grow if the supply constraints are removed and many competitive players are active in the field. In the life insurance business, risk coverage and savings are bundled together unlike in a bank where money can be claimed on demand from saving deposits. In the case of insurance, savings can be reclaimed before maturity only after a penalty has been paid. There is thus a lockin effect involved in signing an insurance contract.

The savings component and the typically long-term nature of the contract make life insurance an important instrument for mobilising long-term funds from the people. Insurance is an important instrument of saving for households in India and in the financial assets of many households there is a mix of life insurance policies, Provident Funds (PF) and pension funds, small savings certificates, mutual funds, equities and debentures. Life insurance forms around 10 per cent of all financial assets in Indian households. There has been a decline in the PF and pension funds type of savings.

Insurance companies spread their risk by making contractual arrangements with a large number of individuals and organisations. They can make profits depending on the extent of innovations in the range of products offered at fair prices. Secondly, competition brings more products with more complex and extensive risk categorisation, better technology, better consumer services, including faster settlements. The higher the capital base of the insurance companies, the more variety they can offer.

To regulate the insurance business the Insurance Regulatory Development Authority (IRDA) was set up in India in 1999-2000. It aims at protecting the consumer's interests, financial soundness and promoting the healthy growth of the insurance sector. More players could lead to more transparent contracts, lower premium, and better ways of redressing grievances. The IRDA also prevents collusive tendencies so that the prices charged remain reasonable.

The entry of the private sector and foreign companies in the insurance business has been allowed. Foreign investment has also been allowed up to 26 per cent. There is much demand for increasing the cap on foreign investment. Resistance has come from the trade unions in opening up the insurance sector further. They fear retrenchment through extensive computerisation and modernisation. They also say that private investors will ignore rural areas which is to some extent true. Rural and, mostly, agricultural sector insurance is sadly inadequate and will require government intervention in a more strident manner.

The future of the insurance sector is bright because it is largely untapped. The huge middle class and the break up of the joint family system has led to an increase in demand for life insurance cover for the breadwinner. In nuclear families there are many in the older age groups who have to fend for themselves in their old age. Their demand for insurance is likely to be up because by 2010, 10 per cent of the population will be above 60 years of age. Besides, a higher growth rate and greater consumer awareness combined with a higher level of education will raise the demand for insurance.

A huge database will be required to profile customers and assign them the right insurance policy. LIC can sell other products like pension funds and the department of Posts and Telegraphs can be roped in to sell insurance and related financial products in villages. They are already mobilising more savings than all the commercial banks put together. The growth of insurance will not only make available a huge amount of contractual savings for use in infrastructure, but it will also be profitable business for many private sector players entering the business.

Mutual Funds

Mutual funds are extremely popular in industrial countries for individuals as an avenue for investment. They can also be an important source of long-term capital for the stock market. The main function of mutual funds is to mobilise savings from the general public and invest them in stock market securities. Today the mutual funds industry is open to the private sector. These are formed as trusts and managed by a separate asset management company, supervised by a board of trustees. SEBI regulates mutual funds and its guidelines related to advertisements, disclosures and reporting requirements have to be followed.

For many years the performance of mutual funds was not encouraging partly because the stock market conditions were not encouraging. But since 1998-2000, there has been a significant mobilisation of funds. Today there are a number of private funds like Birla, Tata, SBI, Alliance capital, ICICI, Prudential, etc.

The mutual funds industry has been dominated by UTI which ran into trouble in 2001. Its prestigious Unit Scheme 64 had been conceived to mobilise savings from the household sector for the industrial sector in 1964. It was not covered by the regulations of SEBI that governs the mutual funds industry. It was not bound by the disclosure requirements of the industry. The Net Asset Value or NAV of the units of US 64 remained ambiguous and elusive. (NAV is determined by dividing the net assets of the scheme by the number of outstanding units on the valuation date). This brought about a crisis and all purchase and repurchase of units by UTI was suspended in July 2001. This affected about 20 million retail investors who had banked on US-64 for its liquidity. They found their assets frozen. Why did US-64 land into trouble?

It was because UTI made investments in certain stocks in the stock market which rapidly declined. The NAV of US-64 declined below the repurchase price and this generated intense redemption pressure. It led to a panic situation when large corporate sector holders of units were allowed to withdraw their investments in US-64. The mismanagement was visible immediately and repurchase and sale was suspended in June 2001. In August, UTI provided the facility for repurchase of up to 3,000 units of US-64 from each individual portfolio. It also made it a NAV based scheme so as to align the purchase and sale prices with the net asset values of the units from January 2002. For all this UTI took Rs. 3,000 crore credit from a consortium of banks led by the State Bank of India.

The UTI Act was also repealed and UTI was split into UTI-1 and UTI-2. UTI-1 was given US-64 and the assured returns scheme managed by an administrator appointed by the government. The government gave assurance to investors to convert these units into bonds carrying 6.7 per cent rate of interest from May 2003. Thus, US-64 scheme was stopped. UTI-1 was also entrusted with 21 schemes guaranteeing certain high rates of return, with the government paying the guaranteed rate of return. UTI-2 was to become an unencumbered mutual fund with NAV based schemes. In January 2003, UTI-2 was handed over to a new set of owners comprising SBI, Bank of Baroda, LIC and Punjab National Bank.

Since the returns from mutual funds depend on the stock market, they become popular when the stock market is up. It has been observed through surveys that bank deposits remain the favourite choice of small investors because mutual funds scam of 2001 has caused some apprehension about the future of such investments. In 2005, the share of UTI and other public sector mutual funds in total resources mobilised increased to 22.5 per cent. In 2006, 17.8 per cent was mobilised.

The Development Financial Institutions (DFIs)

These finance industrial projects through loans by underwriting and direct subscription of shares and bonds. There are a number of DFIs in India like IDBI, ICICI and IFC. Then there are banks that are specialised in financing special business sectors with long-term loans like the EXIM bank which coordinates the working of institutions engaged in financing exports and imports. NABARD, which was set up in 1982, provides credit for promoting agriculture, small-scale and cottage industries, handicrafts and other rural industries. The Power Finance Corporation, Tourism Finance Corporation and Small Industries Development Bank of India are also functioning as Development Financial Institutions.

15

The Services Sector

The services industry has been the fastest growing sector in recent years. The exports of services from India also has been growing and while it yielded $980 million in 1990-91, it grew rapidly to yield $6,591 million by 2003-04. Service exports grew by 20 per cent in 2003-04. In 2005-06, services contributed 55 per cent to the GDP. The usually asked question is, "Can India leapfrog to become an industrialised country and be in the league of the richest countries of the world on the basis of its service sector growth?" It can happen if the high growth is sustained and the service sector pulls up the rest of the economy into a higher growth trajectory. The developed countries are the most prominent service providers in the world. But gradually, India and China are also emerging as important providers of various services. They include consultancy services, healthcare, entertainment, R&D, ship repair, satellite mapping, educational, accounting, hospitality services and Information Technology—software, and Business Process Outsourcing (BPO) services.

In the last 10 years, there has been a spectacular growth in the software and IT enabled services that have grown at the rate of 36 per cent between 1995-1999 and 2003-2004. But India's market share in the global IT services is only 3.4 per cent. It goes to show that there is plenty of scope for expansion. The total earnings from IT services and software in 2004-05 were $17.9 billion and the domestic market was worth $10.3 billion. The IT industry will account for 7 per cent of the GDP by 2008 and comprise 35 per cent of the exports. According to the Economic Survey 2004-05, by 2008 software and IT enabled services will earn $57 to $65 billion. IT enabled services alone will earn $21 to $24 billion.

India's software exports have been flourishing due to a talent base in South India, especially comprising young men and women who are hardworking, creative and relatively inexpensive to hire. The BPO sector, on the other hand, is making use of India's youth which is English speaking and efficient in rendering computer based services. The developed countries are able to save on costs by outsourcing such services to India.

Software exports, call centres and data transcription have indeed experienced a genuine growth but the demand for such skilled people will not be enough to absorb all those looking for jobs in the services sector. In fact, the Indian software industry has grown by 50 per cent in the past 6 years. The number of people employed has risen from 500,000 in 1999 to about 700,000 persons in 2004 in the software, ITES/BPO services. But employment is confined to those with a technical, especially trained background. Growth of the services sector has to be backed by similar growth in agriculture and industry. It is the low cost, highly skilled human resources which have contributed to the success story as well as the fact that software exports do not use physical infrastructure and financial capital.

The Outlook for Outsourcing

Outsourcing means obtaining goods and services from an outside source through a contract. The British outsourced raw materials and foodstuff to India during colonial times in order to promote their industrialisation. India remained primarily agricultural because it had to supply the raw materials for factories abroad. In the 20th century also, whenever industrialised countries have found locations from where they can get cheap raw materials, spare parts and services, they have gone for outsourcing. In manufacturing, MNCs have established bases in countries that have a skilled and cheap labour force. Many of their factories are virtual 'sweatshops' where the working conditions are very taxing and tedious, especially for women workers who are paid less than men.

In recent times, ever since India's software industry started developing, American firms have found it convenient to outsource some of their important services to India and the time difference between India and US suits the American firms just fine.

As a result, there has been a phenomenal growth in the outsourcing industry in India. This has given rise to a reaction against 'jobs being transported to India' in the US. Many have predicted that

3.3 million jobs would move out of US by 2015. Many states have reacted by enacting anti-outsourcing Bills but these have yet to be passed by the US Senate. In January 2004, however, the Senate approved a legislation that prevents private companies working for government departments of the Treasury and Transportation to outsource to any company outside the US. Such Bills would shut off a huge opportunity for Indians and companies to get projects from the US government which spends billions of dollars on technical services every year.

There is thus much controversy surrounding the phenomenon of 'outsourcing' in the US and the Bush administration, in its second term, has yet to come out with a clear-cut policy formulation. Indians have been glad that the view of President George W. Bush regarding outsourcing was never so strident as the one taken by Senator John Kerry. They expect that there will be sympathetic treatment in the future too. Actually, while outsourcing can hardly be blamed for the unemployment situation in the US (slow growth in the job market), it is becoming a highly emotive issue among trade unions and politicians. For India, outsourcing is contributing substantially to the dollar inflow into India.

The latest data from International Labour Organisation (*World Employment Report 2004-05*) also reveal that the increase in unemployment in general, in the industrialised countries, is not so much due to the fact that jobs have moved abroad to developing countries but because there has been a rise in productivity growth within their own countries. That is why jobs are getting fewer. For example, steel production in the US has increased from 75 million to 102 million tonnes but the number of workers in the steel industry have not increased. In fact, there has been a decrease in the work force from 289,000 to 74,000 employees.

The US department of labour has estimated that in the first three months of 2004, less than 2 per cent of mass layoffs in the US were the result of outsourcing. During that period, out of a total of 239,361 employees, only 4,633 were laid off because of outsourcing.

Various ways can be devised to minimise the loss of jobs due to outsourcing and some firms that are outsourcing jobs are already finding innovative solutions for redeploying workers within the company, especially in the UK.

For India, any curb by the American or European countries on outsourcing will mean big losses in terms of foreign exchange earnings. Indian firms are providing various information and communication technology (ICT) services like back office and call centre operations, long distance sales, insurance and medical data entry services. Currently, the ICT sector accounts for 20 per cent of the goods exported and contributes to over 3 per cent of the GDP.

There are 200,000 Indian expatriates working as ICT professionals in the US as part of the H-1B visa programme. The Indian services industry growth has been powered by the software sector. If anything happens to it, there will be a problem in sustaining a higher GDP growth. The fact remains that the average annual wage for the Indian computer professionals is 10 to 20 per cent lower than the wages in the US. Indian wages are also lower than the wages prevalent in Europe. It is the cheap wages that have contributed largely to the success of software exports.

It all means that while the reason for US 'jobless' growth may be due to other structural reasons like the rise in productivity growth of labour which comes from greater use of technology, the trade unions and politicians erroneously blame countries like India for snatching away their jobs. India's services sector growth, on the other hand, provides the hope for the entire economy being pulled up through faster GDP growth which will ultimately provide more jobs for all. But for increase in the overall employment in the ICT sector from its current 700,000, a higher rate of investment in computer education would be required. Also, implementation of universal primary education would give students the basic English language skills; this has contributed to the success of call centres. Besides, more value addition to the outsourcing programmes would be required in the future to carve out a niche for ourselves and get rid of the label 'cyber coolies' assigned to software service providers from India. Fortunately, the Europeans have declared that they would continue to outsource in the future. Germany and Holland have eased visa restrictions on software personnel. Hopefully, Americans would also work out some plan that would give the Indian ICT sector a chance to grow further. In any case, it will ultimately benefit US industry, help them to save money and sustain their own economic recovery.

On the whole, the share of services in the Gross National Product (GNP) has been rising at a faster rate than of manufacturing. The domestic services sector comprising a whole gamut of services like financial, telecommunications, entertainment, hotels, media, transport, wholesale, sports, government administration, defence, personal and community services (NGOs), and construction has been expanding rapidly. Services account for 5 per cent of the GDP and the sector has been growing at 7 to 8 per cent over the past decade.

The government has especially encouraged construction services trade in recent years because it is labour intensive and the numbers engaged in it have increased tremendously. Many unemployed people from the rural areas have become construction workers and have been engaged in the heavy building activity related to urban development. Many, who have been rendered unemployed from the manufacturing sector, have become petty retailers or repair shop owners. The informal sector in services has been growing rapidly and many manufacturing units have also given various services components to be managed by outsiders. Thus, the services industry growth is not exactly due to the growth in agriculture and industry. Rather it has been absorbing people rendered jobless from these two sectors on account of their stagnation. Restaurants, *dhabas*, corner shops, *kirana* stores and various kinds of trading have absorbed people who have not found jobs in manufacturing. The hotel, restaurant, catering, retail and wholesale trading accounts for 30 per cent of the output of the services sector or 15 per cent of the GDP.

Tourism

Tourism is a service industry that, after languishing for many years, has started gathering momentum with more international tourists arriving in India. Even with a much faster rate of tourist arrival, India is far behind the other chosen destinations in Southeast Asia. It is poor infrastructure that has made the Indian tourism industry suffer. The lack of proper train and air connections between major cities and tourist spots scattered around India is a big deterrent to the expansion of tourism.

India has the seas, mountains, historical sites, flora and fauna which is quite unique. There are new types of tourism emerging in the world like ecotourism, religious tourism and health tourism that have a big potential. Many people are discovering that India has rare types of health services and herbal treatment, massages and cures on offer.

Tourism already employs 20 million people directly, and 1.36 million indirectly. But India's earnings from tourism, though growing rapidly, remain rather modest. They were at $3.53 billion in 2003 with 2.7 million tourists coming in. By contrast, the world saw 681 million international travellers in 2003 who spent $605.7 billion. India's share of world tourism was 0.4 per cent, and in terms of earnings, it was 0.58 per cent. By contrast, much smaller countries like Thailand, Cambodia and Singapore are earning huge amounts from tourism.

The growth of tourism is good for increasing employment but it has to be carefully monitored as too many tourists in places like the Himalayas can cause ecological damage. There are, thus, the benefits of backward linkages in agriculture, horticulture, poultry, handicrafts and construction that would lead to an increase in incomes and jobs but there are also costs in terms of its impact on the local culture and environment. The aim in many countries is to target large budget tourists instead of mass or budget tourists. In such cases, the average tourist spending is higher and fewer tourists bring in more foreign exchange.

Recently, the tourist traffic to India has increased by 16 per cent but it is still puzzling why so few people come to India as compared to the rest of Southeast Asia. Barely three million tourists arrive annually. Thailand and Malaysia, which are much smaller, are able to attract at least three times more tourists.

One should try to double the flow of tourists because the benefits from tourism (apart from earning foreign exchange) are many. Today there is an intense competition among developing countries to attract international tourists and for one-third of the smaller nations it is the main industry. They are spending a bigger proportion of their GDP on promoting tourism than India and they have developed the required infrastructure very fast. In India, even though there is so much to see, the government's spending on tourism is inadequate for developing comparable facilities. (The Central Plan outlay for department of tourism was Rs. 225 crore in 2002-03.)

Though the advertisement budget of the government for promotion of tourism has been recently hiked by 60 per cent to Rs. 65 crore, it is still small considering the amount of work needed to make the latest slogan 'Incredible India' work.

If tourism increased significantly, it would help many ancillary industries like food processing, cottage industries and entertainment. And because it is a labour intensive industry, more jobs, especially in rural areas could be created. And since most of the natural beauty and wildlife are to be found in non-urban areas, with proper training rural people could find employment as guides and transporters. The whole of Bali, Indonesia, for example is involved in the tourism industry. More jobs in rural areas would also help to reduce the continuous migration to towns.

Since tourism depends on a network of communications, clean airports, good roads, uninterrupted power supply and modes of easy transportation are essential. Tourists also like safe short-haul destinations, cheap and comfortable accommodation and hygienic conditions in hotels and restaurants because no one wants to fall sick while travelling.

To double the number of tourists, the needs of small budget tourists have to be addressed also by building more inexpensive hotels and guest houses in towns close to tourist spots. Many people are against mass tourism but allowing more people to come and see India cannot be harmful for the country's income and employment. It will help India to globalise faster because interaction with tourists can bring greater exposure to other cultures for the local people—which is educative. France has been coping with mass tourism for years without any problems. Even for the high spending tourists, hotel rates have to be brought down in order to attract bigger numbers. Five-star hotel rates are too high in India as compared to neighbouring ASEAN countries.

Most tourists want to shop in countries they visit; Thailand and other members of the ASEAN have an attractive VAT return policy. Unfortunately, Indian goods have also become quite expensive and the neighbouring countries have much better shopping facilities and discounts. The same kind of curios, artefacts, textiles and jewellery are being produced by them at much cheaper rates. The quality of Indian goods would have to improve and prices made reasonable in order to make India a suitable competitor and a shopper's paradise.

But India has an amazing variety to offer, especially cultural diversity, wildlife, ethnic, health, religious and ecotourism. Yet some of the best places are so remote that one has to spend atleast a day by train or taxi to reach them (for example, Ranthambore and Sanchi). There are few direct flights to choice tourist destinations and waiting at airports can be tedious and boring, especially when combined with irregular and erratic flight schedules.

The airports also need to be refurbished and upgraded; privatisation of the main gateways, Mumbai and Delhi, as recommended by the Naresh Chandra Committee would help. They have to be made interesting and comfortable with various facilities for transit passengers. Bangkok's perfectly modern airport with its huge shopping arcade has been refurbished as a new 'state-of-the-art' airport. Even in remote Cambodia, which is one of the least developed countries of ASEAN, the airport in Phnom Penh is remarkable.

The big (and only) attraction of Cambodia today is Angkor Wat to which thousands of European or Japanese tourist flock daily (Cambodia gets nearly as many tourists as India). There are many reasons: First, 'Kampuchea' was closed to tourism for years under Pol Pot and in the 1980s, it was a dangerous territory due to land mines. Angkor Wat has now been declared as a world heritage monument and much of its charm has been captured and promoted by the French for years. Andre Malreaux was one of the first to have written extensively on it as well as one of the first to have stolen statues from it!

Even when there are more gorgeous and better preserved temple complexes in India, temple tourism is rather thin. An important reason for the popularity of Angkor Wat is that it has been packaged very well and a modern airport in Siem Riep allows tourists to come from Bangkok and straight away set off to see the temples by car or bus. In three days one can cover the vast temple complex. There are at least 50 to 60 big hotels that handle the heavy tourist traffic. The whole town lives on tourism.

It is the lack of aggressive promotion of Indian art and culture and the absence of good infrastructure which pose big problems in promoting temple tourism in South India. The word of mouth about bad experiences in India can do a lot of harm. Angkor, by contrast, delivers what it promises—a mystique which is quite out of proportion to the architectural and artistic quality of the monuments.

Though Cambodia is quite unsafe even now, Angkor is safe and women play a very important part in promoting tourism. In a similar manner, more women could be employed in the tourism industry in India. The best way to prepare for more international tourists is to encourage domestic tourism which has now reached 30 million. Better services in remote places meant mainly for domestic tourists could create the requisite infrastructure for foreign tourists at a later stage. Even for domestic tourists, lower taxes and better package tours would help. This is how most ASEAN countries and China developed their tourism industry in a few years' time. By 2020, when China exceeds France as the number one tourist destination of the world, (currently it receives more than 32 million tourists), India will feel the need to catch up. China will also be the fourth most important tourist generating country of the world. Starting the direct flight to Shanghai from India is a good beginning. Much tourist traffic could be expected from the neighbouring countries if things improve fast with easy visas and easier access to Buddhist monuments.

16

The Fiscal Policies and Budgetary Finances

India's tax system used to be very steeply progressive which means that income taxes were very high. There was widespread evasion with the highly progressive income tax system where the marginal tax rate, that is increase in tax over the higher income slabs, was around 100 per cent. Tax collections were poor despite the high rates but, on the whole, since 1950-51 there has been a manifold increase in revenue receipts. This shows that new taxes were introduced and the tax coverage has broadened in the last 50 years. It also shows a better tax administration and a rise in both prices and incomes since Independence.

There has been a steep rise in the area of public expenditure mainly because of the expansion of the government machinery, an increase in defence expenditure, a rise in salaries and dearness allowances of government servants that had to be incurred as the cost of living rose. The shortfall in revenues was made up by the central government through borrowing from the market and external assistance. Reliance on external borrowing was at its peak in the 1980s.

The total expenditure of the government is equal to the non-plan expenditure plus plan expenditure. Plan expenditure consists of expenditure on central plans such as agriculture, rural development, irrigation and flood control, energy, industry and minerals, transport and communications, science and technology and environment and social services. Plan expenditure was kept high at 6 to 7 per cent of the GDP throughout the 1980s. Non-plan expenditure has gone on rising sharply without much control over the years.

Non-plan expenditure has been rising because it consists of rigid commitments like defence, internal security, salaries, which cannot be reduced as the population rises and the inflationary pressure in the economy continues to intensify. The government cannot drastically reduce the non-plan expenditure and has had to find ways and means of financing it.

In the 1980s, the government was forced to borrow from the Reserve Bank to meet its running expenses or non-plan expenditure. Increases in such expenditure of the government that were disproportionately large compared to its earnings from taxes and capital receipts, increased the fiscal deficit. The main items of capital receipts are loans raised by the government from the market, borrowings by the government from the RBI and other parties through the sale of Treasury Bills and loans received from foreign governments and bodies as well as recoveries of loans granted by the Centre to the states and union territories. The fiscal deficit is the gap between the government's total revenue expenditure plus capital expenditure and the total revenue receipts plus capital receipts. Capital expenditure is the expenditure by the government on acquisition of assets like land, buildings, machinery, equipment, and other investments in shares, loans and advances to the states and union territories as well as public enterprises.

A high fiscal deficit has been a recurrent factor in India's annual budgets and was a cause for much concern in 1991 for the IMF and the World Bank when it was at 8.2 per cent of the GDP. A high fiscal deficit means that the total borrowing requirement of the government to run the economy is high. It means that the government is borrowing extensively from different sources in order to make payments for various economic activities. It also shows that the government's revenue collection is not up to the mark and the capital receipts are not sufficient to fund government's total expenditure.

In the past, the government borrowed from the RBI in the form of ad hoc Treasury Bills sold to the RBI and the Reserve Bank went on printing notes against government's Treasury Bills which meant that there was an increase in money in circulation. This was a form of deficit financing and it was brought to an end with the government signing an MoU with the Reserve Bank in which 91-Day Treasury Bills were to be sold in the market. Printing money to finance the fiscal deficit led to inflationary pressure and there was a sharp rise in inflation in the 1980s.

The borrowing from RBI became necessary because, over the years, the government has not been able to bring into the tax net those people who have an ability to pay taxes and many who are tax liable are actually evading taxes. This inefficiency to extend the tax net to people who can pay is leading to a loss in revenue collection that could be used for promoting development of the social sector and infrastructure. The second problem is regarding the government's own inability to cut unnecessary spending and to trim down the size of the bureaucracy.

It was only in the 1980s that some tax reforms were started. Personal income taxes were lowered and the income tax slabs were reduced from 8 slabs to 4. After the economic reforms were launched a further reduction in income tax rate took place. Company taxation rate was also brought down. In general, the move has been towards reducing direct taxes and simplifying the tax system so that there is less evasion and more compliance. In the 1980s, a big source of revenue came from customs duties. After the reforms, this source has been yielding less and less revenue as customs duties were brought down systematically under the rules of the WTO. Though the share of direct taxes like income tax and corporation tax has increased since the reforms, the share from indirect taxes like customs duties and excise duties have been declining.

Direct taxes have been buoyant in recent years with an increased share in the GDP. Their share rose from only 1.8 per cent in 1990-1991 to 3.3 per cent in 2002-03. As a result there has been a marked difference in the composition of the central tax revenue in favour of direct taxes whose share rose from 18 per cent to 37 per cent during the same period.

The rising share of direct taxes has made the central government's tax structure a little less regressive as people with higher incomes are contributing more to the total tax revenue. But the ratio of direct to indirect taxes has changed. It was 35:65 in 1950-51 but changed to 26:74 in 2002-03. It shows that the proceeds of commodity taxes have increased both in volume and importance, making the burden of financing government activity fall mainly on the middle and lower income groups. It makes the tax system look more regressive also if you take into account the fact that there is a higher degree of tax evasion among the higher income groups and the benefits of public expenditure are accessed by them more.

Since the beginning of the economic and tax reforms, the fiscal deficit has also not been brought down in a spectacular manner. Reduction of the fiscal deficit has now come under the realm of a law which stipulates that it has to be reduced to zero over a certain specified period. The Fiscal Responsibility and Budget Management Act was passed in 2003 to eliminate the revenue deficit by 2007-08.

The central government's main problem has thus been not being able to control its current expenditure and more and more money is being spent on interest payments. The public debt rose sharply from 58 per cent of the GDP in 1995-96 to 76 per cent in 2002-03.

To understand the government's expenditure pattern, one has to look at the central government's budget. The government's annual Budget, which is watched by almost every one, is divided into two parts—the revenue budget and the capital budget. The revenue account of the budget includes: (a) taxes on income and expenditure; (b) taxes on property and capital transactions and taxes on commodities and services. Non-tax revenue also accrues to the government from interest receipts and dividends, and currency coinage.

From the revenue account the government spends for general services, including police, judiciary, defence and collection of taxes, social and community services, education, medical and public health, labour and employment and, lastly, economic services like agriculture, industry and services.

Under the capital budget, the government accesses capital receipts and incurs capital expenditure. As pointed out above, under capital receipts are included net recoveries of loans and advances to state governments and union territories, and public sector enterprises, net market borrowings, net small savings' collection, provident fund and special deposits.

On the capital expenditure side, the central government gives loans to states and union territories for financing Plan projects and loans to foreign governments. But more importantly, capital expenditure also includes government expenditure on economic, social and community development as well as on defence and general services.

The entire Budget making exercise undertaken every year is aimed at making public the government's revenue earnings and expenditure as well as its capital receipts and capital expenditure. Balancing the Budget means that there would be a balance between the government's total revenue and expenditure. Like in the case of a household, the expenditure should not exceed the earnings greatly otherwise there is a problem. In the past when the government's overall expenditure exceeded its total revenue receipts, the deficit had to be financed by deficit financing or printing of notes. But now to finance the fiscal deficit the government generates a capital surplus.

Since the government has not been resorting to deficit financing anymore, it has had to cut some of its current revenue expenditure and capital expenditure and this has mostly been in the area of essential educational and health services. The capital surplus in the budget, which is generated through loans from the market, accessing small savings of citizens with the government and economising on essential services, has in recent years exactly equalled the revenue deficit so that the overall budgetary deficit is nil. It means that the fiscal deficit has been financed by raising market loans, accessing small savings and by cutting down mainly essential capital expenditure.

The government obviously needs to have a higher outlay on the Five Year Plans in every successive Annual Plan and it has not been able to cut Plan expenditure which has gone on increasing. More money has been going to agriculture, rural development, irrigation and flood control, energy, industry and minerals, transport and communications, science and technology and environment and social services in every annual Budget. The government also needs more money for Plan implementation through the states and has to increase the assistance it gives to states. The way out for the government to fund all these increasing amounts of Plan expenditure is to collect more taxes and to cut down non-plan expenditure. Unfortunately, the government is in a bind because the tax collection is not enough for all its requirements and interest payments are getting higher and higher.

Until the mid-1990s, the interest payments were kept artificially low due to RBI's intervention in the determination of interest rates. With alignment of interest rates to market determined rates since the economic reforms, interest outlay of the government has increased significantly because interest rates have risen. In addition, the government has been borrowing from the pool of small savings at high interest rates and this has proved to be an expensive source. In recent years, the government's increased borrowing from the market has further pushed up the interest rates. Both the volume of borrowings and the quantum of interest payments has increased. Higher interest rates have affected the borrowings of the private sector also.

The government's revenue deficit, which is the main item in the budget to be watched, is the government's total revenue expenditure minus total revenue receipts. This has been increasing every year. It shows that the government's revenue collection has not been rising proportionately to its spending from the taxes collected.

The way to collect more taxes is by simplifying the tax system and by improving the tax administration. Computerisation is helping but much more effort has to go into building up a proper information system about the tax base. Under the direct taxes are income tax, expenditure tax, and corporation tax. These are administered centrally. Property tax and tax on capital transaction also fall under direct taxes. The indirect taxes are taxes on commodities and services, i.e., sales tax, central and state excise duties, service tax and custom duties.

The service tax, which is one of the fastest growing sources of tax revenue and central excise, and customs duties are collected by the central government. The government has not been able to access a much higher proportion of revenue from direct taxes mainly because of lack of compliance.

The revenues of the central government have not been rising faster as a proportion of GDP (tax–GDP ratio) mainly because of the reduction in custom and excise duties on account of fiscal reforms introduced in recent years. The tax-GDP ratio has improved a bit for the state governments taken together, over the last decade. In 2005-2006, tax GDP ratio was 10.3 per cent. But the central government's revenue collection has been higher than that of the state governments, mainly because the important revenue sources like income tax, corporation tax, excise duties and customs duties are collected by the Centre. Commodity taxes now contribute about 62 per cent of the total revenue and taxes on income and property have shown a decline. The most important source of revenue for the central government is the central excise duty.

Various attempts have been made in the past to tax only the value addition and not the inputs that go into making the product. Thus, there have been attempts to reform the indirect tax system in which only the end products would be taxed and not the inputs.

MODVAT or modified tax system was introduced in the 1980s and it covered all the industries. It did not tax inputs. The excise duty structure was also simplified. Most states however get most of their revenue from sales tax. Tax collection however has remained rather poor because of the collusion between the retailers and consumers. (In Delhi, it is very easy to evade sales tax by not demanding a bill from the retailer). The sales tax machinery is reputed to be corrupt and inefficient.

Value Added Tax (VAT)

In 2005, most states switched to Value Added Tax or VAT. It would call for better accounting practices as all business transactions would need to be recorded at each stage of production. The tax would be on the final good only and not at the earlier stages. Traders who are dealing with buying and selling of final products have been objecting to VAT. But VAT is likely to bring about a uniform tax system that would help in making India into a unified common market.

With the introduction of VAT, the origin based Central Sales Tax would be phased out. When many states expressed the possibility of revenue losses in the initial years of the introduction of VAT, the central government agreed to compensate them 100 per cent for such revenue losses in the first year, 75 per cent in the second year and 50 per cent in the third year. States would be allowed to levy sales tax/ VAT on sugar, textiles and tobacco with a ceiling rate of 4 per cent. Since 2000, the government has been trying to introduce VAT but each time there has been strong opposition from some quarter or other. The 'White Paper' released by Finance Minister P. Chidambaram on VAT was the first serious roadmap towards achieving a uniform, state level tax in the future. The process started from April 1, 2005 and Dr. Asim Dasgupta, Finance Minister, West Bengal, in his capacity as chairman of the Empowered Committee of State Finance Ministers, has been responsible for looking into the pros and cons of VAT.

The VAT is a general tax that is collected on the sale of goods. And it applies in principle to all commercial activities involving production and distribution of goods as well as provision of services. It is a tax on consumption and is borne ultimately by the final consumer. It is not charged on companies.

Around 160 countries have introduced VAT successfully and shopping in these countries for tourists offers the added attraction of VAT refunds at airports and seaports. It is considered a major reform of the indirect tax system. These countries have enacted the tax reform and have clearly benefited from it and there is little reason why India should remain isolated from the global trend of making it easier for consumers to pay taxes on goods and services. The US is the lone example where VAT has not been introduced. In the EU, the introduction of VAT was instrumental in cementing the economic union.

The clear benefit from VAT is that it is simple. Instead of having a whole host of taxes—sales tax, octroi, excise duties, entry tax, luxury tax—there would be one tax that would take care of all the stages of value addition. The cascading impact of sales tax is also avoided whereby both the inputs and outputs are taxed.

The second clear advantage would be that the rampant tax evasion, which is a characteristic of third world countries including India, would be controlled because all manufacturers and traders would be required to have their papers in order. VAT collection would involve traders keeping their records and a computerised central system of records would have to be in place. This is needed as only then can the value addition be ascertained and the manufacturers given credit which they can later deduct from the gross taxes to be paid by them.

All business purchases will carry a VAT charge, and VAT paid as input tax can be adjusted against VAT on output. Purchases of raw materials and goods purchased for resale will carry VAT. But the original copy of the VAT invoice would be needed to claim any tax credit for inputs.

It has taken a number of years for VAT to be implemented in any country. It requires that other indirect taxes be eliminated and replaced by VAT. Some states could lose heavily and though the government has promised them compensation, many would find it difficult to eliminate taxes. The multiplicity of taxes raises the cost of compliance while not really benefiting revenue. These cause distortions in internal trade and become impediments in the way of a common market that would facilitate foreign investment inflows.

For India to be able to attract a much greater amount of FDI, simpler tax laws, rules and forms are required. At present, the competition between states in attracting FDI takes the form of tax concessions which only the rich states can afford. A uniform system of VAT would preclude this unfair competition.

Many traders have stated that the VAT regime will bring back the Inspector *raj* and this would mean more corruption. Basically, all the states have to be prepared for the introduction of VAT. Delhi has been vehemently against it because Delhi has a disproportionate number of traders who would have to keep their papers in order for the payment of VAT which would impinge on their margins. Delhi has also been a tax shelter and, given the predominance of the last point levy for most goods, the tax is virtually voluntary except when official and organised purchases are made. VAT would change the scene and the culture of non-payment of taxes. No wonder the traders were up in arms about the reform.

There could however be welfare loss (according to Joseph Stiglitz) if VAT creates distortions between the formal and informal sectors and prevents the emergence of an enlarged formal sector in the economy. In a country with a large informal sector, the entire chain of transactions may escape the tax net, resulting in revenue loss. With the imposition of VAT, there could be a shift of resources away from the formal to the informal economy for tax avoidance. There is also a possibility of significant misuse of the tax credit mechanism and this may negate the advantages of the self-policing nature of the tax.

However, the clear advantage would be that VAT will replace the first point sales tax which has a narrow base, and has multiple rates that are often driven by political considerations like interstate competition, a large range of tax incentives and scope for tax evasion which make the tax system virtually voluntary and highly distorted. The tax-GDP ratio, as a result, has remained low.

With the introduction of VAT, in most cases, the revenue productivity would increase and it would mean additional revenue for some states that would allow them to undertake expenditure on social and physical infrastructure. Most importantly, for the success of VAT, a central computerised system would be of vital importance for monitoring all interstate transactions. It would minimise harassment at inspectors' hands and also reduce physical inspection. Interstate transactions will help in creating a unified common market rather than the current fragmented one.

The rules, forms and procedures, however, have to be kept simple and unambiguous. The Centre has to take the initiative of financing and organising the information system for efficient interstate transactions. It has to help the states with technical assistance. These could be costly.

It has been proposed that the mean rate would be 12.5 per cent but would be lower in the case of life-saving drugs and items of mass consumption; higher rates would be applicable to tobacco and alcohol and petroleum products would be outside the VAT system. The current sales tax is at 8 per cent and though the VAT rate is higher, the benefits of a uniform rate would easily outweigh the difference.

What about services? Since they are basically dispensed at the retail level, should the states be given the power to tax services? In India, the service tax is under the Centre and it may take a while for it to come under the states' authority. The ultimate aim is to move to Goods and Services Tax (GST) in future and, according to the Finance Minister, it will emerge as the national VAT.

It will be paid only at the final point of consumption and would be appropriated by the state that happens to be the final destination of a product. All other indirect taxes would have to be eliminated. The beneficial impact of VAT has to be highlighted and the phasing out of all other taxes would have to be undertaken immediately. Otherwise, the success of VAT will be limited. Most importantly, VAT will lead to greater transparency and encourage disclosure of complete information on business turnovers and that would help in income tax collection.

Tax Compliance

In a tax system where the compliance is low for both the corporate sector and wealthy individuals, it is the middle class, mostly with salaried incomes, which has been bearing the brunt of coughing up higher and higher tax rates. Rich farmers are also escaping the tax net. Self-employed persons with high incomes are also not declaring their incomes fully. They are the ones who are flocking to malls, buying the second or third car and enjoying a high standard of living. The taxes that are not paid become 'black money' in the economy.

People with black money invest in gold and jewellery and real estate. There are houses being bought under false names and the prices of houses are getting hiked. Every house deal has a 'black' and white transaction and house agents unashamedly ask for black money to be paid in cash. If all the black income came under the tax net, imagine how much the government's collection would be enhanced.

The complexity of the tax system aids such evasion. Persons who want to avoid paying taxes are helped by accountants on a regular basis.

When asked why a person does not want to pay taxes, he or she retorts that they see no benefits accruing from the government in the form of public goods. Many people think that paying taxes is a waste and have no 'guilt' feelings if they do not pay taxes or falsely declare their incomes to be smaller than what they actually are. No one frowns at anyone who is evading taxes and the culture spreads rapidly.

The entire tax system has to be modernised for better tax collection and compliance. Direct taxes should be moderate and have less exemptions under which tax evaders take shelter. Indirect taxes like import duties should be uniform and should not (and cannot) be very high because of the WTO norms. The tax administration has to be simplified. Whenever there is a multiplicity of rates there are problems. A single rate of customs duty for all commodities perhaps would be ideal but it would not be possible to switch over to such simple forms easily.

On the expenditure side, since the government has not been able to control the revenue expenditure, it has to apply the brakes on certain areas of runaway expenditure like bureaucratic expansion, foreign travel for officials, lavish functions in embassies abroad and other types of nonproductive costs like refurbishing ministerial bungalows. It has not been successful in downsizing the size of the government bureaucracy. It has not been able to cut subsidies that do not reach the poor. In fact, subsidised items are being diverted to the open market, allowing black marketeers to thrive. The government has tried to control important capital expenditure through reduced spending on important projects for infrastructure development, irrigation and agricultural extension work. It has hit important economic services in education and health. Cutting important expenditure can be harmful and counterproductive but is being done to bring down the revenue deficit.

State Finances

Many of the 28 states have no money in their coffers and are, as a result, spending less and less on the delivery of important public goods. The revenue account of states has been continuously in deficit since 1987-88 but became more pronounced since the late 1990s due to the payment towards revised pay scales, pensions and salaries. The states reached this stage in the late 1990s mainly because they had to make higher payments to the employees due to the Fifth Pay Commission's recommendations. All government employees got a hike of 40 to 60 per cent in pay and pensions. The states have had to increasingly rely on the central government's finances.

Thus, revenue expenditure has been growing in the form of wages, salaries, pensions, interest payments, assistance to public enterprises, mainly state electricity boards which have been in the red for many years.

On the revenue collection side, it has not been possible to collect appropriate user charges for water and electricity. The states have also not been able to charge appropriate prices for the use of water for political reasons. Populism has taken precedence over prudence in state spending for garnering political support for the parties in power. On top of it, the central government's transfer of funds to the states, as a proportion of the GDP, has also been declining. Their tax revenues have been increasing very slowly at around 5.7 per cent in the last 10 years.

The state governments are responsible for most public expenditure and especially for the provision of social services. They are responsible for infrastructural services except telecom, civil aviation, railways and major ports. They are responsible for law and order. The states collect money from the sale of utility services like electricity, water and through the collection of sales taxes and excise duties. All these sources have not been yielding enough revenue in recent years. Electricity and water rates have been kept low to appease the electorate, especially the rich farmers. Secondly, sales taxes have not been extended to cover services and the base has not been expanded to cover a bigger range of goods and services. As a result, their ability to increase revenue has been limited. The revenue decline has been high in the case of land taxes and sales tax. It has become difficult for the states to impose taxes on agricultural incomes. The sales tax base has remained narrow and its collection is full of problems. Though the growth in services has been sharp and they account for 70 per cent of the growth of the economy, they are taxed by the Centre. There is a move to shift service tax to the concurrent list.

Non-tax sources of revenue have been drying up and there is also the problem of inefficiency in the delivery of public services. Besides, the interstate competition to reduce the sales taxes in order to attract investment has led to 'race to the bottom'. States have adopted self-defeating schemes of fiscal incentives in terms of sales tax holidays and deferment of taxes. To meet exigencies they have resorted to turnover taxes, additional sales taxes and entry taxes. All these have contributed to a complicated, cascading, opaque tax system.

The states' ability to invest in productive activities has remained low. Since non-tax revenue, like returns of state public enterprises, has actually fallen over the years, the states have had to tighten their development budgets. The lower revenue receipts have not been able to sustain the Plan expenditure.

Many states have borrowed from the market extensively and, as a result, the interest burden has become heavier compared to other items of expenditure. They often have to borrow just in order to make huge interest payments. As a result of their lack of funds they have been cutting out essential capital expenditure that would go towards more rapid developmental projects and poverty reduction.

The fiscal deficit of the states (total expenditure minus total revenues and capital receipts) has, as a result of lack of adequate revenue sources and continuing rise in expenditure, been increasing. This rise in total fiscal deficit—of the Centre and the States—is a cause for much concern, especially for the World Bank and the IMF. It means that the tax to GDP ratio has been declining but the expenditure to GDP ratio has been rising.

Central assistance for Plan implementation to the states has been decided by a formula devised by Prof. D.R. Gadgil. According to the Gadgil Formula of the Planning Commission (He was Deputy Chairman during the Fourth Five-year Plan: 1969-1974), the central government gives financial assistance to the states according to blocs to be developed, which comprise loans regardless of the end use of expenditures. The state governments have been borrowing from the government on the basis of this formula. The central government borrows on their behalf and disburses the loans. Most states have been borrowing to finance their revenue expenditure rather than capital expenditure which is why there is so much problem in sustaining development.

Many economists feel that making a fetish of the fiscal deficit is uncalled for. It is development that should be the main aim of the government and the taxation. If there is a shortfall, deficit financing should be resorted to in order to create jobs and generate incomes. If development is stepped up considerably, there will not be much inflationary pressure as supply of goods and services will also increase. The conservative economists, on the other hand, maintain that the main problem is excessive government borrowing from the market and its harmful effect on private investment that it 'crowds out'. They are strictly in favour of reducing government's market borrowing and increasing commodity taxation in order to raise more revenue. They also believe that states would benefit greatly if they imposed appropriate user charges for water and electricity in order to garner more non-tax revenue and improve their fiscal health.

Politics rules in the end in determining how the states spend money and the ruling parties in the states look only for votes while conducting developmental projects. They do not go for deep structural improvements but give palliatives that appease the electorate. Corruption and lack of efficiency spoil things further.

17

Role of the State and Centre-State Relations

Has the role of the State changed in recent years in a significant manner? Recently, the government has moved away from exercising a high degree of control over all economic activities to a lesser degree of State intervention. Many activities have increasingly been left to the private sector. But unlike Adam Smith's belief in the play of the 'invisible hand', the government still maintains some amount of control on different sectors and has not resorted to a completely noninterventionist role of benign advisor and spectator. The appropriate mix of public sector and private sector is yet to be attained.

The government at the Centre often shows confusion on how much of the economy is to be opened up and whether to stick to promoting self-reliance or give way to increasing market forces. It does not know whether it should still retain the mixed economy model where the key industries will continue to be in the hands of the government or to privatise many of its enterprises. These policy prescriptions have been influenced by political compulsions and the coalition politics that are an important part of India's democracy.

After Independence, as pointed out earlier, except for a few industries, most basic or economically important industries were in the hands of the government. In order to achieve the goals of higher employment growth, optimum distribution of resources, and promoting equity with social justice, the government has in the past favoured an interventionist, paternalistic role which was in line with the State's role in promoting growth in Japan and South Korea.

But since the economic reforms of 1991, the new industrial policy has tried to de-license certain industries and de-reserve some of the items reserved for the small-scale sector. Industries no longer need a license to create new capacity or expand existing capacity. Only nine industries are now reserved for the public sector. The State's role in the industrial sector has been greatly reduced.

There has been a dilution of the Monopolies Restrictive Trade Practices (MRTP) Act through an amendment bill and the threshold limit with regard to assets that a company can possess has been changed. FDI policy was also changed with more investment allowed through the automatic route and higher amount of foreign equity participation.

The policy framework saw a dramatic shift from 1990s because, if the crisis of the late 1980s was to be avoided, a decentralised route to development had to be followed. Economic reforms meant that fiscal deficits needed to be curbed and the bureaucracy had to be reduced. New fields for investment were opened to the private sector and imports were liberalised so that the private sector had access to cheaper and often better quality capital goods, intermediates and raw materials for enhancing its competitiveness.

International capital was allowed more freely to bring in improved technology. Modern management practices and links with international markets through MNCs were favoured. Tax policies were liberalised and simplified. Since more revenue was not likely to be collected through a reduction in taxes and custom duties, government expenditure on non-essential items had to be curtailed.

The policy of having state ownership of all major economic activities goes back to the Nationalist Movement in which it was decided that the way out of poverty was through State-led industrialisation. To have rapid industrial growth, basic or capital goods industries would have to be started by the State. The nascent industries had to be protected. The whole regime of controls and licenses that formed the core of India's industrial policy was followed for 40 years.

In the 1950s, the example of Soviet Union and its achievements in the fields of science and technology and attainment of power through a heavy industrial base was a role model for many developing countries that had recently gained independence. For 40 years, the same model was followed. India did not do so badly as some of the African countries, but did not do as well as the Southeast Asian countries in transforming a colonial industrial structure into a modern one to create a country that would be ready to compete in the international market and also raise per capita incomes and standards of living.

Today, many of the controls have lingered and reforms have perhaps been too slow according to most western observers. Many bureaucrats have resented losing their clout and authority and have tried to bring back rules and regulations through the back door. These would ultimately put off foreign investors. There are still many clearances required from the central and state governments before a foreign investor can get the manufacturing plant started.

The initial years of the opening up did see a rise in industrial growth and the rise of private banking, both domestic and foreign. It saw a stock market boom but it also saw many scams in the financial sector. Liberalisation was not equipped, in the initial stages, with an effective regulatory framework and clever operators jumped in to make quick money through unscrupulous means and insider trading.

As pointed out above, a number of MNCs came with foreign investment and started joint ventures. Salaries of hired local personnel reached heights never seen before. The ceiling on corporate salaries was also lifted after the reforms began and, suddenly, salaries in some companies were hiked substantially to attract the best talent. Bureaucrats, who themselves never got high salaries, sent their children to work in multinationals. There was much euphoria about the opening up of India and unleashing of the giant within. Comparisons with China became commonplace. The new rich with their fat salaries started living it up by consuming more goods and services of high value.

In foreign journals like *The Economist* India was compared to an elephant whose walk would be slow but heavy so that the forest would shake. But this rosy projection about India's future did not last long because there were many inherent inconsistencies in the system. As a result of huge amounts of temporary financial capital flows which remained unabsorbed in the system, inflation rose rapidly. To control inflation the government raised interest rates. From then (1994) onwards, the country saw high interest rates that clamped down industrial borrowing. Industrial growth was also not sustained at a high level of six per cent because demand for industrial goods became sluggish on account of the poor agricultural performance in 1995. The government has been active in the new millennium in promoting industrial recovery through its policy announcements. Industrial growth has picked up since 2005.

Among the policies that are of importance are the credit policy, the export-import policy that are announced annually and fiscal policies which are announced in the Annual Budget. The government has been active in preventing inflation from rising rapidly but has often failed to do so. Though it has remained in the production of goods in public sector enterprises, it has gradually privatised many of the enterprises that became a burden on the exchequer. It has sold equity shares of some profitable enterprises in order to garner resources in financing its fiscal deficit.

In many ways the government has been very active, in some sectors, even interventionist, but in the social sector, where its role is important, it has remained rather inactive.

That is exactly what Amartya Sen and Jean Dreze have said about the role of the State in India. According to them, the Indian government has interfered too much in some fields of economic activity but has been insufficiently active in important areas like basic education, healthcare, social security, land reforms and promotion of social change.

The ineffectiveness of the government's actions is reflected by the fact that India has 260 million people who are still below the poverty line and are not taking part in the market mechanism or the production process in a significant way. Their potential in contributing to the economy is not being utilised and their lives remain unfulfilled. They are exploited as in the form of child labour and female labour and are not given the market wage. They need help from the government in finding jobs. The main role of the government remains in the area of job creation, education, training and health in the villages because the 'trickle down' has not taken place or is rather slow. There is hardly any way in which the entry of FDI in some chosen sectors is helping to create jobs among those without skills, education and land in the villages.

The government still has a very important role to play in improving rural infrastructure, housing, and in promoting development programmes. Better roads, railways, availability of power and drinking water in rural areas will reduce poverty. The government has to be active in employment generation programmes and through training schools impart skills to the people. It has to promote labour intensive techniques, research and development for the small-scale and informal sectors. It has to make village products marketable by introducing better designs and marketing channels.

It has to remain an important producer of public goods and regulator of the economic system. It has to maintain law and order and dispense justice efficiently and rapidly. It has to reform the public enterprises rapidly so that they can become efficient, autonomous and create wealth and assets instead of being a drain on public resources.

In agriculture, it has to play an important role in guaranteeing secure tenancy rights and better credit facilities to small farmers. It cannot abdicate its role as a promoter of agricultural development which is the key to improving the standard of living of millions of poor in rural areas.

The government also has to maintain urban infrastructure so that private domestic and foreign investment can be attracted. It has to listen to the voice of the people and see to it that their grievances are redressed. It has to pay special attention to women and their role in development.

The private sector cannot be entrusted with encouraging human development in the poorest regions because the returns of such investment are low. Private investment is coming in to education but the fees are high and the schools are exclusive. Similarly, in healthcare, there has been a rapid growth in private hospitals and nursing homes in all major cities and towns but treatment is expensive and, often, not up to the mark. It is the public hospitals that have to be drastically improved so that those seeking medical treatment can get it without having to bribe, wait in queues or get shoddy and appallingly callous behaviour from the hospital staff.

An efficiently managed government which is not ridden with corruption, and the direct involvement of politicians, would transform the economy much more quickly than a society in which the private sector 'pulls up' only the top and creamy layers of society and enables them to enjoy a conspicuously high standard of life. A government that cares, takes important decisions quickly and firmly and is consistent in its policies, can do lasting good to the country where nearly one-third of the country lives in stark poverty.

Centre-State Relations

Under the Constitution of India, while the resources are centralised, the responsibilities for undertaking development activities are decentralised. Thus, most of the social and economic activities fall under the purview of the state governments.

In recent years, the states have not been in the best of financial health. The combination of rising revenue and fiscal deficits, high committed or fixed expenditures like interest payments, salaries and pensions have left state finances in a mess. There are many states that are deeply in debt and they rely on the central government to bail them out whenever there is a financial crisis. Borrowing from the Centre as opposed to taking advances and overdrafts from the Reserve Bank of India, has proved to be expensive as the interest rates are higher.

The states obviously have not been doing their own budgeting carefully because expenditure overflows are frequent. The revision of salaries and pensions of state government employees following the recommendations of the Fifth Central Pay Commission, has added to their woes. They have not been getting adequate returns from their public sector units. All this has raised their current or revenue expenditure and badly affected the delivery of social services for which they are responsible.

Most of the public goods come under the states' realm for delivery and some of the recent surveys point out that no serious effort has been made to improve either the quality or the reliability of the services provided by the states. Some of the states are in real bad shape, particularly their infrastructure.

About 6.5 per cent of the GDP is spent on services yet in all areas like availability of safe water, sanitation, health services and education, the states are underperforming. The quality of health services is so bad in the villages that the rural population has to take recourse to travelling great distances to come to good and reliable hospitals. It also means borrowing money to meet health expenditure.

The states' role in designing and implementing policies for promoting development has always been important. The share of states in the Indian government's total capital expenditure was at 57 per cent in 2000-01. They are almost wholly responsible for the maintenance of irrigation works, and public health services. They are also responsible for the states' education system and 40 per cent of the expenditure on road maintenance. In general, Indian states are responsible for a higher proportion of government spending than in any other developing country except China.

There has not been much success in recent years. There is rampant tax evasion and due to various exemptions the tax collection remains poor. Besides, the erosion of the central tax collection machinery has also led to a smaller pool of resources for devolution by the Centre to the States.

In the 1990s, deficits gradually rose in all the states and they started facing a liquidity crunch. While their own tax revenues have been declining, the revenue expenditure has been going up. In the decline of their development expenditure, the worst affected are health, education and infrastructure development. Their capital assets are also not being properly maintained due to lack of funds and roads, buildings, water works, irrigation systems and rivers are not being properly looked after. The state guarantees for borrowing public sector units, especially in power production, have also been invoked many times and the states have had to pay up in cases of default.

The total transfers from the Centre to the states comprise tax devolution and grant. The formula for such devolution of taxes and grants is worked out by the Finance Commissions. The latest report has come from the 12th Finance Commission. Every year, the total transfer has been increasing and in 2001-02, there was an increase of 17.6 per cent over the previous year.

Some of the ways in which the states can improve their finances are: rationalising taxes like land revenue, vehicle tax, entertainment tax, sales tax, electricity duty, stamp duties, professional tax and luxury tax as well as registration fees. Tax administration reforms are important and hopefully the switch-over to VAT would help in getting more revenue. In the initial years when there would be losses due to the switch-over, the Centre would to compensate them, first fully and then partially.

All economists, except those with Leftist ideology, believe that the only way out is to impose 'user charges' on water and electricity. They also believe that except for the provision of primary education, health and maintenance of law and order, all other services provided by the government should have proper user fees to cover at least the cost of services. But all agree that the State Electricity Boards have to be restructured to make them financially viable. It is however true that unless the state finances are in order, the development programme of the central government cannot be undertaken in full steam. All states have pledged to reform their finances and many are in the process of undertaking steps to contain the burgeoning expenditure.

Regional Disparity

India is not uniformly rich or poor. There are states that are prosperous and those that are poor and it does not seem that anything much has changed in a long time. The 'Hindi' or 'Cow Belt' is supposed to be the one that has backward states characterised by high population growth, poor literacy rates and lack of governance in general. The Centre keeps pouring money into these states to help them meet their expenses through various subsidies and relief programmes but the delivery system in these states is also poor and money meant for the poor does not reach them fully.

Disparities in socioeconomic development across Indian states have been accentuated since the accelerated economic growth of the 1980s and increased participation of the private sector. With the beginning of the 1991 economic reforms that were accompanied by deregulation, there has been a further accentuation of interstate disparities.

Some states have been able to undertake reforms quicker than others. They have been able to attract FDIs. Some states have improved their infrastructure and that has played an important part in their growth. Some states have a high level of literacy and women's education has been given a high place. Others have a high level of illiteracy and the health indicators are also poor.

Thus, some forward or progressive states have better demographic and social development profiles and higher per capita income. They also have a higher level of revenue receipts and their plan and non-plan expenditures are also higher. They also have a bigger amount of private investment and better infrastructural facilities. By contrast, the 'backward' states have higher level of poverty, lower per capita incomes, lower revenue receipts and lower government expenditure on plan and non-plan projects. They have underdeveloped infrastructure and lower amounts of private investment.

Ever since Independence, the government has been concerned about reducing regional disparity. This has not been achieved. The poorer states have got very poor human development indicators. Female literacy is a good indicator of slow progress in the weaker states. Backward states have to improve female literacy and health indicators. Rajasthan has the least number of literate women and female literacy is at 20 per cent. Contrast it with Kerala which has 86 per cent female literacy. Similarly, there are other indicators like the per capita income but it has not much to do with the human development indicators. Even though Kerala is ahead of all states in having low infant mortality rates, and highest life expectancy, its per capita income is lower than many other states that are doing well economically. Prosperous states generally have a high share of manufacturing in the state's domestic product. Gujarat has the highest level of manufacturing activity and, in West Bengal, the share of manufacturing activity has been declining reflecting some amount of deindustrialisation. But some states with high agricultural share in their net domestic product are richer than others, like Punjab and Haryana. All the developed states have a higher share of urban population. Maharashtra is the most urbanised and the least urbanised is Haryana even though it is not a backward state.

Two of the richest states, Punjab and Haryana, have sex ratios that are below the national average. The highest sex ratio is in Kerala and it is favourable to women, which is in keeping with the pattern of industrialised countries of the world. As a country progresses in industrialisation, the sex ratio improves.

Regular power supply, a developed transport system, and modern telecom facilities help to attract private investment into the states. Better irrigation facilities will help to raise agricultural productivity and raise rural incomes. The basic problem with the poorer states is the low user charges and the bankruptcy of their State Electricity Boards, State Transport Corporations and State Irrigation Departments.

In the past, the Central government's investment went to key sectors and it had a positive impact on the transformation of backward states. But, in recent times, due to severe budgetary problems that the Centre has been facing, such central investments have also been curtailed.

How to achieve regional balance has been a perpetual problem for the central government and the pattern for devolution of central funds has been examined and scrutinised several times by the Finance Commissions. The sharing of personal income tax and excise duties collected by the Centre and the States is periodically reviewed by the Finance Commission which is appointed every five years. The Commission also decides the principles and the formula by which the allocable funds are disbursed among the states.

The Finance Commissions have positively discriminated in favour of fiscally weak, backward states. Population and per capita income get high weightage. A state with a large population, and lower per capita income gets a higher share of the central tax revenues. The gap between revenue receipts (other than central tax revenues) and revenue expenditure is another parameter which decides the level of a state's share. As a result, the central tax share constitutes a major revenue source for some backward states.

The states also get assistance from the Centre for the state plans. The state plans are financed partly by their own resources and the balance comes from the Centre of which 30 per cent is in the form of grants and the remaining 70 per cent is a long-term loan.

The distribution of plan assistance to the states is governed by the Gadgil Formula since the Fourth Five-year Plan (1969-1974). The Gadgil Formula (though it has been revised twice) also favours backward states and population and per capita income account for 85 per cent of the weight in the formula. Thus, the state plans of the most backward states are fully financed by central assistance.

Since the 1990s, the states are also making use of aid flows to bridge their resource gap. Most states have been borrowing from the government to meet their growing nondevelopment expenditure. The major reason for the increase in nondevelopment expenditure of all states taken together since 1980-81 has been rising interest liabilities. Both the quantum and the cost of borrowing of the state governments have gone up. Since the reforms began, the ratio of development expenditure to nondevelopment expenditure has come down steeply as compared to 1980-81, which means that the development programmes have often been put on the back burner.

In recent times, new states have been created like Chattisgarh, Uttaranchal and Jharkhand. This movement has been triggered by intra-regional disparities. Maharastra and Andhra Pradesh have extreme regional disparity due to topographical reasons. Other states have very poor regions inhabited by tribal populations. The creation of new states, however, is not a solution to regional disparities.

Problem of Governance

The better-off states are also better governed. Through better governance, better infrastructure, the forward or advanced states are able to attract private investment, both domestic and foreign. It has been found that foreign and domestic private investors are attracted not so much by tax concessions and other incentives as by proper governance. In poorer states, because corruption and inefficiency coexist, things move very slowly, making returns to investment slow.

India would have been able to perform much better on the development and growth front if only there was good governance even for some years. Unfortunately, right from the beginning, problems of governance arose all over India. Perhaps this was due to the unwieldly size of the government and the size of the public sector, so that government at the Centre and in the states became synonymous with delays and corruption.

More than after half a century of Independence there still is widespread corruption and this has only increased over the years despite all efforts to liberalise and privatise. Political violence has also gone up and the judiciary has become clogged. As stated earlier, there are around 26 million cases pending in the courts. It takes years to get cases cleared because of procedural and administrative delays.

From all accounts, India is an example of a malfunctioning state. It could be seen as a systemic problem, but many countries were in the same situation as India is in today. Countries like Malaysia and Singapore have solved these governance issues rather well as compared to India. But India has had democracy for more than 50 years and this makes it more difficult to continue a strong-armed policy of governance.

There is a definite correlation between governance and economic growth and studies have proved that there is a rise in economic growth by around 70 per cent if the quality of governance improves. With the same rates of savings and investment, good governance contributes to a significantly higher rate of growth. Thus, attempts have to be made for correcting the flaws in the political system which are governance related.

First, it is a fact that there is insufficient representation of the public in our democratically elected governments. The governments are also politically unstable and there is a lack of accountability to the legislature. One of the reasons for corruption is the high cost of elections that runs into several crores of rupees. There is also a general non-professionalism pervading ministries and legislatures, and a lack of transparency.

Another reason for the lack of governance is the short tenure in postings of government servants. They are also overloaded with tasks, there is excessive procedural orientation and political interference. The monolithic nature of the Indian State contributes to the difficulties in good governance. The Indian State is highly fragmented and there are different layers like: federal, state and local governments. The central government has 60 odd ministries, 70 special offices like the Archaeological Survey of India and 200 subordinate offices like the National Archives. Then there are departmental undertakings like the railways as well as various schemes, projects and programmes like the Integrated Rural Development Programme and Nehru Rozgar Yojana under the central government.

All these bodies are administered in a similar way despite vast differences in tasks, missions and contexts. Few have professional heads who are selected on the basis of open competition. There is political interference at various levels and each government department is headed by some official belonging to the elite services. About 20 million government servants have 40,000 bosses from the elite services. Most paid salaries are not on par with the private sector. In Singapore, government servants are paid adequate amounts so that they are not easily tempted to resort to graft.

Most government servants tend not to take any decisions because they are scared of Comptroller and Auditor General (CAG) audit and to most retaining their job is the important thing. As a result, they lack all initiative to expedite matters or to be decisive. Conformity of rules becomes important rather than meeting the objectives of public policy. Exceptions can be made but only with the help of bribes. In the past, controls led to the use of speed money imperative for expediting government services.

There can be a workable solution. The legislators can be empowered through training and there can be government funding of political parties in exchange for more transparent management. IAS and other elite services can have fixed tenure postings and there should be lateral entry of professionals for revitalising the elite services. The users of government services should be empowered to take stock of the quality of services provided. Civil society can play an important role in monitoring the quality of services.

Fortunately, there are solutions to the problems of governance, but these can only be attained with higher education levels in the country, because then people would demand transparency. A rise in political consciousness can be seen in the 21st century and people are voting corrupt and inefficient governments out of power. All over India, educated civil society is demanding its right to information. Coalition politics is helping the process and with the increase in the participation of ordinary people in the political process, there would be more checks and balances.

Black Money

Corruption and tax evasion are endemic to the Indian economy and have come to be accepted as a part of life. The cult of accepting bribes and using public office for private gain is woven into the fabric of Indian society, perhaps for centuries. Call it greed, deep attachment for family or clan or plain lack of ethics, bribe taking goes up from the bottom to the top layers of society. Similarly, tax evasion does not lower the status of an individual and there is much tolerance about those who do not pay taxes and use the money for various other purposes including charity. There is no public display of anger against people discovered with assets that they have accumulated disproportionate to their incomes while in office. No wonder India ranks rather low (73rd) in the Corruption Perception Index published by the Transparency International, Berlin. Undoubtedly, India is one of the most corrupt countries in the world.

Various finance ministers have tried to unearth the money from the parallel or black economy through voluntary disclosure schemes but these did not prove to be very successful. Besides, the tax rates of some of these schemes were lower than those that honest tax payers had paid. It was as though the government gave a premium for dishonesty!

The individual's sense of values, the values upheld by society and the system itself are all responsible for the huge black economy in India. The organisation of Indian society based on caste and kinship and the differences in the state of development between different states provide a strong rationale for corruption. Caste and nepotism become the basis for the distribution of patronage. Attachment to families and clans brings about a feeling of not being responsible for other fellow citizens and a feeling of being alienated from others. And this feeling of belonging to a small group makes people insensitive to a sense of responsibility towards any but their own clan. People are interested in benefiting only their children and family and a deep sense of insecurity—perhaps because of the lack of a social safety net—often makes them corrupt so that their children and grandchildren can be well looked after.

No one also questions how wealth of certain conspicuously rich persons has come about or has been accumulated. Like the robber barons of England, corrupt officials, businessmen, stockbrokers and politicians find ready entrance into high society. Under globalisation anyone who can give a party in five-star hotels and flaunt fancy cars, a high lifestyle and smart clothes, is acceptable to society and appears on Page 3 of national dailies. The stockbroker Ketan Parekh, who was later booked for huge fraud, was a 'regular' in the party circuit in Delhi and Mumbai.

Provision for a daughter's marriage is another reason for corruption, especially because appropriate dowries are required from increasingly greedy grooms and their families. Another craze is getting their children educated abroad and is a reason behind corruption because of the premium attached to a foreign degree in most job selections. Corruption exists not only in government offices but also in educational institutions, judiciary, and hospitals.

Bribing in prestigious and well-known educational institutions, right from kindergarten to college, is common. Colleges often charge donation fees and most of it is collected in the 'black'. Medical colleges have huge black market fees. Good schooling and college education guarantees good jobs in the future and parents feel obliged to 'invest' by giving bribes.

All the black money in the Indian economy which some put at Rs. 70,000 crore or even Rs. 100,000 crore could be put to much better use than being spent in high level consumerism or being taken out to foreign countries.

Corruption in the public services is well acknowledged and, as Rajiv Gandhi observed, out of every rupee, only 15 paise go to the beneficiary. Around 31 per cent of the foodgrain and 36 per cent of sugar meant for public distribution go to the black market. Hawkers pay crores of rupees as bribes annually to corrupt policemen across the country in order to retain their little selling spaces.

Corruption is widespread in the customs department. According to a survey by the Exim Bank, 64 per cent of the exporters they interviewed faced major problems with customs clearance processes and with port authorities. Exporters spend 1 to 4 per cent of export revenue to grease the corrupt machinery. The impact of corruption is thus systemic. It is deeply ingrained and perhaps keeps the machinery of the economy well oiled and functioning.

But it leads to favouring inefficient producers, distorts the allocation of scarce public resources and leads to big leakages from the revenue collection of the government and the transferring of these resources into private hands. Large-scale tax evasion by prominent business persons is often held as a role model for those aspiring to save money by not paying taxes. Corruption in the economy leads to inflated government expenditure and public money is siphoned off by corrupt officials from infrastructure projects meant for the poor, for their own gains. Many village and municipal schools are without teachers, hospitals without doctors and medicines.

Corruption has often been attributed to an overregulated government system. Economic liberalisation has reduced some of the controls and licenses and, thus, there are fewer avenues for corruption. But it has not led to greater tax compliance or a significant reduction in corruption in the provision of vital services. Corrupt politicians are still being elected. They are still collecting money for the 'party' and much of it finds its way into their own pockets. Black money is thriving in real estate and the film world financing big projects.

The simplification of rules and procedures is, no doubt, very important for reducing corruption and for garnering more tax revenue. But certain supplementary steps have to be taken to reduce corruption. The Right to Information Act is the first important law that will help reduce corruption because it will ensure transparency of public action, its expenditures and policies. The public and civil society have to be empowered suitably to make the government more accountable.

Another important step would be to mete out drastic punishment to those found guilty. The legal system should be overhauled so that the corrupt cannot take shelter behind lengthy court trials and deferred prosecution. Prosecution is pending for around 4,000 cases in the courts. The corrupt officials, armed with money, can also engage the best lawyers and escape the clutches of law. This should be prevented, if at all possible.

18

The Social Sectors

Health

Health and education come under the social sector and they have a big impact on the productivity and output of a country. A prolonged neglect of these would lead to a low quality of life and a lower ranking in the United Nation's human development index. One thing that strikes anyone visiting India is the large number of malnourished people all around. They are present in both urban and rural areas. Official statistics give a dismal picture of the widespread prevalence of malnutrition because half of the children under five years of age are malnourished. Women's health statistics corroborate the same neglect of the girl child and adult pregnant women and this is reflected in the relatively high maternal mortality numbers. Most women suffer from anaemia also due to lack of proper nourishment and neglect during pregnancy. The large number of problems that relate to women's health show the relatively low status of women in Indian society where they have to work hard and eat last and least. They are also not shown to qualified doctors in time.

In villages, since health is a state subject, the state governments keep cutting their budgetary allocations for health because of limited resources. As a result, the state government's primary health centres are extremely ill-equipped with both medicines and qualified personnel and there are hardly any facilities for looking after and curing the initial stages of any of the major illnesses and ailments, locally. That is why people from villages crowd around the corridors of public hospitals in big cities, leading to overcrowding and lack of proper care by the hospital staff who are overstressed and hassled.

Most people unable to avail of public health facilities resort to private healthcare at exorbitant costs and often have to incur heavy debts for treatment of diseases. It is also one of the reasons for making ordinary people sink below the poverty line.

On the infant mortality front, some progress has been made at reducing the number of children dying at birth and the number of children dying immediately after birth. This rate has been reduced over the last 50 years due to a slight improvement in prenatal and post-natal healthcare of babies. In 1970, the infant mortality rate per 1,000 live births was 127—it was brought down to 67 in 2001. If the infant mortality rate could be reduced to 12, life expectancy at birth could be increased from 62 years to 66 years.

The high infant mortality rate reflects the poor state of public health, inadequate medical attention during pregnancy and during birth and poor post-natal care. To reduce infant and child mortality we need nearly 100 per cent immunisation, supply of clean drinking water and provision of sanitation facilities to prevent infections, and professional attention during childbirth.

Around 58 per cent of children of between 12 to 23 months went without immunisation in 1999. As compared to the fact that more than half of the child population in India in 2004 was not immunised, 90 per cent was immunised in China and 99 per cent in Iran.

Maternal mortality has still been high at 540 per 100,000 live births as compared to 50 per 100,000 in China. Around 60 per cent of women are anaemic and 216 million women are undernourished at the beginning of the 21st century. The coverage of ICDS or the Integrated Child Development Services Programme is required. According to Indira Gandhi Institute for Development Research, India loses about Rs. 36,600 crore a year due to water related diseases. The quality of water in most of our rivers is unsatisfactory and large stretches are not fit for even bathing let alone drinking. The lack of resources for improving the quality of water supply is the result of not charging an appropriate price for water. But surveys have shown the willingness of people to pay for clean water.

Access to clean drinking water is a key to good health. Around 62 per cent of the households in rural India collect drinking water from outside their household premises; 1,410 hours per household in a year is spent at the task. Only a small percentage of people did not have access to safe drinking water. In rural areas only 7.5 per cent of the population did not have access and in urban areas, 9.8 per cent of the population did not have access to safe drinking water.

Due to neglect of the health sector and cost cutting in state governments' expenditures under whose domain health expenditure falls, the number of hospital beds per thousand of the population is much smaller than in countries of the ASEAN. In any case, 57 per cent of hospitals and 32 per cent of the total number of hospital beds are now in the private sector. Only 4.8 per cent of the total public expenditure is spent on health and the proportion of GDP going to the health sector is as small as 1.3 per cent. There is an urgent need to increase the expenditure on healthcare—both curative and preventive because the demand is increasing rapidly. This is because in recent years there has been a big increase in noncommunicable diseases like diabetes, hypertension, cancer, cardiovascular diseases as well as AIDS. The control of AIDS has become important considering that it has spread to many of the southern and north-eastern states. Already, there are 5 million people infected by HIV/AIDS. About 25 million are expected to have the virus by the end of the decade. There has to be a more focused effort on preventive measures as in Thailand. It is still not a widely discussed issue and has been, unfortunately, kept under wraps. The campaign for preventive measures has to be more vigorous and focused.

Higher user fees has been suggested for public hospitals but as seen in many other developing countries, high fees means that many people are not able to avail of hospital services for treatment. Public health services have to be upgraded and expanded to cater to a much larger section of the population. In the absence of adequate public health facilities, private healthcare is burgeoning; to keep the quality of services from deteriorating, some evaluation of quality and costs is required. Already 80 per cent of allopathic doctors are working for private hospitals. The government has facilitated their functioning efficiently by a reduction of duty on medical equipment.

Many patients from neighbouring countries are coming to India for private healthcare treatment because even after meeting the transportation costs, hospitalisation costs and cost of surgery are cheaper. But for India to become a health hub of the region, on account of the cheap charges, it may need many additional services.

For example, for postoperative care to be infection-free, there has to be proper garbage disposal, hygienic hospital food preparation and contamination-free water supply. The hospital staff would also have to live within the premises where there are fewer chances of their catching infection from unhygienic dwellings and family illnesses. Basic healthcare has to be provided in the villages and there is no substitute for investing more on the health delivery system.

Education

Another area of neglect for centuries has been education. While crafts and textiles flourished and prospered during Moghul times, education was neglected and especially the education of women. Literacy is still not as high as in China and even after 50 years of Independence, there has been only a little progress. Forty per cent of the population remains illiterate. In absolute terms, India may have the largest number of illiterates in the world because one-third of the world's illiterate population resides in India. The main reason for lack of literacy is the unavailability of good primary education. Since the primary schools are so ill-equipped and inadequate, there is a high dropout rate. Only 71 per cent boys and 56 per cent girls in rural areas attended school, according to the National Sample Survey 1993-94. In urban areas, 85 per cent boys and 80 per cent girls attend school. This means that even in urban areas 20 per cent of girls were not in school and the proportion was twice as high in rural areas. Enrolment may be high but the dropout rate is also high as a result of which completion rate of school education is not high. For the population above the age of 25, for example, the average years of schooling was 2.4 in India as compared to 5 years in China, 7.2 years in Sri Lanka and 9.3 years in South Korea.

A high dropout rate is usually due to poor teaching facilities. About 20 per cent of primary schools were single teacher schools in 1993 and 0.8 per cent had no teachers at all. But in Kerala, 99 per cent of schools had three or more teachers. In 1994, India had a pupil-teacher ratio of 63.5 for primary schools compared to 13 in Cuba, 19.8 in Thailand, 20 in Malaysia, 22 in China, 39 in Nepal and 50 in Pakistan. Overcrowded classrooms mean lack of attention and poor learning by the students. Many children stop going to school out of boredom.

The high dropout rate is also due to the fact that parents do not see the value of sending their children to schools because they seem to be learning little that they perceive as useful for their jobs or work later in life. Many parents send their children to work instead, either in their own farms or workshops or outside their homes. There are 10 million child labourers in India. But according to some, there are around 100 million children working in different occupations. The main reason is the poor state of primary education and the high dropout rate.

To eradicate child labour the best solution is to have compulsory education. But to implement the concept of universal and compulsory education, a huge amount of money would be required. Sarva Shiksha Abhiyan was launched in September 2001. To have properly functioning schools, around Rs. 136,822 crore would be needed over a period of 10 years.

With universal education girls would most probably be kept in school rather than withdrawn to help at home. The impact of education on girls will yield long-term benefits like lower fertility and morbidity. It has been observed in Kerala that there is a direct and positive relationship between the education of girls and the fertility rate decline in the state. Educated girls also take better preventive care of their children's health. They can understand and read instructions better for a more hygienic home environment which does a lot to prevent infectious diseases.

In any case, the education system has to be greatly improved with proper classrooms, buildings, teachers, curricula and books. Otherwise, out of the 239 million children who are in schools, many thousands would be inclined to drop out and add to the 7.5 crore. (The official figure according to Economic Survey 2006-2007 is 70 lakhs.) children who are out of school. Obviously, the crying need is to improve the quality of primary education rather than increasing the number of new schools.

The quality of teaching has to be improved, otherwise children will spend less time in school and seek tuition outside in order to pass exams. The proportion of expenditure as a percentage of GDP going towards education has to be raised from 3.6 per cent to 6 per cent in order to make schooling worthwhile for children.

Unless there is real teaching going on in schools which is evidently beneficial to both students and the parents and the curricula are suited to the job requirements in the market, parents will continue to withdraw their children from schools. Basically, all parents would like to see their children educated but they want proper teaching. They are prepared to pay more money towards the education of their children if proper education is ensured. The tuition fees can sometimes be raised if better education is guaranteed.

The mid-day meal system has helped to control the dropout rates because, often, the meal in school is the only proper meal that the children have in the day. It is important, especially for girls because at home they may not get the best foods. There are many states in which the mid-day meals have been successful and these can be copied in other states also. The pupil-teacher ratio has to be brought down drastically. No school should be a single-teacher school. School buildings, toilet facilities, water, should be improved as well as teaching aids and books. Education has been made a fundamental right and eight years of education should be compulsory.

Private sector initiatives can be encouraged in education. All entry-exit restrictions on schools and colleges from the private sector should be abolished because it would only increase competition. However, autonomous public schools have to be made accountable for their performance.

Subsidising higher education can only be at the expense of primary education. It is much better to improve basic education than subsidise college education heavily. Many parents are willing to pay high amounts for their children at the school level and they should be made to pay higher college tuition fees also.

19

Globalisation and Economics of Environment

Globalisation basically means opening the economy to international trade, capital (investment) and migration flows. The opening up of the Indian economy was carried out due to the new economic policies of the government following the crisis of 1991, and India began to globalise rapidly. Also as a member of the WTO, India has undertaken to open up trade and increase imports by reducing tariff barriers.

Globalisation was in a sense inevitable for India; it has its benefits and negative points. Since the opening up of the economy, more MNCs have come to India and they have set the pace for new standards for corporate salaries (with many perks), and a high lifestyle that was not evident. Foreign capital has been attracted to India for its cheap production costs and skilled labour force. India has, however, received very little foreign investment as compared to China because of certain other advantages that China has. As pointed earlier, the latter has a skilled, educated and disciplined labour force and a superior infrastructure and more attractive business incentives as compared to India. In any case, the race for attracting foreign capital is a tough one and the initial resource endowment of the country is all important. But India is receiving more BPO jobs because of the English language skills that many Indian youth have.

Globalisation has also seen greater inflows of Foreign Institutional Investments—capital which moves from country to country in order to get the highest returns. India too has benefited from such inflows. Their entry boosts up the stock market and the value of stocks goes up. But in return, the receiving countries also become vulnerable to sudden withdrawals that can result in the collapse of the country's financial system. This happened in Mexico and in Southeast Asia. India too has been witnessing upheavals in the stock market periodically due to sudden and bulk withdrawal of FIIs. A bigger stock market has, however, benefited business and has increased the incomes of many.

The software industry has benefited most from globalisation with a large number of software engineers traversing between US, India and other industrialised countries. They not only bring back foreign exchange but also work ethics and experience from abroad. The families of software engineers have become rich (almost overnight) and have invested in property, cars and other consumer durables. Their attitude towards their children and women has also undergone change.

Western clothes are allowed even by traditional families though the eating habits and marriage patterns have not changed much. Traditional values seem to be unchanged whereas eating, drinking, dressing and entertainment patterns seem to be undergoing transformation. There is also a great urge to display the new wealth of the IT industry and other successful industries in lavish parties and marriages.

In many ways, globalisation is evident in all big Indian cities especially in the new pattern of consumption. It has brought into the Indian markets a huge number of consumer goods which are often branded—imported items much advertised in the western media and cinema and sported by world famous people. In most cities, young men and women are wearing western clothes and talking on mobile phones, much like in more industrially advanced countries.

Globalisation is also evident in the number of cars on the road and the familiar traffic jams of the big cities of the world.

People are buying new lifestyle gadgets and consumer durables and in the internet cafes, and in their homes, the young and old are surfing the Internet happily. Even in villages, globalisation has arrived and is evident in the numerous phone booths, beer shops and in the sale of new types of consumer goods like shampoos, toothpastes and soft drinks. In small towns, beauty parlours have sprouted and women are driving mopeds and cars.

Connecting with the world through Internet, satellite TV, foreign travel and mobile phones is a sure sign of globalisation. Many Indians can afford imported goods not only because of the high salaries of the corporate sector but because they also regularly receive foreign exchange remittances from their relatives working abroad. The increase in the amount of black money in circulation has also led to a boom in fancy imported consumer goods.

Indians are becoming more consumerist no doubt and there are so many temptations to do up the house in the latest styles, wear trendy clothes and have more holidays. Many goods are now available through the Internet and there are newer and fancier holiday packages. In many cases, the availability of so many goods and services has triggered new ambitions and aspirations among the youth and they are busy in 'the race to the top'. Reaching global salary levels and having a high lifestyle comparable to foreign CEOs of rich countries is driving the ambitions of many 'high flyers' though it is also increasing stress levels. Reducing stress has become big business through yoga and all other kinds of alternate lifestyle therapies. Losing weight and reducing stress is one aspect of globalisation that has come to India in a big way. More people are also getting stress related diseases and private healthcare is a big business in India today.

More people are also getting used to buying on credit and are spending much more than before, though the spending pattern has yet to reach that of US. But having one or two credit cards gives the consumer a freedom and taste for spending whenever he or she wants and it is much better than having to count the cash at every counter. This could affect the savings habit of the nation in the long run. The number of credit card holders is still small, however, and people in small towns and villages still save a good proportion of their incomes regularly.

India has a much lower rate of savings than China and other Southeast Asian countries where it is in the range of 35 to 40 per cent. A rise in the rate of saving would be good for raising the rate of investment that India badly needs. Buying luxury goods is hardly going to foster a higher savings rate, especially if such goods are imported. Besides, easy loans for cars and consumer goods are now available through various schemes. People are tempted to borrow to buy more.

There is also a craze for exotic food and Indians are getting exposed to world cuisines. Pizzas, Thai and Mexican food are getting popular in the cities. Dining out has accompanied globalisation and in some of the eating joints each item on the menu is more than Rs. 500, which is equal to a few days' wage for an average city labourer.

Globalisation has increased both exports and imports. The export boom as experienced by countries that globalised in the 1970s and 1980s has not fully taken place in India as far as manufactured goods are concerned. Traders are however thriving—those who import shoddy goods and sell them in the domestic market. The jobs in the export sectors have not grown fast enough to employ all the school leavers and young women who are seeking work.

Globalisation has heightened competition and it has led to a much better quality in Indian products. While the quality of many domestic products has improved remarkably, beating some cheap Chinese imports still remains a challenge. China is not only making household gadgets and crockery for the Indian home but also *Ganesh* idols and *Banarasi saris* for women.

There is no doubt that globalisation has favoured the rich, educated and skilled and people with assets. It has marginalised the weaker sections further and sharpened the difference between various social classes. Casual, unskilled, migrant labourers are lured to the big cities by high salaries that they would get but have to sleep on the pavements at night because of scarce and expensive accommodation. And every so often, luxury cars driven by rich kids or drunken truck drivers kill them by running over them while they sleep.

The disparity in lifestyles and the growing inequalities in incomes and opportunities are being noticed by the urban unemployed youth and many are resorting to criminal activities to emulate the rich and the trendy. But they cannot find jobs as they do not have the requisite education, accent, connections, savings and demeanour. Unemployment is rising, especially among youth who are school dropouts, who hang out in *bazaars* and public places ready to be recruited by criminal gangs.

Globalisation however is irreversible now and people are conscious of the benefits of globalisation and the variety and spice it offers. But since millions have been left out, a growing sense of resentment is being felt in manifold ways among the poorer sections of the population. If the government is not prepared to make globalisation more inclusive by having a social safety net for the poorer sections, there could be resistance from the deprived and underprivileged in a more vocal and disruptive, even a violent, manner.

For example, the deprived sections belonging to SC/ST and OBC categories of people are being left behind because they have been disadvantaged for years and have lower levels of education and skills. Globalisation has resulted in the rise of big cyber cities like Bangalore but they are surrounded by slum clusters and shanty towns. The people who are service providers to the new rich remain mere spectators of all that goes on in the big cities. The truth that hurts is that around 350 million people still live on less than $1 a day as compared to only 20 per cent of the population living with much more money and enjoying a global lifestyle.

Giving 'Jobs for all', has remained a slogan with the government at the Centre and the realisation of this goal remains elusive because of the slow down in investment in agriculture and other critical sectors. Unless the problem of reducing rural poverty can be addressed immediately, there will be more armed conflicts in the countryside. Already out of 593 districts, 160 are affected by Naxalite violence. Unemployed youth are easily drawn into terrorist activities and because of globalisation and more liberalised trade, access to weapons is easier. This enables them to take up armed struggles. The challenges before the government are many, especially in smoothening the harsh edges of globalisation and making it more inclusive.

Maybe it is too early for a dramatic change over because, after all, the forces of globalisation are not even two decades old. It is also true that women are getting many more opportunities to work outside their homes since more menial and clerical jobs are open to them. Starting from becoming petrol station attendants to waitresses in restaurants and beauticians in beauty parlours, the average middle class girl before marriage can earn her dowry. Forbidden by law, dowry nonetheless is present in different guises. It could be a car rather than simple cash in globalised India. Single women living on their own are still not as common as in western countries. The patriarchal and male dominated society has not changed much under the impact of globalisation. The successful woman still has to adapt to societal norms and continue with her role as a housewife and mother in the traditional way. This puts a lot of pressure on the life of women executives, clerks, teachers and nurses. Globalisation has not led to gender equality either. The overall sex ratio at 927 girls to 1000 boys remains skewed in favour of boys. Women continue to be harassed and discriminated in the workplace.

For globalisation in India to be beneficial to all, education and skill development, healthcare and more jobs will have to be given prime importance. To protect one's cultural heritage is a lot more difficult because American and western icons and their lifestyle have entered and filtered through the homes of many, especially when the Indian idols are copying that lifestyle. Globalisation has been synonymous with 'Americanisation' all over the world and the resistance to it is mainly from the old guard trying to preserve the country's cultural heritage.

On the surface at least, Indian heritage does not seem to be threatened. The popular TV shows and Bollywood films, despite the heavy emphasis on make up and western outfits, still have stories built around traditional family values, girls becoming good housewives and mothers and respect for elders. But values are also fast changing. With the break up of joint families and with women going out to work there is more emphasis on the individual. Yet the old order clearly remains in many forms with women being subservient to the husband and his family though she may be earning a good salary. In making various important choices women are still weak and are the last to give up old customs for a globalised outlook which might include iconoclastic behaviour.

More than anything else, the entertainment pattern of children has changed. There is a lot of pornography around in the Internet and films. Parents who are critical of such exposure would have to spend more time with them from their busy schedules to see what the children eat, read or watch. Those who are interested in preserving their culture must point out to the children the best aspects of western culture. Copying the worst aspects of western culture is typically easier than copying their work habits and the discipline they follow for keeping fit or in doing their assignments and tasks.

All over the world, with the forces of globalisation becoming important, there have been conflicts and civil wars because there has been an increase in the inequality of incomes. Globalisation has increased the opportunities for making money and has also increased greed and illicit trade, especially in prized commodities like diamonds and tiger skins, *shahtoosh* wool, and drugs. It has also led to a rise in human trafficking.

The differences between countries are getting accentuated because the developing countries are far behind the industrial countries in resources and production capabilities like technology and capital. Unless all countries are more or less equally endowed, globalisation is likely to favour different nations differently and unequally, with very little benefits accruing to nations with a few exportable commodities or natural resources.

Globalisation has brought to the fore a few prominent and powerful MNCs whose individual incomes are bigger than many of the developing countries' total GDP. They have tremendous clout in world affairs and they readily shift their production base from country to country in search for the cheapest supplier of raw materials and labour. In their search for profits, they are impelled to produce more and more without much regard to either overexploitation of natural resources or contributing to and increasing environmental pollution. Exploitative practices by MNCs in their factories have to be checked in order to give labour a fair deal and fair share in the profits. Special mention should be made regarding their hiring of women labour in SEZs in which women are kept in difficult working conditions, paid less than men and dismissed once married.

Although capital has become very mobile and trade has been opened up in most countries, labour is still not allowed to move from poorer countries to richer countries. Globalisation in the 21st century is different from that of 19th century when mass migration took place between continents. Most industrialised countries today actively discourage immigrants from poorer countries and allow only' guest workers' who are allowed to work with permits under special quotas. Usually only the highly skilled labour force is allowed to migrate to the rich countries because it helps the 'host' countries reduce costs and gain efficiency in their own production systems. Thus, while the industrialised countries have pushed globalisation in order to increase their own flow of exports to the rest of the world, they themselves have been busy erecting new types of hidden barriers (non-tariff barriers) in order to stall and stifle imports and immigration flows from poorer countries. Even in the case of outsourcing of software services, whereby the US and EU have clearly benefited from the services rendered by Indian personnel, there have been protests and strong resistance from trade unions and politicians to hiring more workers from India.

Environment

Globalisation has led to the production and consumption of a lot more goods. The number of cars and factories have increased manifold. India and China have increased their consumption of oil and petroleum products over the last 10 years. There has been a big increase in population in the cities. The result has been congestion, the growth of slums and shanty towns in the outskirts of cities and sometimes within the cities, and general increase in squalour, dirt, garbage and people living in inhuman conditions. The quality of air and water have been degraded due to rapid urbanisation and there is a serious problem in the management of solid waste.

If alongside the increase in population and rise in the consumption of goods and services, various precautions had been taken to contain the increase in solid waste and, the amount of atmospheric carbon monoxide, as well as prevention of deforestation, the problem would not have assumed such serious dimensions. The first environmental concern confronting all cities is the problem of solid waste disposal. Access to sewerage and proper toilets is still not 100 per cent in most cities. On an average, in a city of one million people, the refuse generated per day is 500 tonnes. In any of the big cities, garbage can be seen lying around, uncovered. It is an ugly sight for foreign tourists. Exposed garbage causes the spread of diseases through rodents, flies and pests. Plastic bags clog drains, rivulets and water bodies. In some of the scenic spots in the Himalayas, plastic bags clog the free flow of water. Himachal Pradesh has now banned the use of plastic bags.

The informal sector contributes to garbage disposal in a big way. Through waste gatherers or rag pickers some of the stuff is recycled. It also creates a source of income for the unemployed. But it exposes the people, especially children, who are rummaging through garbage, to terrible diseases. Urban waste can be used for energy generation, composting, and vermicompost. It is estimated that urban municipal waste—both solid and liquid, have a potential of generating upto 1,000 mk of electricity. But burning can cause air pollution. Uncollected rotting garbage emits disgusting odours and methane gas which is harmful for the atmosphere as it creates the green house effect.

The proper disposal of sewage is another problem. The water treatment plants are not efficient enough to get rid of various bacterial microorganisms that are carried into rivers and into drinking water. The result is that potable safe water availability has suffered greatly. Water quality has suffered enormous deterioration in the past few years and even water used in soft drinks and in bottles is not entirely safe from contamination.

Water is going to be a scarce commodity because rivers are being polluted by industrial waste and effluents and other solid wastes that, even when treated, still contain unhealthy and dangerous substances. The deteriorating quality of water is affecting the lives of people and leading to the spread of diseases.

The growth of population has led to a decline in the per capita annual availability of water. Agriculture uses 85 per cent of the water and households use 4.5 per cent of the total water supply in the country. Industry uses 3 per cent and power generation plants use 3.5 per cent of the total water available in the country.

The major sources of water pollution are industrial water waste, effluents, domestic water waste and agricultural runoff. When domestic and human water waste are mixed with the drinking water system through rivers and lakes, it can result in severe waterborne diseases. Industries that are polluting by nature like leather, pulp and paper, textiles, chemicals, have all been growing at a rapid pace in recent years. They have not undertaken sufficient care to treat the effluents they discharge and, as a result, there has been an increase in water pollution.

Only 72 per cent of the urban areas get piped water supply. The rest have to rely on underground water supply. In the villages the situation is much worse and piped water is available to about 30 per cent of the population. Most of the rural population depends on the availability of surface and underground water. But all surface water sources are contaminated and unfit for human consumption. The result is that about 21 per cent of all communicable diseases in India are waterborne. They are caused by the presence of fecal matter, chemicals, heavy metals and effluents. Even the fish and shellfish living in the rivers and lakes are getting contaminated and that makes them unfit for consumption. Water contamination is leading to high infant mortality and the abundance of intestinal diseases among children and adults.

In agriculture the excessive use of pesticides and fertilisers after the Green Revolution is causing groundwater contamination. In a rich state like Punjab much of the underground water is unfit for human consumption.

Vegetables grown in these areas also suffer from contamination. Forests are being cut down to make way for new settlements. Though efforts are being made to conserve and expand forest cover, cutting down of trees is rampant. It is a threat to the environment. Much more attention has to be paid by the government and NGOs to establish watershed development and social forestry programmes that would save rainwater for agricultural use.

India is one of the fastest growing countries in the world and its population is the second largest in the world. Its natural resources are not unlimited and if proper care is not taken about how we live and how we spend the resources, there would be severe problems in sustaining development in the future.

India is going to be the most populous country in the world by 2050. It will have 1264 million people by 2016 and by 2051, 66.2 per cent of the population would be in the working age group. India will not only have to provide employment for one billion persons by the mid-21st century, but it would also be using up more fuel, water and other natural resources and these are not available in unlimited amounts.

India occupies 2.45 per cent of the earth's terrestrial surface and has 4 per cent of global precipitation but it is inhabited by 16 per cent of the global population. This shows the limit on natural resources in India.

In big cities, pollution has been rising though people have become very conscious of its consequences and have forced local governments to take remedial steps. It has led to many dramatic decisions by municipal and local governments. Still, the number of cars are too many and multiplying daily. This is adding to air pollution. The only way to control air pollution, which can cause various respiratory diseases, is to go in for rapid mass transit systems. Kolkata and Delhi have got the metro rail in recent years. It will reduce vehicular traffic and pollution.

Vehicular pollution is the most important source for the deteriorating quality of air in the cities. Delhi changed over to CNG for 9,000 public buses in May 2003 and got the Clean City International Award. It also dispensed with old taxis. But various studies have found that CNG conversion has reduced pollution only to some extent. There has not been an all round improvement in the ambient quality of the air because the only parameter that has shown a significant decline is carbon monoxide. This is because vehicular pollution is a complex and dynamic problem and it depends mainly on the number of cars on the roads and the speed at which they are running. Exhaust fumes are influenced by the vehicle speed, road conditions, traffic management, etc. The problem gets complex when the total number of road vehicles increases daily and the emission performance of those on the road already keeps deteriorating. To counter this problem, less vehicles should be on the roads each day and more people should be travelling by mass rapid transport.

Vehicular pollution is also causing heavy metal contamination of vegetables growing near major highways. These, when taken raw or unwashed, can cause serious diseases.

In villages, biofuels (cow dung cakes, wood, twigs, hay) are the most important cause for atmospheric pollution and ill health in rural areas. Women cooking with biofuels suffer most and many have lung and eye diseases. With a switch over to cooking gas, the quality of air in rural households will improve.

Atmospheric pollution and noise pollution are causing a huge amount of stress to people living near main roads and they are also developing hearing and respiratory ailments.

Conserving Forests, Flora and Fauna

India has a huge amount of animal and plant species. Overall, about 8 per cent of the world's species are found in India. It has the 10th rank among 'plant rich' countries in the world and 11th in terms of endemic species of higher vertebrates. It has the 6th rank among the centres of diversity and origin of agricultural biodiversity. The total number of living species identified in India are 200,000. Out of 12 biodiversity hotspots in the world, India has two, one in the northeast region and the other in the Western Ghats.

Unfortunately, environmental degradation has damaged a lot of flora and fauna. When forests are being cut down, many plant species which have forests as their sustaining source also disappear rapidly. There is need for more active conservation and bio research. In the Himalayas, wood was cut at a rapid rate in the past and entire mountains were cleared of trees and now it has been banned— perhaps when a great deal of denudation has already taken place.

It is the increasing population pressure and poverty which are disturbing the ecological balance; the demand for more farm-land is leading to encroachment on forestland.

The natural habitat of animals is also being destroyed by growing urbanisation, industrialisation, poaching, trapping and killing of animals. There is no way of recovering lost biodiversity. The way out is to reduce poverty in the countryside through rapid economic growth so that jobs are created and people become aware of the need to preserve India's vast flora and fauna. Economic growth alone can reduce the pressure on the environment. More parks and wildlife sanctuaries are needed to protect rare species. Educating children from school to look after the environment would also go a long way in protecting the flora and fauna of the nation.

20

Economic Reforms and their Future

For more than a decade, the progress of economic reforms in India has been a matter of concern for foreign investors because the speed with which they are undertaken would determine the future pace of growth. The slow pace of reforms has been blamed for India remaining a laggard as compared to China. In fact, the World Bank and the IMF provided the blueprint for economic reforms when the 1991 crisis struck India. From all fronts, India seemed beleaguered and trapped in a financial crisis. Around 1990, the Soviet Union, one of India's major trading partners collapsed, the Gulf War took place and remittances from Indians in the Gulf area were cut off. Then, there was the third big oil price hike by OPEC.

India faced a huge balance of payments crisis as export growth turned negative and foreign exchange inflows dwindled. It was heavily indebted to international financial institutions. Industrial growth had turned negative and declined by 1.3 per cent. India verged on default in its debt repayment and had to mortgage its gold.

The inflation rate was high at 17 per cent and foreign exchange reserves dipped to the dangerously low level of $1 billion which hardly could pay for two weeks' imports. The rupee was overvalued in terms of the five major foreign currencies. The fiscal deficit was at 8.2 per cent of GDP in 1990-91. A mind-boggling number of legislations existed to curb trade, industrial expansion and foreign investment, which in turn gave rise to rent seeking, corruption and inefficiency. The need for economic reforms was obvious. In this horrendous situation, the bail-out came from the IMF in one of its historic loans of $6 billion.

The opening up of the economy was initiated by the Congress government under the premiership of P.V. Narasimha Rao. For many, the meaning of economic reforms remained elusive for quite sometime because the real implications were not explained to the common man. There was no consensus, nor was there any public debate. Initially, only a small section of the people stood to benefit from the economic reforms directly when suddenly, the licence-permit *raj* was dismantled, the MRTP Act was modified and the capital market opened up. Foreign investors were invited in many more sectors than before and clear incentives were offered to them to set up businesses in India.

The arrival of several multinational companies to establish their factories and production bases in India and the availability of a variety of goods with foreign brand names marked the beginning of economic reforms. This opening up to foreign investment and the new job opportunities it offered was understood by most people. Foreign direct investment (FDI) up to 100 per cent foreign ownership was permitted in most manufacturing sectors.

The rupee was devalued by 23 per cent and this gave an immediate boost to exports. Thus, trade was one of the first areas of reforms. Custom duties were reduced and the quota system of import control was to be completely dismantled by 2001. The system of import licensing was virtually abolished for capital goods, raw materials and intermediate goods. Custom duties were brought down from their peak level of 300 per cent in 1991 to 85 per cent, within two years. As a result, imports of goods rose and foreign goods never seen before appeared in the local markets in a big way.

The rupee's exchange rate was to be determined by the market instead of being pegged to a basket of currencies. The two-tier exchange rate system—official and market—was abolished and a unified exchange rate was established. The rupee was also made convertible on current account in 1994—exporters bringing in foreign exchange could get their money converted in rupees or keep their money in dollars. But though there was much pressure to make the rupee fully convertible—that is on capital account—it was not done, mainly because the government was afraid of massive capital flight. Since there was a large amount of black money in the economy, the danger of wholesale and substantial transfer of funds abroad could not be ruled out. In fact, when in 1997 the East Asian Financial Crisis took place all over Southeast Asia, India remained relatively untouched mainly because it had not made the rupee convertible.

To many, who had the right qualifications and skills as well as connections, reforms meant new opportunities and a huge rise in salaries in the newly established foreign companies that flocked to India. There were many such companies in the initial years, eager to set up their factories in order to tap the huge market.

FDI approvals up to 51 per cent of equity in a large list of industries was made automatic. The Foreign Investment Promotion Board was constituted for expediting approvals in other sectors and for investments above 51 per cent equity participation. The archaic Foreign Exchange Regulation Act (FERA) was amended and subsequently replaced by the Foreign Exchange Management Act in order to liberalise the operating environment for firms with foreign equity and also to make it easier for Indian business to operate from abroad.

High level bureaucrats and high-ups in the armed forces flaunted their children's astronomical salaries (which were considered synonymous with high achievement) in society parties and clubs. Connections and recommendations by influential persons definitely got children from bureaucratic families high paying jobs soon after college. A new crop of management schools sprang up and companies scouted and still scout around campuses for talented young men and women offering handsome incomes in the future.

The past 'industrial licensing' process was more or less abolished except when relating to location and environmental concerns. Only a few sectors were kept for the public sector. Some that were exclusively reserved for the public sector, such as power, airlines, telecommunication and mining have, in recent years, been opened up to private investment.

The opening up of consumer goods and consumer durables to foreign investment meant the market for the first time saw many Japanese and Korean, German, American and British car brands. There was a deluge of Japanese and Korean refrigerators, washing machines and French cosmetics made in Indian factories. Women loved the availability of all the famous brand names in the shopping malls that sprang up in towns and cities. Along with cosmetics and imported fabrics came the new crop of Indian fashion designers. India suddenly was on the world map of fashion with noted international personalities flaunting Indian designer clothes at parties and special occasions abroad.

The winning of two important beauty pageants by Indian women soon after the economic reforms also marked the beginning of a new era of Indian fashion and style. The new Indian women are well groomed and use foreign branded cosmetics.

People working in big MNCs had the spending power to go for holidays abroad and spend on consumer goods and real estate. The media was agog with stories of successful executives and their lifestyles and the 'reformers' within the bureaucracy were universally glorified and feted. The pink business papers were agog with the rise of the market and the end of the shabby government controlled era.

Rents in metro cities went up and also real estate prices. The black money component of rents reached new heights and landladies clutching handbags full of cash rushed to buy gold and diamond jewellery. Economic reforms ushered in the lust for gold like never before. There was much speculation, especially in property prices in Delhi and Mumbai, and they have been skyrocketing since. To some extent the big property bubble burst when new apartment blocks near metro cities increased the housing supply. But prime land has experienced an irreversible increase in the price per square foot.

Foreign institutional investors flocked to India with its huge consumer and industrial base and well established stock market. The stock market flourished as never before. As pointed earlier, the capital market was liberalised, the control of Capital Issues Act was repealed and SEBI was given a statutory basis. The NSE was set up as a fully electronic order book type of exchange with a clearing corporation. A global share depository was also introduced. It gave NSE a greater degree of transparency in its operations. In addition to this, mutual fund operators and Indian firms were allowed to raise funds from offshore markets through global depository receipts. Private players were allowed in insurance with foreign equity capped at 26 per cent. There was an additional provision of 14 per cent for NRI investors.

But the huge amount of foreign exchange inflow that came *via* the route of foreign institutional investors could not be absorbed by the market and the result was excessive foreign exchange deposits with banks. They expanded their lending, causing a rise in inflation in the mid-1990s. The government took measures through its monetary policy to control inflation. Interest rates were hiked and this led to a few years of tight money policy that resulted in the industrial slow-down after 1995.

Since many restrictions were removed for the corporate sector's access to funds, big companies were able to borrow abroad easily and expanded their operations. Many industrial houses borrowed from public sector banks and, of course, many did not pay back and their loans became NPAs. Many companies began with fanfare only to disappear months later. The list of 'Disappearing Companies' is long. A lot of small investors burnt their fingers investing in fly by night companies. The opening up of the capital market was quite obviously not accompanied by strict legislative and vigilant practices. Checks and balances could have weeded out the good from the bad investors and the number of stock market scandals could have been minimised.

Reforms were directed at the government's finances and the fiscal deficit which had ballooned over the 1980s, due to careless and irresponsible government policies, had to be brought under control. The IMF is paranoid about high fiscal deficits and it quickly pointed out that it was the twin deficits in the fiscal and balance of payments front that led to the financial crisis of 1991.

Control of fiscal deficit meant a cut in non-Plan governmental expenditure which is the current expenditure of the central government. The government was advised by the IMF to cut its subsidies, keep its finances under tight control, shed flab and reduce its mammoth bureaucracy. Unfortunately, the government could not cut down on its current expenditure due to political compulsions. Because there was a minority government in 1991, it had to continue with the populist policies.

Instead, the government cut down on capital expenditure or the expenditure which goes for investment in agriculture, education, health and infrastructure. This cut in the critical expenditure necessary for growth proved to be the bane of reforms as it hit the poor people in the countryside most.

The government's investment in agriculture, health and education fell in the initial years of reform, and agriculture, which needed to be revitalised through heavy investment in rural infrastructure, irrigation, fertilisers, better seeds and extension work, suffered. The tightening of the government's finances also meant that the public sector had to be pruned, especially the public sector enterprises. The siphoning off of funds from the public exchequer to resuscitate them periodically had to be stopped. Throughout the 1980s, eminent economists had pointed out that the government had no business to be in business and that it should not be involved in commercial activities like making watches and running hotels. These had led to a huge amount of rent seeking, lack of accountability and political patronage. Disinvestment, through which public enterprises would be able to sell off its equity to the private sector, was introduced. Wholesale privatisation of public enterprises was not considered a suitable alternative as it would give rise to much discontent.

Disinvestment was carried out with much fervour during the NDA led government and crores of rupees were realised through the sale of government equity. Complete sell-outs were also resorted to as in the case of the Centaur Hotel. The money ultimately went to finance the fiscal deficit rather than being used to retire public debt and to promote infrastructure development.

Out of all the sectors adversely affected by the economic reforms, infrastructure was in the forefront and its decline marked a big failure. Though infrastructure remained a priority area, there was not sufficient progress because private sector investment and FDI did not come in sufficient amounts to upgrade it.

Economic reforms were introduced in the banking sector and the bank rate was left to be determined by the market instead of being set by the RBI. Priority sector loans meant for agriculture were reduced.

Reforms and globalisation have gone together because the opening of the economy to global trade and capital marked the beginning of economic liberalisation. There have been many big time gainers but the reforms have also benefited the middle class. Someone or other was able to make more money than before in each family, either through trade or the stock market or even manufacturing. But the promised trickle down to the lowest income groups has not happened. Many blame it on the slow pace of reforms the trade unions and the Left forces that have not allowed labour laws to be changed.

In a democracy, it is difficult to change the style of work rapidly, especially in the public sector. In the corporate sector, much has changed and modern management styles, that make for more efficient production, have been introduced rather fast. Though the labour laws affect only eight per cent of the workforce, the corporate sector, especially those production units with foreign partners or wholly owned subsidiaries of foreign firms, have gone in for more capital intensive production. Food processing and packaging companies have resorted to machines and boast of the 'untouched by hands' label. Automated production methods have been favoured because production units have more flexibility and they do not have to deal with hiring, firing, strikes and lockouts.

The reforms have been popular with corporate business in general because their profits have been soaring with new technology, know-how, marketing methods, franchising and acquisition of brand names through joint ventures with foreign companies. The new methods of management and manufacturing have led to an expansion in exports as well as domestic sales.

The reforms have been unpopular with those who have lost their jobs. Even though the hiring and firing is formally difficult for the corporate sector to undertake on a mass scale, it has protected itself by hiring workers on contract who can be fired with a month's notice. This is a relatively new phenomenon in India. There is no social safety net available in the country by way of unemployment insurance and other subsidised amenities. Joint families and relatives have been taking care of the unemployed. It has been a shock to many who were hired at high salaries and ended up being fired in a short span of time. Many holding high profile corporate jobs could never find similar jobs later.

Even so, corporate sector salaries being much higher than government salaries, government jobs, which attracted the best talent earlier mainly because of the security of tenure and the authority that the officers wielded, have become less attractive. Today, instead of top bureaucrats, the newsmakers are media barons, Bollywood moghuls, film stars, designers and corporate chiefs (CEOs and COOs). The drive to do as well as newsmakers has permeated to the middle class and fired their aspirations. There is a new awakening in all sections of the population and people constantly compare their salaries, perks and lifestyle with each other. Perhaps the opening up of the economy has stirred up the values of traditional India irrevocably and the sense of contentment and fatalism (the old thinking of accepting one's fate as given) has declined sharply. Perhaps that is why India has awakened to its own potential and is considered a serious contender to China's manufacturing success. It is moving ahead as though driven by its own steam and every educated young person is dreaming of making it big in the corporate world or the media world. The private sector now dominates industrial production and 75 per cent of all production is in private hands.

Thus, reforms that have led to the opening up of trade, investment, capital markets and increase in privatisation, have got big votaries among the affluent and the urban elite. Indian corporate sector employees have the lifestyles of corporate executives abroad complete with work outs, golf, holidays, 'retreats' and a tight, stressful schedule of work. There is much pressure to open up foreign investment further. Areas like retail trade that have been still not opened would be opened up sooner or later. In telecom, though the cap on foreign investment has been raised from 49 to 74 per cent, foreign investors want more freedom to invest.

Trade barriers have gone down though India's trade partners complain that invisible barriers still exist. Competition from foreign goods and locally based foreign subsidiaries has led to an improvement in lifestyle and consumption pattern. Indian designers are copying fast the fashion trends abroad in textiles and garments, gems and jewellery, for the home market and for exports. They are also developing a distinct style of their own. Only a few snags that continue to slow down reforms remain.

It is still not easy for a foreign firm to exit from a venture. Legal procedures take long time. The law courts are a veritable maze and it takes years to conclude a deal or solve a dispute. The law and order situation is also not very reliable, especially in certain states that are bankrupt and cannot afford a vigilant police force. Strikes and lockouts, though less frequent, still take place. Trade Unions have not been banned though they are not as strong as before. The infrastructure is still inadequate. Bureaucratic hassles still exist but to a lesser extent. Clearances of all kinds are required before the foreign investor can actually start operating from India. Corruption exists in all forms and guises and at all levels. All these reasons are contributing to a slowdown of foreign investment in India.

The main adverse fallout of economic reforms related to budgetary cuts by the government was on agriculture. Agricultural output fell in the years following the reforms. Agricultural growth has not kept pace with the changes that have been occurring in the rest of India. As a result, the rural people have not been affected much by economic reforms. For them life is still as dreary and has as little prospect as it did before. In some prosperous states, the village youth are getting computer savvy and aspiring for jobs abroad. But in the big states that are poor there are no such opportunities available in the villages.

The contrast between the city glitterati and stylish people and those living in urban neighbourhood slums has sharpened a thousand times. This contrast translated into anti-Congress votes in the 1995 elections and people showed that they wanted a more people friendly government.

The saviour of the Indian economy in recent years, in terms of getting it noticed in the world and making it self-sufficient in foreign exchange, has been the software sector growth. It is also the BPOs which have made outsourcing a big business that have attracted world attention. Foreign exchange has kept flowing in because the demand for software personnel has gone on increasing in the US and EU. Software exports have grown at the rate of 50 per cent and the services sector has increased its share in the GDP to 51 per cent while the share of manufacturing sector has declined. Indian project and mechanical engineers have made a mark in all parts of the world. Remittances still play a very important part in the growing foreign exchange reserves.

On the whole, though the Congress Party initiated the economic reforms, they were not abandoned by the BJP led NDA combine. On many fronts, they seemed to be more enthusiastic about pushing the reforms agenda. Over the years, a consensus has thus been attained about the relevance and irreversibility of economic reforms and their importance for linking up with the global economy. No economy is hiding behind protective barriers any more and all developing countries are striving to increase exports and attract foreign investment.

The real test of economic reforms lies in their benefits reaching the common person. How have these reforms affected the lives of the rural poor? The most obvious answer lies in looking at the poverty ratios and examining the profile of rural consumption expenditure. If there are millions still eking out a miserable existence and if periodically many are committing suicide, then there is something wrong with the system at the top. The trickle down has to be faster and the social safety nets have to be in place for the poorest section of the population in order to enable reforms to make a difference to village India.

Foreign investment, as well as private domestic and public investment has to benefit the rural people through agriculture and manufacturing industries in villages. Otherwise, those pushing for reforms will continue to be seen as pro-rich and at the next general elections those hit by the opening up of the economy and inflation would vote against the reform policies of the government. Those who still remain unemployed will also not see any benefits coming to them as a result of economic reforms. To many they have meant only privatisation of public enterprises and foreign investment in consumer goods meant for the rich.

Second Generation Reforms

The advocates of economic reforms are vocal about privatisation more than any thing else. They want a bigger role of the private sector and the withdrawal of the public sector from manufacturing activities. They want that no subsidies should be given that are not reaching the poor. They also want all utilities to have proper 'user charges' and all the foreign investment 'caps' to go and the retail sector to be opened up. They want to change the labour laws and have a clear 'exit' policy. By increasing the role of the private sector, they think that many problems would be solved. But who is going to solve the problems of 260 million people who are earning a paltry amount and have no future to look forward to? The private sector will definitely not come forward to educate them, feed them, give them jobs and give them healthcare and hospitals. The government cannot really limit itself to a small insignificant role because in a democracy all have an equal vote. Policies that are obviously pro-rich cannot be adopted, especially by a coalition government.

Then there is the big debate about opening up the retail trade sector. Wal-Mart, Carforre, MAKRO, 7Eleven all want to come to India; the government also wants to open up the FDI in this sector.

The advocates say that these giant retail chains will bring technology and quality control. They would source their products from Indian manufacturers and farmers and Indian exports would get a big boost because they would then sell these in outlets abroad. China's example is given as having benefited enormously by allowing FDI in the retail trade. Wal-Mart, for example, has helped to boost China's exports and the promoters of Wal-Mart type of stores say that they would do the same for India. They would bring strict quality control and standardisation that are badly needed. They would invest in storage and transport of produce from farms to retail shops and the small farmers would benefit.

But the question is what happens to the 15 million small retailers in the country? Who will give them jobs when they are displaced by giant retail chains. Adjustment will take time and only the really competitive ones would be able to survive. More studies are needed about the exact nature of the operations of these foreign retailers. Will they undertake investment in infrastructure and quality control or be inclined to sell products sourced from other countries from their shelves? The job creation aspect also is important, especially when the young jobless are growing in numbers. Will they, also, really improve the farming methods and impart knowledge to the farmers? How will the farmers cope when large quantities are rejected because they do not conform to the standards?

Instead of more sectors being handled entirely by the market mechanism, the government will have to improve its own role in poverty reduction, in education, health and in infrastructure. Enormous reforms are required in agriculture and in agricultural marketing, in the public distribution system, in improving banking and credit facilities and housing for the poor. Unless these reforms take place, there is not much scope for policies favouring faster reforms in other sectors to be successful.

21

India and SAARC

Problems of Regional Integration

For India to be an emerging economic power in the Asian region, its relations with its neighbours are of the utmost importance. India is the biggest and the most dominant member of the South Asian Association for Regional Cooperation (SAARC) which has seven members—India, Maldives, Sri Lanka, Bhutan, Nepal, Pakistan and Bangladesh. SAARC was formed in 1985 and there have been 12 summits already in which heads of States of the region met and discussed common problems. But very little progress has been made in having an economic union like the European Union with a common currency, open borders and synchronised macro policies. There are still many barriers to the free movement of goods, services, people, and investment across borders. The governments talk in terms of treaties but much of the promised cooperation does not get translated into action.

Yet, a South Asian Free Trade Area or SAFTA has been contemplated and designed for many years; it came into force in 2006. It will entail a progressive reduction in tariff barriers as well as non-tariff barriers between all the member countries. All members want India to make the deepest tariff cuts and give most generous concessions to the less developed members. Weaker members are also demanding compensation against import revenue losses due to trade concessions. India has made the deepest tariff cuts to less developed members already and given many duty concessions to others.

South Asia has the lowest level of intra-regional trade as compared to ASEAN or NAFTA (North American Free Trade Agreement). There is however a huge amount of informal trade (smuggling) taking place between India and Pakistan as well as between India and Bangladesh. If this trade could be legalised and conducted along official channels under SAFTA, more employment could be created and governments concerned could earn more customs duties. Bilaterally, India has been active and has signed free trade treaties with Nepal, Sri Lanka, Bangladesh and Bhutan. A Free Trade Agreement is already there with Thailand and Singapore.

India's neighbours are all economically insecure, some poorer than India. Poverty reduction is of great concern to SAARC members and it has appointed an Independent South Asian Commission on Poverty Alleviation (ISACPA). South Asia accounts for 20 per cent of global poverty and 40 per cent of the world's poor live in the region. In absolute numbers, more than 400 million people who are very poor, who add up to more than all the poor of Sub-Saharan Africa, Arab States, Latin America and the Caribbean, live in South Asia. The second report of the ISACPA has been presented and it has made some concrete suggestions for poverty alleviation in the region.

The South Asian region has 1.5 billion people and has 22 per cent of the world's population. Yet, it accounts for only 2 per cent of the world's total GNP. The average per capita income is only $441 which makes it one of the poorest regions in the world. It also has the most malnourished people in the world. Sri Lanka has done better than other members in reducing infant and maternal mortality rate but the others have dismal record in human development. About 37 per cent of the region's population lives on less than a dollar a day. Yet both India and Pakistan have to spend huge amounts on defence due to cross-border conflicts and terrorism. Unless there is a reduction in mistrust between India and Pakistan, India cannot reduce its defence expenditure. The huge amount that both spend could have been deployed in increasing the well-being of their people.

In the area of poverty alleviation, there can be cooperation in giving access to health, education and credit facilities to the unempowered, especially women. There are millions of women working in the informal sector in these countries. Through better infrastructure and credit facilties, the informal sectors in these countries could be improved and mainstreamed. A social safety net for the poor in the informal sector could greatly reduce gender inequality.

There can be close cooperation between the members of SAARC to reduce transport costs. This would benefit business between the countries. There can be renewal of the railway links of the past and new roads and rail lines can be built to improve economic development. Better transport links would help to attract greater amounts of FDI. The main reason why surface connectivity is not improving is political.

In any case, border crossing of goods could be made easier so that the rigmarole of documentation, customs inspection and informal payment systems are eliminated. Better transport would lead to more employment opportunities for small traders and vendors.

Cooperation in the field of energy would allow the SAARC members to reach a higher rate of economic growth. South Asian countries are characterised by lower per capita consumption of energy and poor quality of energy infrastructure, skewed distribution patterns and a relatively high cost of energy as compared to Southeast Asian countries. All SAARC countries except Bhutan have remained energy importers and many are facing an energy shortfall. Lack of access to power and commercial energy has adversely affected all productive activities, the social development of the region as well as its investment climate.

With greater cooperation in the field of energy it could be possible to have a common energy grid across the region with integrated electricity and gas systems as in the case of Europe. Interconnection of power systems of contiguously located countries and their coordinated operation can bring immense economic benefits to the region. It would contribute to the quality of electricity supplied and reduce environmental damage. There is bilateral hydro-energy trading between India and Bhutan and between India and Nepal at a government to government level. More private sector involvement is urgently needed.

Gas lines from outside the region can also solve energy problems but there are some political ramifications that may turn out to be difficult to handle. This is because huge financial resources are involved; there is geopolitical apprehension and the problem of pricing of the supplied gas. There is also the question of third country approval for transits that could involve an environmental fallout. Gas pipelines from Bangladesh, Myanmar and Iran have all been considered by India as viable options. But no clear outcomes have emerged and all are at the negotiation stage. The energy projects need to be depoliticised through the spread of information about the mutual benefits by the media, seminars and workshops. The perceived loss of sovereignty is actually standing in the way of enhancing cooperation in the field of energy. There is a need to be convinced of the benefits and revenues more clearly.

In the area of foreign investment also there can be cooperation that will increase the per capita income level and promote growth. Preconditions would have to be created so that perceptions of hostility and security threats do not enter the minds of investors too much. The host countries would have to give assurance to investors about the safety of their capital. But investments would have to be underwritten by international insurance firms. India has invested in Bhutan, Nepal and Sri Lanka and there is evidence of private investment from India going to Bangladesh also. There is very little investment from India to Pakistan. The scope for investment is vast but certain steps would have to be taken to harmonise policies between the different countries of the region to promote FDI.

Basically, political issues have to be addressed first so that the other aspects of cooperation can be followed up in order to promote faster economic growth in the region. For India, it is important that the neighbourhood is peaceful and conducive to development and cooperation, otherwise much of our own effort will be diverted to keeping the borders secure and much human capital and financial capital will be deployed for defence and control of cross-border terrorism. The increasing amount of money spent for border security could be diverted for developmental use and spent much more effectively in making the lives of the people better.

It is also important that there is political will behind all the SAARC agreements; these seem to be full of rhetoric and do not translate into actual actions that benefit the people.

22

Conclusion

India is a country which is going through a difficult patch because millions of people wanting to do well and enjoy the benefits of higher economic growth are, unfortunately, not getting included in the transition of India into a richer country. People with low incomes are acutely aware of how the rich and upwardly mobile are enjoying life as it is reported in the media and films and through the *bazaar* gossip circuit. While a large majority, mainly the urban population, is visibly enjoying the fruits of globalisation, many more are finding it difficult to survive in congested city spaces lacking in basic amenities. The poorer sections want more help from the government in giving them basic public goods like water, power and cheap housing, while the rich and upper middle classes want the government to withdraw from interfering in economic activities and open up the economy to private sector and foreign investment.

Many of the technocrats in government ministries are themselves returnees from the World Bank and IMF as well as the Silicon Valley and they want economic reforms to speed up, especially in the area of labour reforms. They want the opening up of key sectors like retail trading and further liberalisation of investment in the insurance and airlines sectors. The educated, vocal and visible elite is supported by the western press like *The Economist* and the *Financial Times* in the demand for more foreign investment and greater freedom to do business in India. The Indian pink (economic) newspapers, in which articles appear regularly about the virtues of the free market and the benefits of foreign investment, welcome reforms that would benefit the business elite. India has many 'rupee' and even some 'dollar' billionaires and the numbers are increasing rapidly. A section of the population has attained a globalised lifestyle and even the most prestigious manufacturers of luxury consumer goods from Europe, US, Japan and Korea want to establish their shops in India. The most famous film stars are the brand ambassadors of their products. The small but prominent creamy layer has growing spending power and they have a great urge to copy the lifestyles of the western elite.

The Leftist intellectuals, on the other hand, keep talking about the people left behind in the race for greater globalisation and the need to bring them also into the fold of rapid economic transformation. They are an important force as they are supporting the current Congress-UPA government from outside since 2004. They have always been an important force in guiding the direction of economic and social policies whenever they have been coalition partners. Thus, while politically it is becoming increasingly difficult to carry out further reforms, the economy is continuing to grow at its own momentum reaching GDP growth of nine per cent in 2006. Mostly it is the people within the middle income groups who are aspiring for a higher standard of life and working hard to attain it. They are also willing to spend foreign exchange in trying to send their children abroad for higher education. Many from the corporate sector can afford to educate their children abroad. Many young men and women are busy improving their career prospects by job hopping; gone are the days when people stuck to one job for life.

It is village India one must return to whenever one wants to assess the benefits of growth and whether they are reaching the poor, 70 per cent of whom reside in villages. Are they getting anywhere regarding their own (much smaller) aspirations? Are the state governments doing enough to make village schools and hospitals better? Also, are people aware of what they are entitled to because they seem to tolerate incredibly poor quality social services.

Even when there is awareness, there is a lack of empowerment and most have to wait till the next elections to air their grievances with the hope that a change of government would do wonders. But it doesn't, because politicians get a short-term in power and they are busy garnering resources during that period for themselves.

It is the duty of the State to see whether all the children in rural and poorer urban areas are in schools and not working away their childhood in menial, tedious and oppressive jobs. Also, it has to ensure that women are being treated well in remote villages. Considering the increase in the crime rate against women in the cities, is enough being done to prevent such crimes being committed also in rural India?

Like Gandhiji, one would like to see that every person's face is happy, especially the faces of the most deprived sections of the population; but it is an enormous task because the government has limited resources and is faced with huge problems.

Probably, the government would be able to have enough money to carry out all the reforms if only people pay taxes. Issues in fiscal reform and unearthing of black money remains a daunting task. Better management of the banking system, increased access to credit for farmers, and a well functioning infrastructure would make many of the deprived a little better off. Should not the government seek these small-scale reforms in every village rather than the sweeping ones that would open up the economy to the already rich MNCs who want to operate in India? If their operations benefit a small section of the people only, naturally there would be resistance. People would like to know how many jobs they are creating and what is the net gain that India is deriving from their presence.

India's own industries are capable of rising to great heights as shown by several prominent industrialists and their expanding worldwide operations in recent times. They could be more involved in the development of roads, power production, transportation and an increase in their investment could give more jobs in the countryside. It has been pointed out that industrial development has been constrained by lack of efficient infrastructure.

Agricultural reforms are most needed in order to raise agricultural productivity. First of all, tenurial rights to farmers have to be granted and there has to be a smooth marketing supply chain in which the producers benefit and not the middlemen. All reforms in agriculture would require additional investment by the government. Food processing industries in the villages can change the life of village India and they can be established by encouraging contract farming with the private sector. Private investment is needed to set up such industries and other types of industrial clusters in the rural areas and yet all these important investments are not coming forward at the requisite pace. Perhaps this is because of the number of regulations and controls on the movement and processing of agricultural goods, and the hassles of doing agribusiness. If all the controls on agricultural marketing and processing by the Indian private sector could be removed or reduced, more investment would flow in. The government at the Centre has to make the roads, provide better credit and irrigation systems in order to increase the flow of agricultural goods from rural to urban areas.

Unlike the ASEAN countries, India is huge in terms of population, heterogeneity, geographical size, linguistic diversity; it is bound with age-old traditions and an ancient civilisation. Indians cannot easily be disciplined and the population cannot be regimented into doing something that the government wants them to do. Indians are highly individualistic in many respects. They are also more conscious of the wrongdoings of the political leaders though the average rural inhabitant may seem and probably is semiliterate and very poor. Their tolerance level may be high but, sooner or later, Indian democracy has shown that the corrupt are ousted.

The export led growth of China cannot be used as a role model in India because unlike China, people in India are unionised and the discipline of the labour force that China has, is missing. Besides, China has already become the dominant player in the world market in manufacturing and for India to enter in a big way and compete would require a real revolution in education, skills and work discipline. The manufacturing sector accounts for only 17 per cent of the GDP whereas it accounts for 35 per cent in China and 25-35 per cent in ASEAN countries. India can only capture niche markets, which it is already doing in gems and jewellery, certain raw materials and garments. To make these items more competitive is one way to spread prosperity to the villages where some parts can be outsourced by bigger business concerns and multinational companies. India can compete in IT, software and other services for years ahead. This offers hope for a quicker transformation of India than would be possible if it relied only on agricultural and industrial growth.

Agricultural exports can be another option because of India's huge horticultural production, much of which goes waste. India is the world's biggest vegetable producer and the 10th most important fruit producer. But 40 per cent of all the fruits and vegetables go waste. It would require a big flow of investment from both the public and private sectors to collect the produce and process it for sale in the home and export market.

In the financial sector, there is need for a better regulatory mechanism which will ensure that scandals that scare away small investors do not break out in the stock and money markets. The country's savings rate has been rising a little. It will have to be encouraged through the availability of financial instruments; and savings could be mobilised for infrastructure development. The financial system's smooth functioning is vital for the growth of the entire economy.

The government's role at the Centre and state level lies in promoting welfare for the poorer sections of the population by investing more in the social sector. It includes the provision of low cost housing and relocation or restructuring and refurbishing of slums, making safe drinking water available to all, education for all, better public healthcare system, eradicating child labour, and guaranteeing jobs for the unskilled and landless. These are some of the functions that the government cannot ignore any longer.

The private sector's role is equally important in promoting growth in the manufacturing and services sector and creating more jobs, especially in the factory sector. It has to become more competitive and use more labour intensive techniques so as to absorb the regular flow of labour from the countryside. Expanding job opportunities can come only through the private sector.

The main points are:

- The focus should be on agriculture because it has been seen over the years that whenever agricultural growth falls, the GDP growth also gets affected adversely and is lower than the targeted growth. A more productive agriculture is the key to the rapid transformation of village India and its transition to a modern economy. It is also very important for the industrial sector because rural demand for industrial goods pushes up industrial growth. Though some states are ahead of others in agriculture, the universal use of better inputs and techniques has not happened in the form of a full-fledged agrarian revolution. Use of the latest technology in harvesting and post-harvesting operations as well as application of new research in biotechnology and tissue culture, seeds and fertilisers, have to be encouraged in order to bring India on par with countries like Brazil and Thailand that have become major exporters of agricultural products.

- Continued focus on infrastructure is important because it is the main bottleneck India is facing in making a rapid transition to a more urbanised economy. A special emphasis is required on rural infrastructure that will enable the rural population to increase their incomes by travelling to nearby towns for work and trade. Roads will make villages connect to a more globalised India.

- A much bigger budgetary allocation for human development, especially healthcare and education, is necessary in every state. This is sadly lacking in many of the most populous states. Reducing the interstate differences in human development should be an important priority; raising the overall Human Development Index of India is extremely important for the nation.

- Computer education will have to be given to students in all rural areas; computer literacy even among adults in every state has to be promoted in order to raise efficiency. IT is the fastest growing sector and the urban and rural youth should have easy access to computers. The telecommunication revolution and the growth of the IT industry can transform India rapidly.

- The government could help in making Indian industries more efficient and competitive by streamlining its policies that still interfere with their functioning. This could increase industrial growth. The financial sector has to be reformed so that the banking sector is more competitive and efficient in meeting the needs of industry, agriculture and the services sectors. Stock markets have to be better regulated so as to make them attractive to domestic and foreign institutional investors. Various safe and reliable instruments for investment for small investors have to be nurtured.

- The fiscal side of the economy has to be changed, both with regard to revenue and tax collections, and in trimming government expenditure in non-productive areas. The size of the government bureaucracy has to be trimmed and retraining of redundant employees should be encouraged so that they can find jobs in other areas. More retraining facilities would make disinvestment easier.

- The huge amount of black money that is being generated every year should be tapped somehow and the resources used for development. Better governance of all government sponsored poverty alleviation programmes would reduce corruption. Less bureaucratic paper work and need for various permissions and approvals of government ministries in trying to do business would cut the cost of starting business in India. The vestiges of the 'inspector *raj*' have to be eliminated. The number of permits required for foreign investment is still high and the median time taken for completion of formalities is 90 days as compared to 30 in China.

- The informal and small-scale sector, with its huge employment potential, should be mainstreamed with proper safety nets and facilities, because it employs 93 per cent of the workforce.

- Foreign investment should be encouraged in priority areas like airports, roads, power, telecommunications and ports. Caps on foreign investment have to be examined carefully to assess their impact on the potential gains for the private sector in having greater access to capital and more job opportunities. For example, in the case of insurance, the options of raising the cap from 26 per cent to 74 per cent has to be examined in order to assess the impact of the opening up on the total funds that can be collected from the public. Foreign investors could tap a wider market by giving them a variety of new products.

- India can become a favourite tourist destination through better facilities for tourist travel and stay. Encouraging eco-tourism and religious tourism as well as offering other new types of tourist packages, would yield more foreign exchange and generate many more jobs. Yet, preserving the environment should be priority at all times.

- India should become the main player in SAARC and help to build bridges with all its neighbours. Peace on the borders will help India most by keeping defence expenditure down. The SAARC could be involved in solving common problems of poverty alleviation and low levels of social and human development.

- India can transform into an economic power once the transformation of the rural economy to a modernised economy is complete through rural industrialisation, better infrastructure and communications, empowerment of women, more access to capital and better education and health facilities. The benefits of globalisation and economic reforms would then reach the ordinary person in the cities and towns and the common farmer.

- The working of the Indian economy cannot be entirely left at this crucial stage to the market forces alone. The State's functioning has to be guided by a number of competent and dedicated people at the helm who are interested in seeing that the benefits of rapid growth reach all and not just a few.

Appendices

A. Employment and Growth Rates across Different Sectors

Sector	Employment in Numbers (million)		Annual Growth (%)	
	1993-94	1999-2000	1983 to 1993-94	1993-94 to 1999-2000
Agriculture	190.72	190.94	2.23	0.02
Industry				
Mining and Quarrying	2.54	2.26	3.68	-1.91
Manufacturing	35.00	40.79	2.26	2.58
Electricity, Gas and Water Supply	1.43	1.5	5.31	-3.55
Construction	11.02	14.95	4.81	5.21
Services				
Trade, Hotels and Restaurants	26.88	37.54	3.80	5.72
Transport, Storage and communication	9.88	13.65	3.35	5.53
Financial, Insurance, Real Estate	3.37	4.62	4.60	5.40
Community, Social and Personal Services	34.98	30.84	3.85	-2.08
All	315.84	336.75	2.67	1.07

Source: Ministry of Finance, 2004.

B. Life Expectancy and Mortality Rate across Some Asian Countries and South Asia

Country	Life Expectancy at Birth (Years)	Infant Mortality Rate (per 1,000 live births)		Maternal Mortality Ratio (per 100,000 live births)
	2000-05	1990	2003	2005
China	71	38	30	56
India	63	80	63	540
Nepal	61	100	61	740
Pakistan	63	96	81	500
Sri Lanka	74	19	13	92
Bangladesh	63	96	46	380
South Asia	63	84	66	NA

Note: NA: Not Available.

Source: UNDP, *Human Development Report 2005*

C. Trends in Deficits of Central Government

Year	Revenue Deficit (As per cent of GDP)	Fiscal Deficit
2001-02	4.4	6.2
2002-03	4.4	5.9
2003-04	3.6	4.5
2004-05	2.5	4.0
2005-06	2.1	4.1

Source: Ministry of Finance, *Economic Survey 2005-06*

D. Real Gross Domestic Capital Formation

(as per cent of GDP at market prices, 1999-2000 prices)

	2000-01	2001-02	2002-03	2003-04 (P)	2004-05 (Q)
GDFC	23.9	22.3	25.0	26.7	28.5
Public	6.9	6.8	6.1	6.3	6.8
Private	16.4	16.2	18.2	18.6	18.9
Private corporate	5.6	5.4	5.7	6.9	8.2
Household sector	10.8	10.8	12.5	11.7	10.7
GFCF	22.4	22.4	23.7	24.4	24.6
Public	6.4	6.3	6.3	6.6	6.6
Private	16.0	16.0	17.5	17.8	18.0

Note: GDFC: Gross Domestic Capital Formation, GFCF: Gross Fixed Capital Formation
P: Provisional Q: Quick Estimates

Source: CSO; Ministry of Finance, *Economic Survey 2005-06*.

E. Select Indicators: Output

	1950-51	1970-71	1980-81	1990-91	2000-01	2004-05
(a) Food grains (million tonnes)	50.8	108.4	129.6	176.4	196.8	204.6
(b) Finished steel (million tonnes)	1.0	4.6	6.8	13.5	30.3	39.3
(c) Cement (million tonnes)	2.7	14.3	18.7	48.8	97.6	133.6
(d) Crude oil (million tonnes)	0.3	6.8	10.5	33.0	32.4	34.0
(e) Electricity gene rated (Billion kWh)	5.1	55.8	120.8	264.3	499.5	608.6
(f) Coal (million tonnes)	32.3	76.3	119.0	225.5	332.6	412.9

Source: Ministry of Finance, *Economic Survey 2005-06*.

F. Foreign Direct Investment in Some Asian Developing Countries

Country	Foreign Direct Investment Inflows (billions of US $)			Share in World FDI Inflows (percentage)		
	2002	2003	2004	2002	2003	2004
China	52.74	53.51	60.63	7.36	8.46	9.35
Hong Kong	9.68	13.62	34.04	1.35	2.15	5.25
India	**3.45**	**4.27**	**5.34**	**0.48**	**0.67**	**0.82**
Indonesia	0.15	-0.6	1.02	0.02	-0.09	0.16
Korea	2.98	3.79	7.69	0.42	0.6	1.19
Malaysia	3.2	2.47	4.62	0.45	0.39	0.71
Philippines	1.79	0.34	0.47	0.25	0.05	0.07
Singapore	5.82	9.33	16.06	0.81	1.47	2.48
Sri Lanka	0.2	0.23	0.23	0.03	0.04	0.04
Thailand	0.95	1.95	1.06	0.13	0.31	0.16
Developing Countries	155.53	166.34	233.23	21.74	26.29	35.98
World	716.13	632.6	648.15	100.00	100.00	100.00

Source: UNCTAD (2006), *World Investment Report 2005*, United Nation and Academic Foundation.

Select Bibliography

3iNetwok (2002). "Governance Issues for Commercialization", *India Infrastructure Report 2002*, Infrastructure Development Finance Company. Ahmedabad: Indian Institute of Management, Kanpur: Indian Institute of Technology and New Delhi: Oxford University Press.

Acharya, Shankar (2003). *India's Economy–Some Issues and Answers*. New Delhi: Academic Foundation.

Agarwal, A.N. (2003). *Indian Economy—Problems of Development and Planning*. New Delhi: Wishwa Prakashan.

Agarwal, Manmohan, Alokesh Barua, Sandwip Kumar Das and Manoj Pant (1998). *Indian Economy in Transition—Environmental and Development Issues*. New Delhi: Haranand Publications Pvt. Ltd.

Agarwala, Ramgopal, Nagesh Kumar and Michelle Riboud (2004). *Reforms, Labour Markets and Social Security*. Oxford University Press.

Alternative Survey Group (2002). *Alternative Economic Survey 2001-2002*. Noida: Rainbow Publishers.

Bagchi, Amiya and Nirmal Banerjee (1981). *Change and Choice in Indian Industry*, Calcutta: Centre for Studies in Social Sciences.

Bajpai, Peeyush, Laveesh Bhandari and Aali Sinha (2005). *Social & Economic Profile of India*. New Delhi: Social Science Press.

Bardhan, Pranab (1985). *The Political Economy of Development*. New Delhi: Oxford University Press.

Bhaduri, Amit and Deepak Nayyar (1996). *An Intelligent Person's Guide to Liberalization*. New Delhi: Penguin Books.

Bhagwati, J. and Padma Desai (1970) *India: Planning for Industrialization*, Oxford University Press.

Bhattacharya, B.B. (2001). *Mid-Term Review of the Indian Economy, 2000-2001*. New Delhi: India International Centre.

Burton, Stein (1998). *A History of India*. Malden MA: Blackwell Publishers.

Chandra, Bipan, Mridula Mukherjee and Aditya Mukherjee (1999). *India After Independence*. New Delhi: Penguin-Viking.

Chandrashekhar C.P. and Jayati Ghosh (2002). *The Market that Failed*. New Delhi: Left Word.

Chatterjee, Partha (1997). *State and Politics in India*. Oxford University Press.

————. (1997). *A Possible India*. Oxford University Press.

Corbridge, Stuart and Harris John (2000). *Reinventing India: Liberalization, Hindu Nationalism and Popular Democracy*. New Delhi: Oxford University Press.

Das, B.L. (1999). *The World Trade Organisation—A Guide to the Framework for International Trade*. TWN Third World Network.

Datt, Ruddar and K.P.M. Sundharam (2004). *Indian Economy*. New Delhi: S. Chand & Co.

Davidson, Alexander (2005). *How to Understand The Financial Pages*. Kogan Page.

Debroy, Bibek (2004). *India: Redeeming the Economic Pledge*. New Delhi: Academic Foundation.

Debroy, Bibek and Mohammed Saqib (2005). *WTO at Ten*, Volumes I & II. New Delhi: Konarak Publishers.

Department of Public Enterprises (1999). "Highlights", *Public Enterprise Survey 1998-1999*. New Delhi: Ministry of Heavy Industries and Public Enterprises.

Dhar, P.N. (2003). *The Evolution of Economic Policy in India*. New Delhi: Oxford University Press.

Dreze, Jean, Ehtisham Ahmad, John Hills and Amartya Sen (1999). *Social Security in Developing Countries*. Oxford University Press.

Frankel, Francine R., Zoya Hasan, Rajeev Bhargava and Balveer Arora (2000). *Transforming India*. New Delhi: Oxford University Press.

Guy, John (1998). *Woven Cargoes: Indian Textiles in the East*. New York: Thames and Hudson.

Habib, Irfan (1997). *Essays in Indian History*. New Delhi: Tulika Books.

Jalan, Bimal (1992). *The Indian Economy*. New Delhi: Penguin-Viking.

———. (2005). *The Future of India*. New Delhi: Penguin-Viking.

Jenkins, Rob (1999). *Democratic Politics and Economic Reform in India*. Cambridge: Cambridge University Press.

Kapila, Uma (2005). *Indian Economy since Independence 2004-05*. New Delhi: Academic Foundation.

Khilnani, Sunil (1997). *The Idea of India*. London: Penguin Books.

Krueger, Anne O. (ed.) (2002). *Economic Policy Reforms and the Indian Economy*. Oxford University Press.

Mahbub-ul Huq Human Development Centre (2004). *Human Development in South Asia 2003: The Employment Challenge*. Oxford University Press.

Mathew, P.M. (1993). *Informal Sector in India*. Vennala, Cochin: Institute of Small Enterprises and Development and New Delhi: Khama Publishers.

Ministry of Finance (2001). *Economic Survey, 2000-2001*. Government of India.

———. (2003). *Economic Survey, 2002-2003*. Government of India.

———. (2004). *Economic Survey, 2003-2004*. Government of India.

———. (2005). *Economic Survey, 2004-2005*. Government of India.

———. (2006). *Economic Survey, 2005-2006*. Government of India.

Nayyar, Deepak (2002). *Governing Globalization*. Oxford University Press.

Parekh, Kirit (eds.) (1997). *India Development Report: 1997-1998*. New Delhi: Oxford University Press.

———. (1999). *India Development Report: 1999-2000*. New Delhi: Oxford University Press.

Parekh, Kirit and R. Radhakrishnan (eds.) (2002). *India Development Report: 2002-03*. Mumbai: Indira Gandhi Institute of Development Research and New Delhi: Oxford University Press.

————. (2004). *India Development Report: 2004-05.* Mumbai: Indira Gandhi Institute of Development Research and New Delhi: Oxford University Press.

Patel, I.G. (1998). *Economic Reform and Global Change.* New Delhi: Macmillan India Limited.

Patel, Surendra J. (1995). *Indian Economy—Towards the Twenty First Century.* Oxford University Press.

Planning Commission (1996). *Report of the Working Group on National Policy on Public Distribution System.* Government of India, June 30.

————. (2000). *Mid Term Appraisal Ninth Five Year Plan 1997-2002.* Government of India, October.

————. (2001a). *National Human Development Report.* Government of India.

————. (2001b) *Report of the Task Force on Employment Opportunities* (Chairman: Montek S. Ahluwalia). Government of India.

————. (2002). *India Vision 2020* (Chairman: S.P. Gupta). Government of India, December.

————. (2002). *Report of the Special Group on Targeting Ten Million Employment Opportunities per Year over the 10th Plan Period,* Government of India, May.

Mattoo, Aditya and Robert M. Stern (2003). *India and the WTO.* World Bank and Oxford University Press.

Mukherjee, Neela (2000). *World Trade Orgranisation, India's Trade Policy in Services.* Vikas Publishing House.

Radhakrishnan, R. and Alakh Sharma (1998). *Empowering Rural Labour in India.* New Delhi: Institute of Human Development.

Rao, C.H.H., B.B. Bhattacharya and N.S. Siddharthan (2005). *Indian Economy and Society in the the Era of Globalisation: Essays in Honour of Prof. A.M. Khusro.* New Delhi: Academic Foundation.

Shariff, Abusaleh (1999). *India Human Development Report—A Profile of Indian States in the 1990s.* New Delhi: National Council of Applied Economic Research and Oxford University Press.

Singh, Kavaljit (1998). *Globalisation of Finance.* Delhi: Madhayam Books.

Sinha, B.K. (1998). *The Indian Economy in the 21ˢᵗ Century.* New Delhi: Ajanta Books International.

Subramanian, Swamy (2003). *Economic Reforms and Performance, China and India in Comparative Perspective.* New Delhi: Konarak Publishers.

Vaidanathan, A. (2003). *Economic Reforms and Development.* New Delhi: Academic Foundation.

Vyas V.S. (2003). *Indian Agrarian Structure, Economic Policies and Sustainable Development.* New Delhi: Academic Foundation.

World Bank (2000). *India Country Framework Report for Private Participation in Infrastructure.*

————. (2005). *State Fiscal Reforms in India— Progress and Prospects.* New Delhi: Macmillan India.

WTO Secretariat (1999). *Guide to Uruguay Round Agreements.* Kluwer Law International.

Index